James Clare

Life of the Venerable Servant of God Julie Billiart

James Clare

Life of the Venerable Servant of God Julie Billiart

ISBN/EAN: 9783743372658

Manufactured in Europe, USA, Canada, Australia, Japa

Cover: Foto ©Lupo / pixelio.de

Manufactured and distributed by brebook publishing software (www.brebook.com)

James Clare

Life of the Venerable Servant of God Julie Billiart

LIFE OF THE

VENERABLE SERVANT OF GOD

JULIE BILLIART

*FOUNDRESS AND FIRST SUPERIOR GENERAL OF THE
INSTITUTE OF SISTERS OF NOTRE-DAME*

By a Member of the same Congregation

EDITED BY
FATHER CLARE, S.J.

Mulierem fortem quis inveniet ?
Filiae ejus surrexerunt, et beatissimam praedicaverunt.
(*Prov.* xxxi)

London and Leamington
ART AND BOOK COMPANY
New York, Cincinnati, Chicago: BENZIGER BROTHERS
1898

WHENEVER the words "Saint," "Miracle," "Revelation," etc. are used in the following Biography, they are to be understood in a purely historical sense; conformably to the decree of Pope Urban VIII.

PREFACE.

AMONG the remarkable servants of God who in recent times have exercised signal influence in the cause of religion, and who, by their labours in the education of the young, have promoted and extended the knowledge and love of our divine Lord, and formed loyal children of holy Church, a primary place must be assigned to the Venerable Servant of God, Mother Julie Billiart, the Foundress and first Superioress-General of the distinguished Institute of "the Sisters of Notre-Dame de Namur." In the following pages the reader is made acquainted with the leading events of her life from A.D, 1751 to A.D. 1817, in which latter year it pleased God to crown her arduous labours by a holy death.

Few persons have been endowed with a character and personality so strongly marked, or with qualities so admirably adapted to the great and noble work which Almighty God called upon her to perform. That work was nothing less than the establishment of a society of holy religious consecrated to Him by vows, and devoted to the promotion of his greater glory by the education of children of all classes, training up school-mistresses, and by aiding the clergy in their apostolic labours according to their institute and calling.

In reading the life of this Venerable Servant of God two great truths are forcibly impressed upon us; truths often inculcated in the sacred writings of the Old and New Dispensations, and exemplified in the lives of the great and good, the special friends of God, as well before as since the coming of our Blessed Lord into the world.

The former of these truths regards the merciful and loving Providence of God towards His chosen people under the Old Law, and towards His holy Church, the Kingdom of His well-beloved Son, in the New Dispensation.

This He manifested in an especial manner, by raising up in times of great danger or adversity those who under His guidance, and endowed by Him with the necessary qualifications repelled the dangers, and successfully converted adversity into prosperity and glory.

This truth will not be called in question by any one who is even slightly acquainted with the action of God in regard to His people; but we may illustrate by one or two instances.

Six hundred and fifty-seven years before the coming of Christ, the Almighty chose His servant Judith, a holy widow, who by penance and prayer, and much fasting, prepared herself to carry out the work, to fulfil the destiny for which He called her, namely that of being the saviour of His chosen people.*

* Judith c. viii.

She went forth from the city of Bethulia, strong in her confidence in God, undaunted by the appalling difficulties of the undertaking, faithful to the call of heaven, and cut off the head of Holofernes, the leader of the army of Nebuchadonosor king of the Medes.

Dismayed and panic-stricken, the soldiers fled, and in their wild confusion fell to mutual slaughter, from which but few escaped to tell the story; and thus her people were freed from the Medish yoke.*

One hundred and fifty years later, when Assuerus was king of Persia and "ruled the nations from Ethiopia even to the Indies," his wicked minister Aman concerted a plot for the destruction of the Jewish nation, in the twenty-fourth year of their captivity at Babylon. It was then that the Providence of God made use of Esther in order to frustrate the impious designs of the enemies of her nation and save them from annihilation. †

If the Almighty gave such striking proofs of His protecting providence in the Old Law, and chose even frail women to be the instruments for the preservation of his chosen people, what wonder if in the New Dispensation He has given us equally striking and more frequent proof of that same all-wise and all-loving providence in regard of His chosen people by excellence, the children of the holy Catholic Church?

---

* *Judith* xv.   † *Esther* iii.-ix.

The enemies of Israel were many and formidable, but not so terrible, nor so persistent in their efforts as those against whom the Church has to contend, of whom St. Paul writes: "Our wrestling is not against flesh and blood, but against principalities and powers, against the rulers of the world of this darkness; against the spirits of wickedness in the high places." * The powers of darkness, the spirit of the world with its false principles and its pernicious examples, the waywardness of human nature, combined with the disloyalty and contumacious perversity of those who have made shipwreck of their faith—all these are ever striving to allure the children of the Church from their allegiance to her authority. This is clear in every epoch of her history. To the executioners of the early ages of Christianity succeeded the heresiarchs of the fourth, fifth and sixth centuries. Then came the period in which the barbarians from the east and north-east of Europe for well-nigh an equal space of time spread havoc and desolation over the fair fields of Christendom. Against the heresiarchs the Almighty raised up a body of great, holy and learned men, whom He endowed with those qualities and graces by which they were enabled to refute and confound the enemies of truth. Such were Athanasius, Jerome, Ambrose, Augustine and a multitude of others.

---

* Eph. vi. 12.

Against the barbarous invaders who left their passage strewn with ashes or encumbered with corpses, and who seemed to have inflicted a mortal blow on Christian life, the same Almighty Providence raised up the glorious family of St. Benedict. Armed with the crucifix, filled with the Spirit of God, they stemmed the torrent of barbarism, tamed the unbridled passions of these wild hordes, taught them to adore and love the Crucified; and Christian life, which seemed to be hidden in death, sprang up with renewed spiritual energy and fervour throughout the states of Europe. So too in the thirteenth century, when the children of the Church were exposed to a new and double danger, on the one hand from the violence and craft of fresh heresies, and on the other from the luxury and sensual indulgence which pervaded the higher classes and threatened to invade even the Sanctuary, we find that same loving Providence selecting a Dominic, a Francis and a Clare, to found religious orders which should repel the threatened dangers, and by means of their followers become instruments for the salvation of souls in generations still unborn. Again, in more recent times, a new danger, and a new phase of hostility to the Church, and one in some respects more formidable than any which preceded it, was the revolt of the human intellect against the divinely constituted authority of the Church. Its leaders, undermining the very foundations of faith, substituted in its stead human reason and human authority. By flattering the passions, perverting the sacred names of liberty and progress, falsifying history, aspersing with calumny the Vicar of Christ, and invoking the Sacred Scriptures against Him who inspired them, they summoned the Church before their impious tribunals, found her guilty of blasphemy and of seducing the people, and pronounced her worthy of death. In this extremity God was pleased to call forth Ignatius, Teresa and a host of others, who have rescued thousands from spiritual ruin. In our own times another and an appalling effort is being made to undermine and ruin the mystical Body of Christ, by robbing it of that portion which is the most dear to His Sacred Heart, and which is the weakest and least protected, namely the young of all classes, especially the children of the poor. By corrupting the waters of human life at their source the enemies of God and of His Church flatter themselves that they will at length, surely though gradually, succeed in destroying the kingdom of Christ on earth.

From the beginning of the present century this has been in France the persistent effort of wicked men, who have striven to wrest out of the hands of the pastors of the Church the education of youth of both sexes, and to appoint as professors and teachers of the young, persons who, if not openly hostile, are at least indifferent to all religion. The same efforts, but by means if possible more unblushing, are being exerted to the same end in Italy, where not only the faith but the morals of youth are being undermined and destroyed. In England and America the enemies of the Church are energetic and persistent in their endeavours to secularize education, to prevent the teaching of religion, to banish the name of God from the schools, to blot out the thought of Him from the minds, the love of Him from the hearts of children. Were they to succeed, it is clear that the result would be universal corruption; the passions of the soul would be let loose, and men would cease to worship God or practise any religion. To counteract this danger, to prevent this calamity, it has pleased His Divine Majesty to choose, among other instruments of His merciful and loving Providence—and that in an especial manner—the Venerable Servant of God, Mother Julie Billiart. She was called to form a body of religious who by their Institute were to devote their lives to unremitting labours and self-sacrifice in this noblest of causes,* the education of girls of every station, and especially to the instruction of the children of the masses. They were in fact to fulfil the duties in the education of girls, which are being performed by the followers of St. Ignatius and St. Joseph Calasanctius for boys and youths, and in this way to maintain and extend as far as possible the knowledge and the love and service of God.

We also find a second great truth illustrated in the life of Mother Julie. This is the law of suffering. The Spirit of God teaches us that suffering is a

---

* Of all divine work, the most divine is to labour with God in the salvation of souls. (St. Dionysius.)

pledge of our being pleasing to God: "Because thou wast acceptable unto God, it was necessary that temptation should prove thee;"* and St. Paul instructs his disciple Timothy, saying that, entering into the service of God, he must prepare himself for many trials, "for all that will live godly in Christ Jesus shall suffer persecution." † Moreover, a greater than St. Paul, our Lord Himself, proclaims and blessed all those who for His sake suffer persecution and are the victims of men's malice and evil tongues. "Blessed are ye when they shall revile you, and persecute you, and speak all that is evil against you untruly for My sake." ‡

Accordingly we find that the history of all those who have been distinguished for sanctity and for the promotion of God's glory in the world, is invariably marked by one characteristic—it is a history of suffering and of opposition. Like their grand Original, "they are all placed as a sign of contradiction." We may say with all truth that the law of sanctity is the law of suffering. More especially is this the case when, in addition to the labour of securing his own perfection, the person devotes himself to the sanctification of others.

How thoroughly this law was verified in the life of Venerable Julie Billiart is made clear in the following pages. We may say that her whole life was made up of sufferings, was one long martyrdom. As she

---

* *Tobias* xii, 13. † 2 *Tim.* iii. 12. ‡ *Matt.* v. 11.

advanced in years, so also did her sufferings increase in their intensity.

In early youth she was deprived of the comforts of a home: to this trial was added for two-and-twenty years another, by which she was deprived of the use of her limbs through a paralytic stroke. In addition, her life was exposed to imminent danger from the persecutors of the Catholic Church.

But of all her sufferings the greatest were those reserved for her later years, when she found that the chief opponents to the work which our Lord had destined her to do, were the very persons from whom she might reasonably have expected the staunchest support and encouragement, who by their profession were constituted the guides and directors of souls, and whose sacred duty it was to promote whatever might conduce to the honour and glory of God or the salvation of souls. Our Blessed Lord had to suffer from the high-priest and the priests of the synagogue, and this it was that filled up the cup of His sorrow, and made it run over: so too it was the will of God that His Servant should share in this His sorrow by permitting her to suffer opposition, persecution and calumny, from those dedicated to the Sanctuary. Yet never a sign or expression of murmuring or impatience escaped her, but with unswerving courage she bravely and cheerfully accepted all for the love of our Blessed Lord. There was no betrayal of a shadow of doubt, or wavering, but an unshaken confidence in the protection of her Heavenly Spouse, " in whom she believed, whom she loved, and in whom she placed all her trust."

It was by these her sufferings that God prepared and perfected Mother Julie Billiart for the work He had assigned to her; and how perfectly she co-operated with Him and corresponded with the abundant graces which He bestowed upon her to fit her to carry out His design, is seen clearly in the history of her life. In it we observe with what extraordinary firmness, energy and perseverance she overcame all kinds of difficulties, whenever there was question of God's glory and the salvation or perfection of souls. Her uninterrupted union with our Lord and her profound spirit of prayer developed in her singular generosity, fearlessness and magnanimity, qualities necessary in one who was to found an Institute such as hers, and who was to become the Mother of the Society of the Sisters of Notre-Dame.

In those who sought admission into her Congregation she required a serious resolve to devote themselves to a life of recollection and prayer, to give up their own wills, to cultivate detachment from all which is not in God and for Him. The true Sister of Notre-Dame was to be prepared to leave country and friends, to go to any place or country, to accept any office assigned by Superiors, if it be for God's glory and the salvation of souls; nay, she must moreover be content to be employed in any menial or domestic duties at the call of obedience or the expression of the Superior's will.

In order to keep alive this spirit of prayer and self-sacrifice, and this detachment from creatures, she prescribes daily meditation in the morning and evening, frequent visits to our Lord in the Blessed Sacrament, and also scrupulous observance of silence and recollection, as far as is consistent with the duties of teaching or instruction.

Of course for such an exalted vocation, in which the active life is combined with the contemplative, from which it must derive its main force and efficacy for a vocation in which to the labours of evangelizing others is added that of securing one's own sanctification, there is required in all who would aspire to embrace it, great freedom or largeness of soul, a manly and courageous disposition (*cor magnum et anima volens*), a steady, firm and uncompromising character. These qualities the reader will find in an eminent degree in Mother Julie Billiart, or, as she called herself, Sister Ignatius, and through the grace and special blessing of our dear Lord, she has handed them down to those who glory in the great privilege of being members of her Society. And if we may judge the spirit of the Mother by that of those whom, under God, she claims as her children, if their virtues and labours redound to the honour and glory of her whom they call their Mother, what must have been her spirit, and who can say the height of her honour and the greatness of her glory in the sight of our good and generous Father in heaven? Within the short space of time during which this Society has been established, we find that it has multiplied its foundations in Belgium, in England, and especially in America. Further, we also find that it has opened two houses in the Congo State of South Africa; that in Belgium it counts above 1,300 members, in America above 1,150, and in England between 500 and 600; that from one establishment alone the Sisters have trained and sent forth apostles of education in the shape of lay mistresses to the number of 2,000, who are employed in all parts of Great Britain in teaching the rising generation.

Well then may we apply to Mother Julie those words with which the citizens of Bethulia greeted the heroine Judith on her return from the destruction of her country's foes: "*Tu gloria Jerusalem, tu lætitia Israel, tu honorificentia populi nostri.*" *

Surely it is a glory for the true Jerusalem, the Holy Catholic Church, that she can point to her as one who in her own person, as also in her children, has done such glorious deeds for the promotion of the knowledge and love and glory of our God against His and our enemies. Truly she is the "lætitia Israel" in giving true joy to the souls of all those whom she has been the means of preserving from the pollution of sin, and inspiring with a love of Him who is the only source of true joy. She is "honorificentia populi nostri," the honour of all those

* *Judith* xv 10.

who are of the household of the Faith, for her spirit survives in those hundreds of virgins, who, following in her footsteps, are zealously carrying on the work which she so nobly began.

In conclusion, the author acknowledges her great indebtedness to the Rev. Père Clair, whose admirable Life of Julie Billiart has been of much service in the production of the following pages, and from which some chapters have been borrowed and translated.

JAMES CLARE, S.J.

ST. BEUNO'S, *October, 1897.*

CONTENTS.

CHAPTER	PAGE
I.—Childhood	1
II.—Julie's First Trials	14
III —Persecution	24
IV.—Julie's First Companion	36
V.—The Hôtel Blin de Bourdon	52
VI.—Laying the Foundations	70
VII.—The Great Missions	85
VIII.—Religious Training	102
IX.—First Foundation in Belgium	113
X.—The Beginning of Sorrows	125
XI.—Expulsion from Amiens	150
XII.—Into Exile	188
XIII.—The Mother-House at Namur	200
XIV.—Notre-Dame at Ghent	217
XV.—Rehabilitation of the Foundress in France	238
XVI.—Rapid Spread of the Institute	267
XVII.—The War	304
XVIII.—The Last Cross	323

CHAPTER	PAGE
XIX.—THE SOUL OF MÈRE JULIE	338
XX.—JULIE'S HAPPY DEATH	358
XXI.—HER SEPULCHRE SHALL BE GLORIOUS	386

LIST OF ILLUSTRATIONS.

THE VENERABLE JULIE BILLIART	*Frontispiece*
BIRTHPLACE OF THE VENERABLE JULIE BILLIART AT CUVILLY	3
MONSIEUR L'ABBÉ DANGICOURT	7
FRANÇOISE, VICOMTESSE BLIN DE BOURDON	36
PÈRE VARIN, S.J.	74
MONSEIGNEUR PISANI DE LA GAUDE	150
NAMUR	200
HIS HOLINESS POPE PIUS VII.	265
THE MOTHER-HOUSE OF THE SISTERS OF NOTRE-DAME, NAMUR, 1897	333
CHAPEL SHRINE OF THE VENERABLE JULIE BILLIART AT NAMUR, GARDEN OF THE MOTHER-HOUSE, NAMUR	395

THE

VENERABLE JULIE BILLIART.

CHAPTER I.

CHILDHOOD.

The Venerable Servant of God Julie Billiart, destined to become the foundress of the "Sœurs de Notre-Dame de Namur," was born in an obscure village of Picardy. Cuvilly is in the department of Oise, France, only a few miles from the historic town of Compiègne, memorable for the siege in which Joan of Arc was made prisoner by the English. The whole province is full of souvenirs of the Hundred Years War between England and France. One of the later Lords of Séchelles perished on the scaffold during the French Revolution. A daughter of the house married M. de Pont l'Abbé, and became a kind friend and protectress to Julie Billiart.

The plain on which Cuvilly stands is traversed by the high road to Flanders; it is bounded on the north by the wooded slopes of Séchelles, and on the south by the ridge of hills rising above the valley of St.-Maur. The landscape is of a peaceful, pastoral character, dotted with rural hamlets, each with its church steeple and its Calvary. Every village of Picardy, as well as every spot where the roads meet, has its wayside cross. The emblem of man's redemption stands half hidden in the shade of ancient trees, often surrounded by a hedge or trellis covered with honeysuckle or traveller's joy. In those happier days when France was still a land of faith and love, the villagers took a pride in arranging and ornamenting their Calvary, and placed their hearths and homes with touching Christian instinct under the protection of the Cross of Christ. Many and many a time Julie must have gazed upon that sacred emblem, many and many a time knelt and prayed before it as a child. The pilgrim who visits the early home of Mère Julie, entering the village by the Calvary, cannot fail to notice the interesting parish church dedicated to St. Éloi. It is of considerable size, bearing traces of different periods of architecture, chiefly sixteenth century Gothic, though the apsidal chancel, curiously deviating from the line of the nave, is probably of earlier date. In the Rue de Lataule a house is pointed out as that in which the Billiart family formerly lived. A gate in the low stone wall leads into a courtyard, which is bounded on the right by a long low building with a thatched roof, while opposite the gate a little straw-covered shed separated the yard from the garden—for in Cuvilly no cottage is without its sunny garden, bright with

gay flowers. The room occupied by the Servant of God during her long illness is distinguished by its boarded floor, and is just as she left it. The whole of this interesting little domain became in July 1882 the property of the Institute of the Sisters of Notre-Dame. To the spiritual daughters of Mère Julie the cottage of Cuvilly is not only a precious memorial of the past—it is a sanctuary and a shrine.

The Billiarts were a family in which piety and virtue were hereditary; they had been settled in the district for a long time, for the name occurs in the archives of the Commune for generations back. The family enjoyed a fair measure of the goods of fortune; they made considerable gifts to their parish church, and one of their number was "lieutenant de justice du dit lieu." In 1751 the homestead of the Rue Lataule was the abode of an industrious couple, Jean-François Billiart and Marie-Louise-Antoinette Debraine.

Their circumstances were then comparatively easy, for in addition to the produce of their small plot of land, they derived some income from keeping a little shop.

Married in 1739, they had already had four daughters and one son before the birth of Julie. Two of the girls, Louise-Antoinette and Marie-Rose, died in infancy; two more children, Marie-Louise-Angélique and Jean-Baptiste, barely outlived childhood, so that in a few years there remained only

Julie, a sister, Marie-Madeleine-Henriette, her elder by seven years, and a younger brother, Louis-François, born in 1754. In course of time Madeleine and Louis-François married and brought up good Christian families; they are now represented by descendants at Paris, Beauvais and Cuvilly.

Julie Billiart was born on July 12, 1751. She was taken the same day to the parish church of St.-Éloi, where with the names of Marie-Rose-Julie she received at the baptismal font that robe of grace which, we may well believe, she carried unspotted before the throne of God. This happy day was always remembered by her with special thanksgiving. Writing in the decline of life to one of her spiritual daughters, Sister Anastasie, she says: "You will receive my letter on the anniversary of my baptism. Surely I ought to die of shame for not having long since died of love for God, of gratitude to my good Jesus!"

More richly gifted with the treasures of Heaven than with those of earth, the parents of Julie were noted for their simple-hearted piety and solid virtue, and their unpretending household was of that patriarchal type now alas! almost unknown amongst us. In this quiet Christian home Julie grew up in happy ignorance of the world, and seemed daily to advance "in wisdom and grace before God and man." The Holy Ghost became her first master,[*] charming her by the sweetness of His love. When

---

[*] Process of Information at Namur.

missed from the family circle she was often to be found in some hidden nook, saying her childish prayers with a gravity and devotion far beyond her years.* And even at this early age she was wont to deny herself in many ways, practising in secret acts of penance and voluntary mortification.

The village school was kept by her own uncle Thibault Guilbert. She was very soon sent there, and she eagerly profited by the opportunity given her of learning to read and write, for little else was taught at Cuvilly. But her intelligence developed of itself, and in after years people used to admire in the unlettered peasant a certain loftiness of thought, and a distinction of manner and of language, which spring from innate nobility of soul. As if some foreshadowing of her future work had fallen on her young life, the child's favourite lesson was the Catechism. By the time she had reached the age of seven, she knew it perfectly, and had mastered not only the words but their meaning. After school hours it was her custom to gather her companions round her, and if any were absent she would send for them, crying out, "I want plenty of little souls, to teach them how to love and serve the good God." Then with her bright and winning manner she kept them attentive while she explained the Catechism, and wound up with an exhortation on the love of

---

* Evidence given in 1820 by M. Trouvelot, dean of Ressons-sur-Metz who died head-priest of St.-Jacques, Compiègne.

God or the hatefulness of sin, so earnest, we are told, as to captivate all her listeners whether young or old. It was the future foundress unconsciously practising the special work of her own Institute, the instruction of the children of the poor. For, as Mère St.-Joseph, her co-foundress, loved to repeat, "The Sisters of Notre-Dame are made for teaching the Catechism." In this employment Julie seemed supremely happy. Her heart even then was that of a little apostle, already burning with that zeal for souls which consumed it all through her life. As she grew older she kept her early love for teaching; she would assemble the neglected little ones whose parents were too poor to send them to school, and teach them the chief mysteries of our holy faith with as much of the Catechism as was necessary for them to know to prepare them for the reception of the sacraments of Penance and the Holy Eucharist. She seems to have added to her religious instructions in some cases lessons in reading and writing. Amongst her little scholars, writes Mère St.-Joseph, "was a little beggar boy whom she instructed so patiently and well that she managed to refine away his native roughness and made him fit to take a place. From this first situation he rose to a better one, and so to a third; and at last was able to set up in business and realize a modest competency. Thirty years later, I was touched to see a letter, very well composed and filled with sentiments of piety and gratitude, which he wrote to our Mother to thank her for the good

MONSIEUR L'ABBÉ DANGICOURT.
From an Oil Painting in possession of the Sisters of Notre-Dame, Namur.

fortune of which he regarded her, after God, as the chief cause."

Julie's childish efforts to win souls to that God who was secretly drawing her own heart to Himself, attracted the attention of the saintly Curé of the parish. M. Dangicourt, who in the designs of Divine Providence was destined to guard and guide this privileged soul, was no less remarkable for his solid virtue than for his profound learning; he had won the confidence of the neighbouring clergy, while his own little flock loved him as a father and venerated him as a saint. He first came to Cuvilly in 1759 as curate to his uncle M. Pottier, upon whose death he took charge of the parish. Father Sellier, the Jesuit, in his notice of the Servant of God, thus speaks of her holy director:—" Cuvilly had for Curé at that time an ecclesiastic of rare merit, M. Dangicourt, noted for his piety, zeal and learning. Madame de Pont l'Abbé thought so highly of the pastor of Cuvilly that she used every effort to obtain him as tutor for her son, and after many entreaties the Bishop of Beauvais acceded to her wishes. Whenever the pious châtelaine went to her country seat, she was in the habit of inviting a circle of congenial friends to enjoy his society and profit by his counsels."

Under the direction of this holy priest the simple peasantry of Cuvilly found in the practices of piety their truest happiness. After their hard day's toil they loved to collect in the church, where the zealous pastor used to read the *Night Prayers of the late Monseigneur the Marshal of Bellefont*,* followed by a hymn which the *Magister* entoned. It is doubtless from this time that we may date Julie's love for the singing of hymns —a love which she kept all through her life, and which she has bequeathed to her daughters.

Enlightened by the spirit of God, M. Dangicourt judged from Julie's apparently infused knowledge of the truths of faith, and her singularly delicate appreciation of Divine things, that God had great designs upon her soul, and he was jealous of her correspondence with them. He therefore initiated her into the method of mental prayer and the practices of a devout life. By his advice, she set herself to conquer that natural impetuosity of character in which her director foresaw dangers to her soul. So frequently did grace triumph over nature, that although she was often tried by the boyish freaks of her brother Louis, who took a mischievous delight in disturbing her pious solitude, no sign of ill-humour ever appeared. If she sometimes considered herself to have been wanting in gentleness, she at once asked pardon with touching sweetness and humility.

Seeing how visibly God was drawing the child

---

* The manuscript, in a large, clear hand, bears the signature of the schoolmaster, Thibault Guilbert, with this quaint note: "The late Cardinal de Bouillon thought them so beautiful that he wished to have them, to make use of in his own house. It is certain that anyone who reads them slowly will find them full of unction."

to Himself, M. Dangicourt resolved to allow her to make her First Communion when she was but nine years old — a rare privilege in those days, when children in France were not admitted to the Holy Table till they were thirteen or fourteen. But, no less prudent than clear-sighted, he wished this favour to be kept secret, permitting her to communicate on all the great feasts and sometimes oftener, but always very early in the morning, when the Church was empty. He admitted her publicly to Holy Communion with the other village children two years later.

Meanwhile Julie rapidly advanced in the path of solid virtue. None but God knew the ardour of her love, and the generosity with which she offered herself to Him, in those happy moments when, kneeling alone and unseen in the old village church, she possessed within her Him whom her soul loved; but all could bear witness to the spirit of self-sacrifice which marked her daily life. From the time when she left school, her one thought seemed to be to devote herself to her parents; and, as she was blessed with good health, she cheerfully undertook the most laborious duties about the house and garden. Like Martha she was "busy about many things" in the service of her Lord; but she did not forget "the better part." She began the day by an hour's meditation, and always managed to give some time to spiritual reading. Her favourite books were the Gospels, the Psalms, the Epistles of St. Paul, and *The Following of Christ*. Later on, she added a few other chosen works, such as Rodriguez on *Christian Perfection*, *Les Pensées Chrétiennes* of Father Bouhours, and the writings of St. Teresa. Every day she paid several visits to the Blessed Sacrament, even in seasons of the heaviest labour in the fields. Rather than omit the least of her exercises of piety she shortened her sleep; it was at the foot of the altar, or in her room if the church was shut, that she found — as she herself owned — "rest, strength, and courage." In the sacristy at Cuvilly several interesting memorials have thrown light on the special devotions of the servant of God. The manuscript of "Night Prayers" already mentioned contains a résumé of the "Rules and Practices of the Confraternity of the Sacred Heart of Jesus, established on the 15th of April, 1738, at the Monastery of the Visitation Sainte-Marie de Compiègne." Two lists of names follow, in the handwriting of M. Dangicourt, enumerating the members of this pious Association at Cuvilly. The tenth name on the first list is that of Marie-Rose-Julie Billiart, and a little further down appear the names of her sister Marie-Madeleine, her brother Louis-François, and several members of the family. The rules assigned to each associate an hour's adoration before the Blessed Sacrament, to be made once a year. The hour chosen by Julie was from two to three on Good Friday. A grandniece of the servant of God, in a deposition made at Beauvais in 1882, declared that devotion to the Sacred Heart was hereditary in their family. Her mother used to say, "My children, it is to the Sacred Heart that I pray ;—keep up this practice, it is a family devotion."

The Sisters of Notre-Dame have a custom instituted by their pious foundress of reciting a daily Act of Reparation to the Sacred Heart of Jesus. That said every Tuesday begins with the these words :—"O Jesus, Son of the living God, Who, by an incomprehensible effect of the love of Thy Divine Heart, hast willed to hide Thyself beneath the mysterious veil of this august Sacrament," etc. Not without emotion do we read in the little manual of Cuvilly a prayer beginning with the same words. The paper, worn with age and stained with drops of wax, tells how frequently the prayer must have been said : Julie had doubtless carried it away engraven on her heart.

In addition to the memorials of her devotion to the Sacred Heart the sacristy at Cuvilly gave evidence of her love of the Immaculate Mother of God. A white satin banner, said to have been embroidered by her hands, and now kept at the Convent of Notre-Dame at Namur, bears the monogram of Our Lady with the inscription " *Tota pulchra es, Maria, et macula non est in te.*" Later on we shall hear of the vow Julie made to propagate the devotion to " Mary conceived without sin." Cuvilly still preserves the tradition that when

Julie had finished her daily devotions to Our Lord in His Sacrament of Love, she never failed to kneel at the Lady Altar to ask the blessing of her heavenly Mother before going home. In 1764 Julie received the Sacrament of Confirmation. The Cardinal Bishop of Beauvais, Mgr. Étienne-Réné Potier de Gesvres, visited Cuvilly that year for a double ceremony. On the morning of June 4 he confirmed the village children. On the list of names discovered in an ancient antiphonary of the church we find that of "Marie-Rose-Julie Billiart, aged 13." In the afternoon of the same day the Cardinal blessed with great pomp the chapel erected in honour of St. Barnabas by the Knights Hospitallers of St. John of Jerusalem on their estate at Bellicourt. They had brought from beyond the sea relics of this saint and other sacred treasures. One of these was an authentic relic of the true Cross, set in a large cruciform reliquary, and the esteem in which the holy child of Cuvilly was held is shown by the fact that this was presented by one of the Knights to the little Julie, who labelled it herself:—"Given to Julie Billiart by a Knight of Malta." The child generously deprived herself of her treasure in favour of the parish, and up to the Revolution the sacred fragment was exposed every year on the days which commemorate Our Lord's Passion. The reliquary may still be seen in the Mother-House of the Sisters of Notre-Dame at Namur.

About a year after her Confirmation, urged by

her desire to belong entirely to God, Julie, with the approval of her director, made a vow of perpetual chastity. From that time her love for the Divine Spouse of Virgins increased yet more. She approached the Holy Table as often as possible, and at the age of twenty obtained the signal favour of daily Communion. Long years afterwards she owned to her first companion, Mother Blin de Bourdon, that "never in her life had she experienced so deep a joy as when her confessor allowed her daily Communion, and that her soul had then been seized with a mingled feeling of happiness and wonder which it would be impossible for her to express." No one else marvelled that this privilege should be granted to her who was already known as "the Saint of Cuvilly."

Such was Julie's childhood, seeming to promise a life of peaceful happiness and yet marked with prophetic indications of the career which in later years was to be hers. Grace had already planted in that young heart the germs of the virtues which were specially to characterise the future foundress, —love of God, zeal for souls, power for good over others. Julie was already practising the active combined with the contemplative life—a life specially characteristic of the Sisters of Notre-Dame. Sufferings and trials of all kinds were to complete her preparation for the apostolate. The instrument was to be reduced to a state of utter helplessness that the work might be attributed to God alone.

CHAPTER II.

JULIE'S FIRST TRIALS.

"When God has great designs on a soul," says St. Vincent de Paul, "he tries it in the furnace of tribulation." Julie Billiart was to be no exception to this law by which the saints are fashioned. She was only just sixteen when the first of a series of trials came suddenly upon her. Up to that time her family had enjoyed a modest competency, and had never known privation or want. Her father's character had won the esteem of his neighbours, and all had prospered with him. Now, one after another, came heavy losses, and worse still he had to suffer from the slanderous reports of those who are ever ready to attack the unfortunate.

One night, when Jean-François Billiart and his family were asleep, thieves broke in and carried off the best part of their small stock of merchandise. In their haste they dropped some pieces of linen and lace into a disused well, but these, when found, were completely spoilt. The loss was a serious one, and bankruptcy was inevitable. To satisfy his creditors, M. Billiart was forced to sell nearly all the land which formed his little patrimony, and now that his last resource was gone, he found himself face to face with poverty and want. It was then that the full strength and beauty of Julie's character manifested themselves. Not only did she console her suffering parents by lavishing on them the riches of her filial love, but with a courage and devotion far beyond her years she set to work at once to provide for their support. It was harvest time, and without a moment's hesitation she went out into the fields to seek employment. There, we are told by M. Trouvelot, she surpassed all her companions in dexterity and industry; her powers of labour seemed supernatural, as though she drew from Holy Communion strength of body as well as vigour of soul.

There was something in her manner which commanded almost involuntary respect; not an unbecoming word was ever dropped, even by the most thoughtless, when Julie was present. At meal time, while the reapers rested, she taught them to sing hymns, or engaged their attention by reading aloud some pious book which at once instructed and interested them. They wished for no other amusement when they could have Julie with her book, or her still more captivating conversation, and even petitioned her to assemble them on Sundays also. But on that day she gave herself entirely to God and her family.

When the harvest was over, Julie undertook other labours, making many long and trying journeys, both on foot and on horseback, in order to sell off the remainder of her father's stock to the best advantage. Her efforts were sometimes rewarded with unexpected success. Upon one occasion, when her father was bemoaning the hard necessity he was under of parting with some of his goods for the tenth part of their value, Julie, with the quiet decision of manner which characterised her, packed up the material and carried it off to Beauvais, a distance of over twenty-four miles. She had never before been in the town and knew no one there, but trusting to Divine Providence she walked into the first shop she saw open and offered her goods for sale. She had met with an honest tradesman, who, touched with compassion, paid her down at once the full price. Thus Julie went on day after day, preserving the amenity of her character amidst her daily domestic cares, the modesty of her demeanour in her intercourse with the world, the peace of her soul amidst endless temporal embarrassments, and keeping up all her devout practices though overwhelmed with occupations.

These incessant labours seemed too little for her vigorous spirit. She found time to visit the sick, and her much needed repose was sacrificed night after night whenever any one among the poor villagers was dangerously ill. Her well-known charity caused her to be chosen for many a little office of trust, and Cuvilly long preserved with veneration the embroidered purse with which she used to make the collection in the parish church on

Sundays.* Father Sellier, S.J., whose connection with the Venerable Servant of God will be noticed later on, mentions in connection with this period of her life a detail worth noting here. Mme. Hérault de Séchelles, to whom the manor of Cuvilly belonged, came every year to spend the summer months in her château there. She was quick to remark the virtues and superior qualities of Julie, and made her the confidante of her good works and the distributor of her alms. But this little distinction, so flattering for her, only made Julie more modest and retiring. She had other friends too—those noble Carmelites of Compiègne whose holy and fervent lives were to merit for them, a few years later, the palm of martyrdom. Julie was skilful in church embroidery, and this employment took her from time to time to the Convent; the annals of her life tell us that she was inspired with new ardour in the service of God by her conversations with these saintly women.

Unremitting toil and the exercises of active charity were now to be exchanged for intense suffering and complete inactivity. The scanty food, the incessant labour, the constant exposure to extremes of heat and cold, gradually told upon the girl's hitherto robust constitution. She began to suffer from violent toothache, and an ophthalmic affection

* This purse is now in the possession of the Sisters of Notre-Dame at Namur. It is worked with the arms of the family of Pont-l'Abbé of Gournay-sur-Aronde, who were the instrument of God for saving Julie at the time of the Revolution.

threatened her with total blindness. To obtain the cure of her eyes she made a pilgrimage to Montreuil, where a copy of the Holy Face of Rome, sent to a Cistercian Convent by Pope Innocent IV., was held in great veneration, and was visited especially to obtain the cure of diseases of the eyes. Julie's faith and devotion were rewarded by the complete restoration of her sight. Her eldest sister Madeleine, who had been blind, if not from infancy, at least for many years, obtained a similar grace on the same spot. The servant of God never lost the memory of this double favour, and many years after related the event to encourage one of her spiritual daughters to address herself to the Holy Face for the cure of her eyes.

But to fulfil the designs of God she had to advance still further on the " King's Highway of the Holy Cross." In relieving and consoling her parents there was much natural and innocent satisfaction, but even this she was now called upon to relinquish. One winter evening in 1774 Julie was sitting at work by her father's side, when the window near them was suddenly broken by a large stone which fell at their feet: immediately afterwards a pistol was fired through the window at Jean Billiart. It missed its aim, but though no one was wounded all were terribly frightened, and Julie's nervous system received a shock from which she did not recover for more than thirty years. Intense pains declared themselves in all her limbs, and little by little reduced her to a state of such utter weakness that she could hardly drag herself from room to room. As long, however, as any power of movement remained to her, she still gave herself to her domestic duties. Every day found her paying her accustomed visits to Jesus Christ both in His Sacramental Presence and in the person of His Poor, and many a night still saw her watching by the bedside of the dying and the dead. No complaint, no passing murmur, ever escaped her lips. The Abbé Dangicourt, an almost daily witness of Julie's heroism, could not contain his admiration, and spoke of his young penitent in such glowing terms to his Bishop, Mgr. de la Rochefoucauld, that the prelate expressed a wish to see "the Saint of Cuvilly."* Julie was therefore taken to the episcopal palace at Beauvais, and there questioned by the Bishop himself in the presence of several eminent ecclesiastics. All agreed that this humble peasant was already far advanced in the science of the Saints, and when she had withdrawn, his Lordship said to those around him: "That young girl seems to me to be inspired by God Himself. I shall be surprised if we do not hear more of her later."

Up to the year 1782 Julie had occasional moments of respite from the violence of her sufferings. But after that date she became a complete cripple, owing, it was thought, to the injudicious treatment of a

* Francis Joseph de la Rochefoucauld succeeded Cardinal de Gesvres in the See of Beauvais in 1772. He showed himself the father and friend of his flock, whose sufferings he tried to mitigate by every means in his power. It was this Bishop of Beauvais who, with his brother the Bishop of Saintes, perished in the massacre of the Carmes, September 2, 1792.

country doctor, who, according to the custom of the times, bled her repeatedly, and so weakened her that she could no longer stir without crutches. At the end of some months both legs were paralysed, and she betook herself to that couch of suffering from which she was not to rise for many many years. Her state was further complicated by violent convulsions, and for a long while she lay between life and death. Five times did Julie receive from her confessor the Sacraments of the dying, but her crown was not to be so speedily won; her soul was to undergo a long purification in the furnace of suffering in order to prepare her for the great work God had in store for her. The grief of her aged parents, whose stay and prop she had been, was not the least of Julie's sorrows; yet her soul was in peace, for the more God afflicted her, the closer did she cling to Him, and the favours with which He rewarded her fidelity far surpassed the sufferings by which He tried her patience. Every day M. Dangicourt brought her the only solace she desired, her Lord in His Sacrament of Love, and she remained for hours afterwards absorbed in prayer. "What struck me most in Mère Julie," says Père Sellier,[*] in writing of this period of her life, "was a quite uncommon gift of prayer, and I believe she was raised to a very high degree of contemplation. She spent in this holy exercise four or five hours every day. At such times she was to be seen perfectly

---

[*] Précis of the Virtues noticed in Rev. Mère Julie, by Père Sellier.

rapt in God, motionless, all use of her senses suspended, and her countenance glowing with heavenly peace and sweetness. The noise made around her was powerless to distract her during these Divine communications. She came to herself from this mysterious state with a visible effort, and only after some one had quietly shaken her or pulled her by the arm. I am speaking of the time when she lay paralysed upon her couch of pain." "Constantly stretched upon her bed of suffering," relates Sister Stéphanie Warnier, quoting the testimony of contemporaries, " our Mother lived in unbroken union with God. Mère St.-Joseph once asked her if those days had not seemed very long and tedious to her; but she answered that during the first eight years of her illness she had never once felt loneliness or *ennui*. If, later on, the cross bore heavily upon her, it was due rather to the intrusion of a schismatical priest at Cuvilly, which deprived her of the Sacraments. At that time, too, God withdrew from her His sensible favours and abandoned His servant to severe interior desolation." Her own sufferings did not cause her to forget those of others; they seemed to increase her compassion for all who were in trouble. After the epidemic which raged at Cuvilly in 1782, she begged Mme. de Séchelles to have a hospital built in a field on the east side of the village, where there was a spring much frequented by the sick and still known as the " Fontaine-Malade."

Meanwhile her time was fully occupied; she daily gathered round her bed the children of the village to teach them their catechism, devoting herself with a special zeal to those amongst them who were preparing for their first Communion. Many long years after the fruits of her teaching were still visible in her native place. A Curé of Cuvilly * relates that he had met with old people to whom he had taken Holy Viaticum, who would say to him: " Wait a little, M. le Curé, till I have said the acts taught me by Julie Billiart." Grown up persons often mingled with the children. She had the art of making them love virtue, so attractive did her lessons render it. To see her, indeed, was to love her; simplicity, kindness and frankness beamed in her countenance, enhanced by an angelic modesty and by the auréole of suffering.

The invalid's little room was very inconvenient and confined. The charitable ladies who visited her, therefore, had the brick floor replaced by oak boards, which are still there. They also had a door made to open on the courtyard, in order to admit visitors without their passing through the house. Mme. de Séchelles frequently came to seek edification from the conversation of the Servant of God. At Julie's bedside she met Mme. de Pont-l'Abbé, who resided at her country seat at Gournay-sur-Aronde, and the Countess Baudoin with her three daughters. This lady's father

* Rogatory process of Beauvais: evidence of M. l'Abbé d'Héry.

was Count d'Arlincourt, one of the "Farmers general of the Revenue,"* and often, when passing the summer near Cuvilly with his daughter, the old Count would accompany her in her visits to Julie. The affection and esteem with which the poor invalid inspired him prompted him to leave her in his will a life annuity of six hundred francs. Little did he or any of Julie's noble friends dream of the troubles in store for them, which were to cost some of them their lives as well as their fortunes. Nor did these pious ladies realize how much they were doing for God in protecting that humble and suffering peasant. She meanwhile remained in her state of lowliness catechizing children and working for the altar.†

But she was about to be called upon to give to her Divine Master a more striking proof of her fidelity, and confess, at the peril of her life, the faith she had taught to His poor.

* Souvenirs of Mère Blin de Bourdon.
† The Servant of God employed her hands, of which she retained the free use, in making lace and altar linen. See letters to Françoise de Bourdon.

CHAPTER III.

PERSECUTION.

The eight years just described—years of solitude, of daily Communion, of almost uninterrupted intercourse with heaven—seemed to have been given to the Servant of God to prepare her for new and more terrible trials. In 1789 the storm of the Revolution burst over France, and in July 1790 the National Assembly voted the Civil Constitution of the Clergy, an act virtually annulling the authority of the Catholic Church. Exile, imprisonment or death were the fate of those faithful pastors who refused to take the oath of submission to the Civil power. In order to be able still to minister to his flock, the venerable Curé Cuvilly was obliged, like so many others, to seek safety in concealment. For six months his hiding-place was a kind of dark hole behind a hen-house. From this he ventured out at night to fulfil his priestly duties, and many a time his mass was said in the little home of Julie Billiart. But he was too well known to be able long to elude the vigilance of his enemies. Though but in charge of a poor country mission, his eloquence had made him a name, and every year he was invited to Paris to preach at Mont-Valérien, where the celebrated Calvary attracted a crowd of pilgrims, his own parish being confided during his absence to the Canons of the Collegiate Church of Rollot. At Mont-Valérien, then, he took refuge, and here very shortly afterwards he died.

His place at Cuvilly was taken by one of the schismatic priests. This unhappy man tried in the beginning to pay visits to the holy invalid, but Julie, strong in her faith, refused all communication with the intruder, and so great was the ascendency which her holiness gave her over others, that many a wavering soul was preserved from schism by her words and example. "We must pray much for him," she would say with characteristic charity, "that God may open his eyes." M. d'Héry, who is our authority for these facts, adds the following remarkable words:— "Julie has left behind her the reputation of a person whose faith was her very life, and she did much to preserve it intact among the people during the troubles of the French Revolution. It is to her happy influence that, on the re-opening of the churches, the faith of her part of the country is to be attributed. I have often heard of her zeal for the salvation of souls,—a zeal which showed itself in her practice of explaining Christian Doctrine, and in her efforts to maintain souls in the true faith at the epoch of the constitutional schism." At the same time that she thus supported the weak, Julie helped to conceal in their midst several good priests and managed the meetings between them and their distressed people.

This was more than enough to enrage the Republican party against her. Their threats were too significant to be mistaken, and Madame de Pont-l'Abbé, who was much attached to Julie, trembling for her safety, besought her to seek shelter in her own château of Gournay-sur-Aronde. She came herself in her carriage to fetch her dear invalid and the niece Félicité, who had long been her loving attendant and nurse. But Gournay was no very secure refuge. Its noble owner with her virtues and her wealth had too many titles to the hatred of the Republicans to be left in peace. To save her life she was forced to join the stream of émigrés, leaving behind her the friend whose infirmities rendered flight impossible, and whose only chance was to remain at Gournay under the care of a faithful dependent of the family, who was to stay to look after the property.

Meanwhile the enemies of God and of His Church had not lost sight of their intended victim. One evening a great crowd assembled near the gates of the château, and called out fiercely for "la dévote;" they declared she had concealed some refractory priests in the house and that unless she were instantly given up to them they would set the whole place on fire. Already had these misguided wretches torn down in their fury the village Calvary, and with its fragments made a pile whereon they intended to burn at one and the same time the image of their Redeemer and the frail body of His suffering disciple. The concierge hastily warned Julie of her danger. There was no means of concealment in the house, but in a lane near there was an open cart. Thither they carried Julie, laid her at the bottom of it, and covered her with straw. The mob soon forced the gates of the château, streamed into the old quadrangle and through the deserted rooms, still calling for " la dévote." From her hiding-place Julie could hear the savage cries of her pursuers, rendered furious when they returned from their fruitless search, and their foul blasphemies caused her intolerable pain. In later years she acknowledged in confidence that she would willingly have made herself known, and delivered herself up to any torment, if by so doing she could have hoped to prevent the offence against God, and she would regret that she had not been discovered and had thus lost the opportunity of giving her life for her faith. At last the mob, wearied with their own frenzy and somewhat sobered by a timely address from the indignant concierge, took their departure, and Julie's friends hastened to her rescue. There was no question of her re-entering the château— the mob might return at any moment, and it was determined to attempt at all risks an immediate flight to Compiègne.

Félicité got into the cart with her aunt, and they

were driven cautiously along, avoiding the high road and making a long round before they reached the town. Julie arrived there more dead than alive. After they had taken her from under the straw, her conductors thought that they had done enough, and, trembling for their own safety, they hurried back to Gournay. She was left alone in the courtyard of an inn, unable to move a step, knowing no one, and compelled to pass the long winter's night in the open air. It was with great difficulty that Félicité could get her to swallow a little wine. "Meanwhile," says Father Sellier, "she awaited with unalterable patience the moment when Divine Providence should come to her aid; nor was she deceived in her hope." Two kind ladies named Chambon took her into their house and gave her all the care which her condition required. But she did not enjoy their hospitality for long; her name of "la dévote" had followed her, and they became with reason alarmed at the danger to which their guest's reputation for sanctity exposed them. Poor Félicité had to look out for another lodging for her charge. Five times during the three or four years of her stay at Compiègne the Servant of God had to change her abode, being tracked like a wild animal by the ferocious hunters of the Revolution. Her favourite aspiration at this time was this filial complaint, "Lord, wilt Thou not lodge me in Thy Paradise, since I can no longer find a shelter on earth?"

No murmur or shadow of complaint ever escaped her lips. She used to say: "For the few short years of life what matters it where we are ? We are sure to find some little corner to wait in. How happy should we be to resemble our good Master who had not whereon to lay His head. We are surrounded by the dying and the dead ; let us then pray to die to all by universal detachment." And again, "I am in God's hands, and you know now entirely I have abandoned my future to Him. By His grace I feel myself an exile as long as my God wills."

Julie's position during these years was peculiarly trying. The privations which her poverty imposed upon her, the continual state of alarm in which she lived, the shocks of every kind in which she had undergone, caused a great increase in her infirmities. Her nervous system was weakened, her jaws contracted in such a way that she became incapable of uttering a single word without the most violent efforts. She was soon reduced to the necessity of explaining herself by signs. In June 1792 the news reached her of the death of her father, whose end was edifying as his life had been. To add to her grief it was impossible for her to go to Cuvilly to console her mother. But these trials were nothing compared with the long privation of all spiritual help. Accustomed from her childhood to frequent confession and daily Communion, Julie pined away far from the Divine Consoler, who to purify still further her strong and generous soul now withdrew from her all sensible consolation, all the sweetness she had enjoyed in prayer, allowing her to suffer that interior anguish of which all the Saints have tasted the bitterness. But the brave heart never flinched. Already Julie murmured to herself those words which she afterwards repeated so often to her spiritual daughters: "How good is the good God who tries us! Let us live for Him, let us die for Him! If we live by crosses, we shall die of love." *

At last sunshine succeeded the storm. God, who seemed to have forgotten His servant, did not allow her to be tried beyond her strength. His messenger of consolation was the Abbé de Lamarche. This worthy priest was a type of the old French clergy, as remarkable for his learning as he was for his personal character and his virtue. A really extraordinary man, he had that intuitive knowledge of spiritual things which may be called the genius of sanctity. He was commonly believed to be gifted with supernatural light for the guidance of souls. There was about him such an air of holiness that all who knew him venerated him as in very truth a man of God. Hotly pursued during the Reign of Terror, he had escaped the scaffold in a way which he was unable to explain.†

M. de Lamarche can best tell us himself his relations with Julie. "It was not till 1793," he

---

* "Si nous vivons de croix, nous mourrons d'amour."
† Mgr. Baunard, *Life of Madame Barat.*

wrote to the Abbé Belfroy, "that I made the acquaintance of Mère Julie. She had left Cuvilly, her native place, and been taken to Compiègne for greater safety in the troubles which at that time agitated France. I was then ministering to the spiritual needs of some faithful souls who dwelt there, notably the Carmelite nuns. Mère Julie was living in retirement in a small room with one of her nieces who took care of her. I went to visit her; she did not speak, or rather she only spoke by signs. When she went to confession, I had to give her an hour's notice. She then prepared herself with intense fervour, and obtained, as she herself owned to me, the grace of articulating distinctly. It was only after absolution that she fell back into speechlessness. It seemed clear to me that it was by no effort of nature that she was able to express herself in confession, but that she obtained this favour by her lively faith. I saw her from to time for about a year; I was more and more astonished at her progress in perfection. She offered herself continually to God as a victim to appease His anger. Her resignation was perfect; always calm, always united to God, her prayer was, so to speak, unceasing." We find this gift of prayer, which dates from her earliest years, alluded to by all who have left us any details of her interior life.

It was in one of these moments of close union with God that He who makes choice of the weakest instruments for His greatest works manifested His

Will to His humble servant. Julie was one day ravished in ecstasy and saw presented before the eyes of her soul the hill of Calvary. Surrounding our Crucified Lord she beheld a multitude of virgins wearing a religious habit she had never seen before. The vision was so clear, the features of some of the religious so deeply imprinted on her memory, that many years after she was able to say to some of those who offered themselves to be her companions, " God wills that you should enter our Society ; I saw you among Ours at Compiègne." Thus she spoke to Françoise Blin de Bourdon, to console her in her trials ; thus to Marie Blondel to strengthen her in her vocation. When the time came for her to choose a religious dress for her Sisters, without a moment's hesitation she gave orders as to the shape and material to be used ; her tone was very calm and recollected as she said, " It was shown to me at Compiègne." At the close of the heavenly vision Julie heard these words, which explained to her what she had seen : " Behold the spiritual daughters whom I give to you in the Institute which will be marked by My Cross."

Meantime the Reign of Terror began, and the worst excesses of the Revolution were perpetrated. In July 1793 came the martyrdom of those dear Carmelites whom she loved to call her true Mothers. They had been taken to Paris to await their fate in the Conciergerie, and the faithful Abbé de Lamarche had followed them in disguise. The whole community of sixteen religious, with their Prioress, who was over eighty, at their head, were led together to the guillotine. As they left the doors of the Conciergerie, they began to chant the *Salve Regina*, and continued singing as they went along the streets; and the strain never ceased till the head of the last of their number had fallen under the axe. The aged mother Prioress, like the mother of the Machabees, saw all her community one after another fall in death, and when her own turn came, assisted by one of the gendarmes, she mounted the scaffold with unfaltering step and laid her venerable head upon the block. The good Abbé de Lamarche was with them to the last. Standing at the foot of the scaffold in his disguise, as each daughter of St. Teresa ascended the fatal steps, he gave her the last blessing, thus completing his faithful service as chaplain to the Carmelites at Compiègne.* Their heroic death left an impression on the mind of Julie which time was unable to efface. Long years afterwards in her spiritual conferences it was her delight to place before her daughters the example of these generous victims of the Revolution, and to praise their courage and their faith.

But the cup of Julie's afflictions was filled to the brim when in 1794 she learned the tragic fate of the Counts d'Arlincourt and Baudoin, the father and the husband of one of the staunchest of her noble

---

* M. de Lamarche spent the latter part of his life at Clermont and died at Beauvais in 1827.

friends. The Count d'Arlincourt, in spite of his eighty-four years and his charity to the poor, was amongst the " Farmers-General " who perished in the hecatomb of which Lavoisier was also a victim. His son-in-law, the Count Baudoin, followed him to the guillotine.

The darkest hour was just before the dawn in the case of Julie Billiart as in that of so many others. She had scarcely recovered from these successive shocks when she received a letter from the Countess Baudoin—her *bonne dame* as she used to call her—begging Julie to go to her. She had reached Amiens in safety with her three daughters; had taken a *quartier* in the house of a noble family; had hired a little set of rooms for Julie and her niece, and she begged her to go and occupy them without delay. In her infirm and suffering condition it seemed to Julie that the removal could hardly be accomplished without a miracle; moreover she felt within herself an unaccountable repugnance to making the attempt. But after a long interior struggle she seemed to see in the reiterated entreaties of her friend an indication of the will of God, and she agreed. A comfortable carriage was at once sent to Compiègne, and Julie set out accompanied by Félicité. They reached Amiens in safety, October 1794. As she passed through Cuvilly, she saw her mother for the last time.

At the corner formed by the Rue des Augustins with the Rue du Soleil there still stands the large house which was once the town residence of the

Viscounts Blin de Bourdon, and in it may still be seen the room so long sanctified by Julie's presence and the little oratory opening out of it, where Mass was so often said throughout those mournful and memorable days. Here for the first time were to meet the humble peasant and the noble lady whom God had destined to be fellow-labourers in the work to which He called them. Before relating how the two foundresses came to know each other, we must go back a few years to learn something of the early life of Françoise Blin, Viscountess de Bourdon.

CHAPTER IV.

JULIE'S FIRST COMPANION.

GÉZAINCOURT, the birthplace and early home of Françoise Blin de Bourdon, is situated towards the north-east of Picardy, near the town of Doullens. The scene of our story is now no longer the sunny, treeless plain of the centre of the province, but a landscape of varied beauty, whose woods are the outskirts of the vast forests of the Ardennes. It is one of those *campagnes ignorées* where deep winding lanes, branching off from the high road on either side, take the traveller to green meadows, plaintive brooks, clumps of ash and alder—a whole world of fields, and trees, and sky, and happy rural life. The village and its castle are nearly hidden in a wooded valley through which the Authie, hardly more than a rivulet, steals its way between banks thick with rushes and yellow iris. The old manorial dwelling has been replaced by a modern edifice, but a picture at the Mother House, Namur, shows us the Château de Gézaincourt just as it was when Mlle. de Bourdon inhabited it.

At the time of which we write, its owner was the Baron de Fouquesolles, into whose family the estate came in 1698. One of his daughters

FRANCOISE, VICOMTESSE BLIN DE BOURDON.

[*To face p. 8.*

married the Viscount Blin de Bourdon. The parents of Françoise, therefore, were Pierre-Louis de Blin, Viscount of Domart-en-Ponthieu, and Marie-Louise-Claudine, daughter of the Baron de Fouquesolles, Viscount of Doullens. She was their third and youngest child, born at Gézaincourt on March 8, 1756. The following day, the feast of S. Frances of Rome, she received in baptism the names of Marie-Louise-Françoise. Her grandmother held her at the baptismal font, and soon became so attached to the child that she could not bear to part with her. Accordingly it was agreed that she should be brought up by Madame de Fouquesolles, and the estate of Gézaincourt was settled upon her there and then. For this reason, up to the time of the French Revolution, Françoise Blin de Bourdon was always addressed as "Mlle. de Gézaincourt."

Every tradition which has come down to us of the childhood of Françoise points to the admirable training she received and the special graces that surrounded her in that truly Christian home. Her grandmother was not only the benevolent châtelaine, loved as a mother by all her dependents, but she was also the "valiant woman," the type of a Christian gentlewoman of the olden days of France. She had received her little god-daughter as a tender plant to be reared up for Heaven, and her training was as firm as it was wise. Françoise was not more than four or five years old when she gave tokens of the impressions produced thus early on her childish mind. Her grandmother had given her a pair of shoes ornamented with the large rosettes of the period, and the child spoilt them by running near the lake in the park. When Mlle. Ursule, the governess, was lamenting over the fallen splendour of the rosettes, and reproving the little girl, Françoise answered: "It is no sin to spoil rosettes, so why should you care about it?" Another day she was stung by a wasp and screamed aloud with the pain, whereupon Mlle. Ursule told her that she had much better be quiet and suffer the pain for her sins. "I have not committed any sins yet," was the quick reply, "but," drying her tears, "I will stop crying for the love of Jesus."

The character of Françoise was a strong one, and it needed all the intelligent firmness of her watchful guide to subdue, without injuring or embittering, that rich and ardent nature. Several characteristic traits are related of the child's determined will. Her grandmother found her one day disobeying her governess, and as a punishment told her to go to the top of the stairs and remain on the landing till sent for. "If I go there, I shall scream so loud that you will not leave me." She knew the Baroness's objection to a noise. "Go all the same." Françoise went up a few steps and began screaming. "Go up

to the top," was the only reply, "and stand on
the landing as you were told." The child walked
up repeating, "I shall not stay, I shall make
too much noise." When she got to the landing,
she set up shrieking at the top of her voice, till
the poor Baroness, terrified lest she should hurt
her chest, sent the governess to bring her down.
Françoise triumphantly exclaimed, "I told you
I would scream." Mme. de Fouquesolles knew
how to touch the child's better nature. She called
her to her side and spoke to her gently and
seriously of the Holy Child of Nazareth, how He
obeyed and how sad He was when children were
naughty. The tears soon stood in the little one's
eyes. "Don't be vexed, grandmamma, I will not
make the little Jesus sad. I am going back to
the landing." She then returned to the stairs
without another word, and stood for half-an-hour,
"to make up," she said, "for displeasing the
little Jesus." Another day she was taken to see
the Carmelite nuns. The sisters at the "turn"
amused themselves by putting her in it. She
stamped her little foot and said, "The good God
is not pleased when nuns tease little children.
Grandmamma gives me a penance when I am
naughty, and I will give you one, to take me
into the Convent and play with me for three
days."

Françoise had been told not to walk on a certain
terrace in the park, and she was bent on going

to the forbidden spot, probably because it was forbidden. She went, and was immediately sent for by her grandmother to be punished. No sooner was the punishment over than the culprit returned to the terrace, exclaiming, "I like to go, and I shall go again because I like." Six times did the patient grandmother repeat the penance, and at last the wilful child gave in. She was conquered once and for ever, and the story was one she was wont to tell her spiritual daughters in her old age, to show, she said, what bad dispositions she had when she was young.

She was but six years old when she made her first confession and was much surprised at having only two *Paters* for her penance. Her grandmother, she said, would have given her a a great deal more. Mlle. Ursule explained that the Precious Blood applied in the Sacrament satisfied abundantly for her sins. "Then let me go again," she answered, "only what can one say the second time? Do people offend the good God again when He has once pardoned them?" It is recorded, in fact, that from this time her attendants never had to reprove her for any obstinate act of disobedience.

The little Baroness was always well managed by her grandmother, but the numerous relations and friends who came to stay at Gézaincourt in the summer were not equally judicious. Their admiration of the child's beauty, grace and wit, and their praises and caresses might easily have turned the little girl's head. Madame de Fouquesolles prudently resolved to send her away to a convent school, and she confided her treasure to the Benedictine nuns of the Abbey of St. Michael at Doullens. Each winter, however, when the château was deserted by its visitors, she sent for Françoise, and kept her with her till the return of spring, when she took her back regularly to the Convent. It was there that Mlle. de Gézaincourt made her first Communion, and she often spoke in later years of the grace it had been to her to be prepared for that supreme act in a religious house. Soon after this she was sent to finish her education under the Ursulines at Amiens.

When she was nineteen, Mlle. de Gézaincourt was claimed by her parents, and lived some years with them at Bourdon and at Amiens. She made her début in society and was introduced into the highest circles of Paris. She was presented at court—the court of Louis XVI. and Marie-Antoinette—and was particularly noticed by the King's sister, the saintly Mme. Elizabeth. The world was at her feet with all that was most alluring and fascinating.

The young Baroness was dazzled, but it was only for a very short time. We have not many details of this period of her life—we only know that she refused several brilliant offers of marriage, giving her family the impression that she was cherishing a religious vocation. Her own notes furnish this short entry:—" 1783. Imperfect light, half conversion."

Just at this time a serious accident happened to her mother; the Viscountess fell from her carriage, a lingering illness supervened, and Françoise took up her place by the bedside of her suffering parent for ten long months. On April 2, 1784, surrounded by her husband and children, the good Viscountess peacefully gave up her soul to God.

Only five weeks previously, at Gézaincourt, the tomb had closed over the mortal remains of the Baron de Fouquesolles, and his widow, crushed by the double blow which deprived her nearly at the same time of her husband and her only child, begged that her granddaughter might return to her. M. de Bourdon was not alone. His eldest girl, Marie-Aimée, had married, but he had with him his son and daughter-in-law with their little boy. So Mlle. Françoise returned to her old home in the early spring of 1784. She was no longer the bright girl who had left it so light of heart seven years before, but the earnest thoughtful woman who had deliberately chosen her path and had devoted her life to the service of God and of His poor. "The dawn of her conversion," as she called it, had turned into day, and we find in her notes of this time, "Conversion entire, unchangeable resolution to avoid everything which might lead me away from my end." Her duties alone detained her in that world which never possessed her heart. Her path was clear before her; she had two special claims on her time, her grandmother, now over seventy, and in failing health, and the tenants on the estate. She took up again the occupation which had been dear to her in her girlhood, and for ten years lived a life of uninterrupted usefulness, which is still spoken of at Gézaincourt. The details recorded here are many of them taken from the account of a venerable octogenarian, Flore Delhomel, seen and conversed with by a traveller who visited the spot in 1879. "La bonne demoiselle," as all Gézaincourt called her, was an example to everyone by her piety and fervour. Her frequent communions were particularly remarked in a district of Picardy which still retained traces of the influence of Jansenism. She spent a considerable portion of each day in prayer, and on Sundays scarcely left the Church. It was her delight to act as sacristan; she dressed the altar, prepared the vestments and contributed both by her taste and liberality to the beauty of God's house. The feast of her special devotion was the "Fête-Dieu" or Corpus Christi, and she organized the procession of that day with minute and loving care. All the altars on the road taken by the Most Holy were richly adorned by her hands, and the *reposoir* at the château was entirely her own work.

Next to her religious duties was the care of the poor. Accompanied by the faithful Ursule, she visited the sick, herself preparing their remedies and dressing their wounds. Flore Delhomel, who, though in her ninetieth year, seemed to recollect everything as if it had happened yesterday, declared that the "bonne demoiselle" had special skill in curing burns and scalds. When she herself was in her infancy, she had her arm very badly scalded, and her mother took her at once to the castle. Mlle. de Gézaincourt kept the little one with her in order to attend to her constantly and gave her back to her mother quite cured. Such was her reputation for domestic surgery that people came to her from all the country round, and all went away blessing the gentle hand that dispensed their remedies so skilfully, and dressed their sores so tenderly. Flore spoke of a well remembered press, where she kept her medicines and ointments, many of which she made up herself. There was a little sheltered parterre near the house which went by the name of "Mademoiselle's garden." She had her own set of tools, and was often found by those who came to her for advice with her trowel in hand. Mademoiselle's garden was gay with the fragrant blossoms she gathered to adorn the chapel and to brighten her grandmother's sitting-room, roses and carnations and lavender and mignonette, but one side of it was set apart for medicinal herbs—basil and sweet marjoram, mallow and coltsfoot, yarrow and feverfew—which the same delicate fingers prepared for her sick poor.

It must not be supposed, however, that Françoise saw no more of the outer world than the peasantry on her own estate. The summer brought her father, her brother and sister with their children, and there was still an annual succession of visitors from Paris and from Amiens, while the neighbouring families often had social gatherings at the château, one feature of which was a noted bowling green, which it was fashionable to frequent for games of tennis. At these re-unions Mlle. de Gézaincourt bore her part with simple dignity. But if she was present at amusements it was only for the sake of others, and whenever she could do so without being noticed, she stole away to her oratory or to her poor.

It may be asked if the pilgrim who visited Gézaincourt in 1879 saw any vestiges of the gracious life led there a century ago. Alas! very few traces remain. The ancestral towers of the de Fouquesolles have disappeared to make way for a modern edifice; the oratory where Françoise knelt and prayed has been replaced by a Gothic chapel, built by one of the Blin de Bourdon family; the park has undergone many alterations; "Mademoiselle's garden" has gone; but the lake is still to be seen beside which she played as a child, the swelling hills are there, and the old woods, and the river lapsing in sunlight and in starlight. There are some things that never change!

In the daily round of her duties Mlle. de Gézaincourt took little heed of the stormy events that began to rage around her. The steps by which the Revolution worked itself out to its bitter end, need not be related here. In 1793 the sanguinary tragedy was at its height, and the terrified *noblesse* were abandoning their country to its ruthless destroyers.

It was a cold dark night in January 1794 when

the usually silent valley resounded with tumultuous cries; the castle was threatened, but the attack was warded off by the devoted peasantry. The Curé, warned of the impending danger, gave his first thought to the safety of the Blessed Sacrament. He carried the ciborium to the château and confided the precious deposit to the care of Mlle. de Gézaincourt. No one but Françoise and her grandmother knew the sacred spot where their Lord deigned to hide from His pursuers. The faithful priest fled into the woods, and the guardians of the Blessed Sacrament trusted themselves to It. A few evenings later, Françoise was in prayer at the feet of the Hidden God, when the tumult was renewed, this time close to the castle walls. She opened a window softly and caught the words, "The Republicans are upon us, arm at once!" One of the servants hurried to meet her, saying that the "Agents of the Nation" were below, asking for the Baroness. Mlle. de Gézaincourt turned to dart one look, and with it a fervent prayer, towards the secret tabernacle, then calmly descended to encounter the gendarmes. Struck by her quiet dignity, they muttered with some hesitation that they bore an order to arrest the Baroness de Fouquesolles and herself. While the furious horde who had accompanied them pillaged the castle, Françoise pleaded for her aged relative. Nor did she plead alone. The villagers who had rushed to the rescue with the first weapons they could seize, declared that as long as there was a drop of blood in their veins, their "mothers" should not be taken from them. The "Agents of the Nation" were forced to pause. They consulted together and then made a proposal to Mlle. de Gézaincourt. If the "Citoyenne Blin" would go with them, they would leave Mme. de Fouquesolles alone, but the peasants must be disarmed and she must hide her departure from them. These hard conditions were accepted. Françoise advanced towards her loyal dependents, thanked them and assured them that their benefactress should not be taken from them. They would oblige her now by retiring, as all had been peaceably arranged. After the poor villagers had taken a reluctant leave, the gendarmes waited till all was quiet, and, at one o'clock in the morning, gave the order to start. Françoise was carried off in an open cart drawn by two plough horses. A faithful man-servant followed at some distance, in spite of the the threats of the gendarmes. The captive ventured to ask whither they were taking her: the only answer was that she was "under the protection of the nation." For a few moments, she afterwards related, the full horror of her situation presented itself to her mind—a violent death was before her, and she felt all the revolt of nature and all the bitterness of a real agony. But this was immediately succeeeded by a feeling of trust in God. She put herself into His hands whether for life or death, and offered herself and her family, the other members of which she justly supposed to be in the same critical position, to the good pleasure of God. When her sacrifice was made, a feeling of profound peace took possession of her soul and the rest of the journey seemed to her no more than an ordinary drive.

Early next morning the party arrived at the gates of Amiens and proceeded at once to a large building used as a house of detention for prisoners, in the Rue de la Marine. On entering "La Providence" Françoise learned that her whole family had been arrested and that her father and her brother with his wife and child were all prisoners. Her entreaties to see them were harshly silenced, and she was thrown into a wretched garret, where the miserable captives were huddled together without distinction of rank or age. Every day the cruel jailer roughly announced to the prisoners the execution of some of their nearest and dearest relatives. No one knew whose turn was to come next. Throughout those terrible days Françoise acted as an angel of consolation. She prayed and wept with the mourners, she poured into their hearts the balm of Christian resignation. She tended the sick, and divided amongst them the little delicacies which an old servant of the family sometimes contrived to bring to her. Some of these unhappy creatures were actually perishing from starvation, fearing to take the food provided by the jailers, lest it should be poisoned. She herself never complained of any suffering or privation. She owned later on that the physical discomforts of the place made little impression on her, and that her chief trouble had been the distraction and confusion of all around her, disturbing the peace of her soul and interfering with her habit of recollection in God.

But a great sorrow was in store for her. On March 18 she received a letter informing her of her grandmother's death. Madame de Fouquesolles had not been told of her grandchild's arrest at the time, but she asked for her continually, and at last the sad truth was revealed. When the extent of her misery was realized, the Baroness's reason gave way. She refused all nourishment, and whenever anyone tried to persuade her to eat, her answer showed that her thoughts were with the beloved child of years ago: "No, no, I shall wait for *la petite.*" *La petite* never came; her aged relative gradually sank and went finally to await in heaven the grandchild whom she had expected so vainly upon earth.

On account of the crowded state of La Providence notice was given that any of the prisoners who wished it might be removed to Les Carmélites. No one but Mlle. de Gézaincourt asked to make the exchange. "Would you like to know," she used to say in relating the story to her sisters in after years, "how many accepted the offer? Your humble servant, and no one else." She was led to her new prison through the streets of Amiens between two gendarmes with drawn swords. From this time forward the captivity of Françoise was like a continual spiritual retreat. The hardships of her daily life were forgotten in the congenial intercourse she enjoyed with the fervent daughters of St. Teresa, and the hours were divided between prayer and holy conversation. For seven long months did she renew each day the sacrifice of her life, when suddenly came the news of Robespierre's advance towards Amiens. A long list of victims was prepared for the occasion, and at the head stood the names of all the Blin de Bourdon family. Françoise read her own name, with those of her father and brother, in a national journal. We find in her notes: "Accustomed though I was to look death in the face, this certainty of my impending execution, together with the thought of my father and brother, whom I should see only on the scaffold, caused me for a time an agony of pain. The bitterness of death passed over me, but it was soon at an end. The mercy of my God delivered my soul from this anguish, and with the aid of His supporting grace I regained, after a few moments, my usual serenity—only my prayers were longer and more earnest for help in the last awful moment."

She was heard in a way she had little expected. Robespierre, instead of setting out for Amiens, had fallen in his turn, and the Reign of Terror was at an end. By degrees persecution ceased and the prison doors were opened. On August 3, 1794, the young Viscount de Bourdon (Françoise's nephew) came to Les Carmélites. He and his parents were already free, and he brought to his aunt the joyful news that she was restored to liberty. They were all waiting for her, he said, at the Hôtel Blin. It was late in the evening, and the calm, patient aunt answered with that look of quiet resignation which the seven months' waiting for death had imprinted on her features : " To-morrow, my boy, I shall be with your father. I have said my night prayers, and I will stay in my prison till morning." How were the intervening hours spent by Françoise ? In pouring out her soul in prayers of thanksgiving for the marvellous deliverance vouchsafed to herself and her family. The next day she was in the arms of her father, and in the joy of that re-union she forgot all the sorrows that had preceded it. After the first outpourings of joy and tenderness Viscount Blin set out for his château at Bourdon, but Françoise remained for a year at Amiens in the family mansion of her brother. Here it was that the Countess Baudoin introduced her to Julie Billiart.

And thus met the threads of those two lives, outwardly so different, inwardly so like—lives kept pure in childhood by the sweet love of Christ, made strong in maturer years by His Cross. He whose hand held the warp and the woof was about to weave them indissolubly together.

CHAPTER V.

THE HÔTEL BLIN DE BOURDON.

How many beautiful meetings have been recorded in the history of the saints! St. Dominic and St. Francis, St. Ignatius and St. Francis Xavier, St. Teresa and St. John of the Cross—souls thrown across each other's paths, apparently by chance, but to those who read aright the workings of God's providence, brought together by His hand for the fulfilment of His eternal designs. The biographer of Julie Billiart loves to linger over that meeting between the two foundresses at the Hôtel Blin in the October of 1794.

Françoise was now about thirty-eight years old, and her thoughtful countenance bore the impress of that deep peace which comes of long suffering endured for God. Julie was at once irresistibly and supernaturally drawn to her. But to the Viscountess herself visits to an invalid whose obstructed speech rendered conversation almost impossible did not at first promise much attraction, and after the death of the Servant of God she many a time confessed that in the beginning she had even to fight against a certain repugnance with which the poor sufferer inspired her. But it was not for long. By degrees, as she tells us in her memoirs, she began to love her visits to the little room, where Julie sometimes passed whole days in solitude; for Félicité was obliged to go out to make the necessary purchases and to sell her work. She read to her, prayed with her, watched her unalterable patience and resignation, and daily learned more of her beautiful soul, her burning love for God and her wonderful prayer. The sojourn of Françoise among the Carmelites had inspired her with a wish to become a daughter of St. Teresa, and she now placed herself under the guidance of Julie, in order to learn from her how to advance in the exercises of the contemplative life.

It was not long before the circle at the Hôtel Blin was completed by the arrival of the holy and learned Father Thomas, afterwards one of the Fathers of the Faith* and eventually a Jesuit. The Abbé Antoine Thomas was a doctor of the Sorbonne, and an old acquaintance of Mme. Baudoin. Arrested during the Terror and imprisoned at Arras, he was already on the list for execution when a dangerous illness caused his sentence to be deferred. In the interval came the fall of Robespierre, and the consequent escape of many of the condemned. The Abbé Thomas fled to Amiens, and was soon found out by Mme. Baudoin and introduced to the Viscount Bourdon. His liberty, however, was still in danger, for, though the

---

* This association, first known as the Society of the Sacred Heart, was formed in Belgium by certain young ecclesiastics, at whose head was the Abbé de Tournély. Their design was to keep alive, under another name, the rule and spirit of the Society of Jesus. The greater number of the Fathers joined the latter Order on its re-establishment.

Terror was over, priests were pursued with unrelenting activity. "The greatest precaution was necessary, and the good Abbé was obliged to conceal his name, his priestly character, and often his person."* Having accepted the hospitality of the Viscount, he now secretly acted as chaplain to the little band of chosen souls in the Hôtel Blin. An altar was soon arranged in the room of Julie; here the Abbé offered the holy sacrifice and gave daily communion to the invalid. The altar was taken down for precaution's sake immediately after Mass.

Françoise de Bourdon and Mme. Baudoin were not the only visitors to the sick room. Lise Baudoin, a bright eager girl of about eighteen, had formed a warm attachment for her mother's friend. With her came four of her companions, girls of her own age and rank,—Josephine and Gabrielle Doria, Jeanne and Aglaé du Fos de Méry. They were all intimate friends of Mlle. Blin, whose piety and good works they shared, and like her they placed themselves under the direction of Father Thomas. Young, ardent and enthusiastic, with their girlish aspirations chastened and subdued by the troubles of the times, their hearts seem to have gone out to Julie with childlike affection. Holiness acts like a magnet, and it is certainly a striking witness to Julie's power over souls that these high-born girls should all have put themselves under her spiritual guidance. By her bedside they prayed and meditated together,

* Memoirs of Mère Blin de Bourdon.

recited the Divine Office, silenced in so many monasteries by the Revolution, and worked for the Church and for the poor. They had chosen as patroness and model her whose sweet name was to be that of the Institute which the little family prefigured. We find in Mère Blin de Bourdon's notes an act of consecration to our Lady in her own handwriting, dated March 25, 1795, the feast of the Annunciation; another to St. Joseph, April 19,* and finally one to the Sacred Heart of Jesus, July 2, the feast of the Visitation, of the same year. This last, signed like the preceding ones, " Marie-Louise-Françoise Blin," is the act attributed by some writers to Blessed Margaret Mary herself : " I give and consecrate to the Sacred Heart of our Lord Jesus Christ my person and my life, my actions, pains and sufferings."† There is another act of consecration to the Sacred Heart, in the handwriting of Mère Julie, which is preserved by the Institute of the Sisters of Notre-Dame with filial affection. It contains the vow to propagate the devotion to the Divine Heart of our Lord and an offering to the Sacred Heart of Mary with the vow to spread the cultus of the Immaculate Conception. The document is undated, but tradition assigns it to December 8, 1794. This act of consecration, known to the public by many thousands of leaflets, was in 1881 enriched with indulgences by Cardinal Dechamps, whose approbation fixes the date attributed

* In 1795 in the diocese of Amiens the feast of St. Joseph was transferred to April 19, March 19 occurring in Holy week.
† See Père Croiset on Devotion to the Sacred Heart.

to it. The recent promulgation of the Bull *Auctorem fidei*, which put an end to all controversy on the subject of devotion to the Sacred Heart, may have had something to do with this increase of generous love for the Heart of Jesus to which the servant of God had already consecrated herself in her very childhood. Affiliated by the Abbé Thomas to the *Pious Association of those devoted to the Sacred Heart in the Holy Sacrament of the Altar,** she wrote with her own hand: " I, M.-R.-Julie Billiart, inscribe myself with all my heart in the confederation of love formed in honour of the Sacred Heart of Jesus." †

Mlle. Blin, being obliged to reside, from 1795 to 1797, sometimes at Gézaincourt and sometimes at Bourdon, only stayed in Amiens at intervals, but she was in constant communication with her spiritual mother, whom she consulted on all occasions. This circumstance led to a correspondence, of which thirty-three letters of the Venerable mother still remain to us. Françoise treasured these letters all her life, and when dying bequeathed them to her daughters. The greater number are autograph, but a few, which contained matters relating to family affairs, have been copied and abridged by Françoise herself. Nothing reveals more fully than this correspondence the soul of Julie, and the religious affection which

---

* Canonically erected at Rome in the parish church of St. Lawrence of the Hill by a rescript of Pope Pius VI., January 6, 1790.

† The original is preserved in the archives of the Mother House at Namur.

united her with her whom she loved to call her
"eldest daughter." "Ah, my dear good lady," she
writes on July 5, " what a balm your letter was to
my heart! I can never tell you how much our separation costs me; yet, by God's grace, I am resigned
and willing to make any sacrifice He asks of me.
I confess I was on the point of being the first to
write, so keenly did I feel your leaving, but I tried
to make a sacrifice to our good God, though I
thought continually of you, and kept thanking Him
for letting me know you. Every day at the
precious moment of Holy Communion I meet my
good friend in our Lord—for I cannot call you
otherwise; you know that it is in God and for
God that I love you so tenderly. I thought of
you very often during your journey; how the
works of the Creator must have raised your soul to
Him! I thank our good God for the favour He
has done you of finding means to make your meditation. You gave me the greatest pleasure by telling
me a little about it. That you may daily advance
in that holy exercise is the grace I ask for you from
our Lord, for it is thus that God fashions His saints.
Oh yes, that we may both be saints! that is what
I beg of Him. I have had no news from Father
Thomas since he went away. I do not know whether
he is alive or dead, but certainly he is not leaving
Montdidier at present. So you see, my dear friend,
that I am quite alone with God alone. Ask Him,
oh! ask Him to grant me grace to wish for nothing

else in the world but this precious treasure—God alone, God alone for ever!"

A fortnight later Father Thomas is back, and Julie announces to Françoise that she hopes to renew with him on the first Friday of the month the act of consecration to the Sacred Heart, reminding her friend to do the same. "You know it is in that blessed refuge, the Heart of Jesus, that we must meet;" and later, thanking her for some little presents: "You know where I place all my gratitude towards the instrument of Divine Providence in my regard? Ah, it is in the Heart of our dear and sweet Jesus that I lay up all your acts of charity so that none may be lost."

The public practices of Catholic worship were still forbidden by law in France. In the country, however, people had more liberty, and non-juring priests said Mass in the churches and chapels, and administered the sacraments to the faithful, whenever they could. Nevertheless Mlle. Blin's frequent Communions at Bourdon drew upon her some criticism, and in one of her letters she half acknowledges to Julie that she is not altogether free from human respect on this point. The servant of God answers on August 16: "I am confident that with God's help you will triumph over these petty troubles. . . . Ah, my dear good friend, what harm can a few mortal eyes do us? If those people only knew Him who gives Himself to us so lovingly, yes, if they only knew *the gift of God*, how they would envy our happiness! Consider it a privilege that God deigns to make use of you to edify the world by your holy example. Courage, my dear good lady." Then she adds with characteristic simplicity: "How grateful I am for all your kindness to me! I am quite ashamed before God that He should give me not only bread but sugar! You wish me to speak to you of my wretched body—it is not worth it, but since you are anxious to know, I will say that it is good for nothing, absolutely good for nothing. I spend whole days, thanks be to God, in great pain, and my nights are sometimes worse. But, my dear good friend, what are my sufferings compared to all that our Lord vouchsafed to suffer for the love of me? When our good God sends me extra pain, I give a share of it to my dear friends in the faith. . . . Mlle. Lise is going on as well as can be; she is becoming more simple. On Thursday last she made a little retreat in my room with the permission of her spiritual father and mine."

How wise are the counsels which her experience gives when, in her turn, Françoise is passing through those interior trials by which God purifies and strengthens His chosen ones! "Yes, my dear friend, this is the true path to Heaven; let us live in the habitual disposition to be victims of God's good pleasure in the different states by which He wills to try us. It is at such times that our Lord expects proofs of our fidelity. You know what we must do in spiritual darkness? *Be ready to bless God at all times*, as the royal psalmist says. You know that the way of prayer is a way of death, especially of death to one's own judgment, which wants to meddle with everything, and arrange everything, even in the spiritual life, after its own fashion. Nothing is more contrary to the spirit of God. However rigorous His conduct towards us may sometimes appear, we know that it is always the conduct of an infinitely wise, just and good Father, who is waiting for His children at the goal to which He leads them by different paths. And then, my dear friend, let us be honest with ourselves. Is it not true that we are quite capable of spoiling the whole work of grace in our souls? So that it is often very good for us to be visited by desolation and abandonment on the part of God. We must just do like little children, who on a dark night keep tight hold of the hand of father or mother and let themselves be led where they will. I bless our good God that all the states of soul through which He wills you to pass do not deter you from making your daily meditation; that perseverance will bring down upon you great graces."

Other difficulties Julie's strong faith and staunch loyalty to the Church settled with equal clearness and authority. The villagers both at Gézaincourt and Bourdon had sunk, since the expulsion of the clergy, into lamentable ignorance, and for a moment Françoise, in the face of their deplorable condition, hesitated as to whether it were not better to let them attend the churches served by the constitutional priests than to be thus entirely deprived of religious instruction. At once Julie answers her: "So they tell you it is better to be a schismatic than to be in such brutish ignorance. My good friend, those who speak thus do not consider that to attend the instructions of a priest who has taken the oath is to put oneself out of the true Church. Now we cannot in conscience leave our brethren in error. Without a moment's hesitation, then, you must say to the mothers of families and others who consult you, whether on their own account or with regard to the education of their children, that no one can in conscience go to the sermons of schismatic priests any more than to their mass, that they have left the bosom of the Church, and that those who follow them are also out of the Church and consequently out of the way of salvation. They tell you it is better to be in schism than in brutish ignorance! But, make it clearly understood, that those good souls who are in the impossibility of having legitimate pastors will not be held responsible for their want of instruction. God will not require more of them. Let them remain all their lives, if you will, without teaching and without mass—they will not be out of the way of salvation. If they are in good faith, God will sooner send them an angel from heaven than allow them to perish. They tell you, my dear friend, that these things are obscure, difficult to harmonize; but please remark that in matters of faith there can be no contradiction. The Church has condemned those who desert from the Catholic, Apostolic and Roman faith; so we have no need of further information on that score. The whole difficulty in point reduces itself to knowing what you have to answer when honest folk question you. This is the opinion of our Reverend Father. Since you say they are absolutely in the dark about the matter, you must prudently explain that they do wrong in listening to the intruder, and lead them gently and gradually to the knowledge of the truth. He says that when a wrong idea about doctrine has once got into their heads, it is very hard to get it out again. And does not *The Imitation of Christ* tell us that there is more good to be got from a poor ignorant peasant than from a proud philosopher full of his own conceits?"

Was not Mère Blin de Bourdon right when, long years after, she invoked Julie Billiart as "virgin diligent in prayer," "sure guide in the path of perfection," "zealous promoter of the greater glory of God and the salvation of souls!"

And now the last ties which bound these two souls to earth were to be broken, that perfect detachment might leave them free for the work of God. Early in September, 1795, Julie wrote to Mlle. Blin: "Félicité is leaving to-day for my old home. Yesterday I had a letter from my brother to say that my poor mother is very ill. He tells me he feels quite forsaken. I am sending him the little that remains to me out of what Providence gave me through you. I will write to you while my little girl is away." And a few days later: "I have lost my poor dear mother. You will understand what my heart feels, though, by God's grace, it is perfectly submissive to the decrees of His Providence. It is by successive sacrifices that He means me to belong to Him, to Him alone. Beg of Him then that I may be immolated to the good pleasure of our Divine Master."

It was not long before a similar cross was laid on Françoise. The Viscount Blin de Bourdon was approaching his ninetieth year. Upright and honourable, he was satisfied with showing himself a perfect gentleman, and stood on the brink of the grave with no thought of God or eternity. The doctrines of the new "Philosophers," whose books filled his library, had darkened his intellect and chilled the faith in his heart. But his daughter had resolved to win him a happy death, and while during these two years she lavished on him every mark of filial affection, incessant prayers and acts of sacrifice went up for him to the throne of God, not only from her own heart but from that of her saintly friend at Amiens. The latter multiplies at this time her counsels of prudence and patience. "Who knows, my good friend, the moments of God? Let us not grow weary of waiting for the Lord, who has waited so long for us. Ah, how good He is!" And again: "God's work in souls is done very gradually; we must not want to outrun grace. A word, a mark of affection, may sometimes do much. Charity will suggest to you a thousand little expedients. Say a few words as if by chance, Providence will bless them. . . To-day after

Holy Communion God brought you before me—you and your dear father, in a very special way, and I was filled with confidence that He would grant you what you are asking Him in the name of His Divine Son. Courage and confidence!" At last the aged nobleman yielded to the loving persistence of his daughter. He returned loyally and wholly to his faith and to his God, received the last sacraments with devotion, and on February 1, 1797, died peacefully, surrounded by his children, in the ninety-first year of his age. Julie writes: "So, my dear child, our good God has at last taken your father to Himself. May our Lord have mercy on him and grant him peace. . . . The goodness of the Lord is an unfathomable abyss."

Not long before, Mme. Baudoin's chequered life had also come to a close. She died full of years and good works, assisted by the prayers of the Servant of God and the ministrations of Father Thomas, and with her last breath commended her Lise to Julie's maternal care. During these two years of more or less continued absence Françoise had seized every opportunity of returning to Amiens to refresh her soul. In 1796 we find her going through the Spiritual Exercises of St. Ignatius for the full space of thirty days under the guidance of Father Thomas. She gave her director an exact account of her meditations, and each day noted down the lights received and the resolutions formed. The journal of this retreat has been preserved, and shows a soul already far on in the way of perfection. The Viscount's death now left her free to return to Amiens for good, and resisting all the entreaties of her brother and his wife, who, warmly attached to her, were eager to keep her with them, she hastened back to the house in the Rue des Augustins. And now this little group of Julie's first disciples organized itself into a species of community, " which gave," says Mère Blin, to whom we owe the details of these early Amiens days, " great edification to the world. They punctually followed a simple rule of life, chanted the office of our Lady, lived in common, and called Julie *Ma Mère*." The rule in question had been drawn up by Father Thomas, who was intimately acquainted with all the six associates, and without whose advice Julie did nothing. The Constitution of the year III. had re-adjusted religious affairs, and in the comparative tranquillity which Amiens now enjoyed it became possible to add to the exercises of the contemplative life works of active charity, to visit the poor and the sick, and to teach the ignorant. Churches and chapels were now once again thrown open, and on August 6, 1797, the Bishop of Saint-Papoul, Mgr. Simon de Maillé, gave confirmation to large numbers in the Church of Saint-Remi. After the ceremony the prelate paid a visit to the little community in the Hôtel Blin, again administering the sacrament in the very room of Mère Julie. The incident shows the universal esteem in which she was held, but it is memorable for another reason. Among the children who received the Holy Spirit by the bedside of the

Servant of God was one destined to be the father of a martyr. This was Isidore Nicholas Daveluy, whose son became coadjutor bishop of Corea and was beheaded for his faith in 1866.

It might indeed have seemed that Julie had now around her the nucleus of that Society which she had seen beneath the cross at Compiègne. But it was not so; and it is noteworthy that though she appears to have known clearly that she was destined to work with others for the salvation of souls, she had no intention at this time of founding a new congregation. " One step enough for me," was all through life her motto, and God had not yet made His voice clearly heard. Nay, He seemed—as He so often does seem to our human eyes—to scatter the seeds just as they were beginning to grow. One by one the five young girls were drawn from Julie's side into other paths. Lise Baudoin was the first to go. Of an excessively sensitive temperament, she passed quickly from one extreme to the other, and Julie's letters allude more than once to her " ups and downs." At one and the same moment attracted by the world and drawn to God, she now yielded to her passionate attachment for a married sister in Paris, who was bent on having her to live with her. They had scarcely been re-united three days, when Lise saw her dearly loved sister snatched suddenly from her by death. But she never renewed the ties with Amiens, which she had so hastily broken. She spent some years in indecision, and died while yet young. Jeanne de Méry made a brilliant marriage, becoming the wife of the Marquis Ignatius de Ferretti, of the family of Pius IX. Aglaè never married. The two Dorias seem to have turned to good account Mère Julie's lessons. Gabrielle married the Count de Cornulier and led a retired life, carrying out the good works begun at Amiens and beloved by all the poor on her estates. Josephine Doria spent two more years with Mère Julie and finally entered the Order of the Visitation. The following extract from the Annals of the Convent at Boulogne, where she died, is interesting as showing the effect of Mère Julie's influence: " God in His love for our sister, (Josephine Doria) gave her an admirable guide in the virtuous Mère Julie Billiart. Hundreds of times this inspired soul repeated to her both by word of mouth and by letter that her perfection depended on the Cross, that she must expect to lead a dying life, that a Spouse of Jesus Christ has no other pledge of His love than crosses, contradictions, humiliations: in fine this good mother was never weary of encouraging her disciple in the road to this mystic death by showing her its advantages and reminding her of the strength which God's graces and His love would give her, in order to attain it."

The peaceful days at Amiens were soon rudely interrupted. The law of September 4, 1797, inaugurated the odious régime which has been aptly termed *Terreur à froid*. Once more priests were required to take the oath of hatred to royalty, and those who refused were hunted, imprisoned, transported to the

Ile-de-Rhé or to Cayenne and treated with the utmost rigour. The very day after the promulgation of the law, the municipal authorities at Amiens were dismissed, as infected with royalist principles, and making common cause with the refractory clergy. The churches of St.-Germain and St.-Remi were closed, domiciliary visits were multiplied, and towards the end of the same year six priests were shut up in the prison of Bicêtre. Father Thomas was of course the object of active search. Twice was the Hôtel Blin ransacked from top to bottom without success,—a third time the man of God only escaped by a kind of miracle. It was night and he had already gone to bed when the alarm came, so that he had not time to reach his hiding place before his pursuers were upon him. He hurried, however, to a hay-loft above the stables, but was perceived by the gendarmes as he climbed the ladder and prevented from drawing it after him. "I've caught my bird!" shouted the half-intoxicated republican, "you shan't escape this time, *calotin*." Just at that moment the man's candle providentially fell and went out—the Abbé leapt boldly over him as he stooped to pick it up, and succeeded, he hardly knew how, in gaining his hiding-place. The infuriated band searched the whole house in vain, and at last were forced to withdraw, swearing that it would not be long before they renewed the attack. Julie and Françoise had passed that terrible night in earnest prayer for their spiritual guide, and as soon as morning dawned a consultation was held as to the means to be adopted for the safety of the Abbé and a more secure retreat for themselves. Gertrude Doria possessed a small estate at Bettencourt, and this she now placed at Julie's disposal. Thither the servant of God was removed, accompanied by the Abbé Thomas, Françoise de Bourdon and the faithful Félicité, on the night of June 16, 1799.

CHAPTER VI.

LAYING THE FOUNDATIONS.

CUVILLY, Amiens and Bettencourt—these three names are especially linked with the origin of the Institute of the Sisters of Notre-Dame. The Picard village had seen Julie's childish apostolate, her first graces and her first crosses; Amiens had witnessed the meeting of the co-foundresses; but it was at the little hamlet of Bettencourt that the first stone of the edifice was to be definitively laid. Bettencourt-St.-Ouen is a pretty village about twenty miles to the northwest of Amiens. A gently rising ground dotted with homesteads and cottages looks down upon a smiling pastoral valley watered by the Nièvre. Towards the south the hill forms a steep and sudden descent, and the view from the summit is singularly picturesque. The Château of Bettencourt, as it was called, was a quaint seventeenth century house with a high-pitched roof and a double row of dormer windows, a courtyard, and a large garden shut in by high walls. Here Julie was to pass two more years of prayer and of patient suffering. She could afford to wait. More than one passage in the Amiens letters makes it clear that God had shown her the destiny of Françoise Blin de Bourdon linked with her own in some life-work for His glory. "I have always present before my eyes what I once mentioned to you—that God will let me end my days with you. You will have occasion to exercise your zeal together with me." Again, and still more definitely: "As my *eldest daughter*, you will share with me all the mercies of the Lord." "I tell you, my dear child, that God has done me the favour of Himself showing me the line you must follow; keep very exactly to what I tell you." "You must, my dear child, unite yourself to me as closely as possible, so that we may enter into the plans of God's providence over us. I have no sort of doubt that He has some special design in your regard; we will take but one step at a time, consulting each moment the blessed Will of God." Finally, on the death of Viscount de Bourdon: "As soon as I learnt your Father's death, I saw you throw yourself into my arms. And I thought the moment had come when God should give you to me and me to you so strongly that death alone should separate us." Yes, Julie could afford to wait. One of the most remarkable points in her ardent and energetic character, is this pausing for the impulse of God's hand before undertaking any work. She was as strong to wait as she was to act, for both the waiting and the action were born of that beautiful faith of hers, which trusted her "good God" through all trials, and followed Him over all obstacles.

We who have traced Julie's life so far, shall not

be surprised that the cross was to mark the first weeks of her sojourn in her new home. Not only did she fall dangerously ill, but Françoise was attacked by small-pox. The latter, however, speedily recovered; and Julie herself, when once convalescent, became so much stronger that she was able to exchange her bed for an invalid chair. Better still, her speech became freer and her use of it more frequent. Here again obedience obtained what natural remedies had been powerless to effect; Father Thomas used to put questions to her and order her to answer; gradually the power of articulation returned, and though she still often kept silence, she was now quite able to converse with those who visited her. The simple words in which Mère Blin de Bourdon's memoirs record this circumstance would seem to imply a supernatural favour. " Towards the end of her stay at Bettencourt, Father Thomas went to visit his old home in Normandy, and during his absence God restored to our Mother the full use of her speech. She required it more than ever for the instruction of her neighbours." There was indeed plenty to be done. Three months after the death of Pius VI. at Valence, Napoleon's powerful hand delivered France from the yoke of the Directory, and the Church, which her enemies had fondly imagined to have buried together with the last Pope, was once again free. The Abbé Thomas could now fearlessly celebrate his daily mass in the Oratory of the château, and exercise his zeal in a parish long deprived of its pastor.*

While he gave himself to the functions of his ministry and to the instruction of the men of his flock, he entrusted the women and children to Julie and Françoise. Every morning the good priest appeared at an open window of the château, and, armed with a speaking-trumpet, summoned the villagers to Catechism. The first indifference soon gave way before the kindness and devotedness of the missionary and his assistants. Young and old obeyed the call, while the little girls trooped around Julie and Françoise and their mothers stood by, with their infants in their arms, to listen to their lessons. The days of Cuvilly seemed to have come back. These scholars of divers ages learnt not only to know, love and serve the God whom they had forgotten, but to read, to write, to cipher and to do different kinds of needlework. Little rewards were distributed from time to time to the most industrious; and one of these souvenirs, a small statue of the Madonna and Child, delicately carved in bone, may still be seen in the house of an old woman at Bettencourt. In a short time the whole face of the village was changed. One touching story which has come down to us shows how deeply the lessons given had taken root. An old republican, who had been brought back to his duty

---

* M. Trinqui, Curé of Bettencourt, had been forced to fly. He returned later on to his parish and died there in 1807.

by the Abbé Thomas, was reduced to beggary. Every day he began his rounds by calling at the château, and as soon as he had received his alms was always seen to hurry away in the same direction. The Abbé, curious to know the meaning of this, one morning followed him, and saw him stop before an old blind beggar, and respectfully lifting his hat, put into his hand what he had just received. The priest asked the motive of this conduct, and was deeply moved at the beautiful reply. " I take off my hat," said the old republican, " before that man as before the living image of Jesus Christ suffering. I am so glad to be able to give him every morning the first alms sent me by Providence. That old man is more to be pitied than I, and does not deserve his misfortunes as I do."

More than one holy priest—among others Julie's old friend the Abbé de Lamarche—came to Bettencourt from time to time; but one day Father Thomas brought to her a religious whose word was not only to decide the future vocation of the former Doctor of the Sorbonne, but to set afloat the barque of Notre-Dame. Father Varin, superior general of the Fathers of the Faith, had come over on foot from Amiens, whither in 1801 he had been summoned by M. Louis Sellier and the Abbé Corbie, to negotiate the transfer into the hands of his congregation of the Oratory School, which these gentlemen directed. M. Sellier, then a layman, was indeed himself called to the religious life and had already

PÈRE VARIN, S.J.
BORN FEBRUARY 7, 1769; DIED APRIL 19, 1850.
From a Portrait taken shortly before his death.

[To face p. 74.

been accepted by Father Varin. But, like so many others, he hesitated to take the final step, and without precisely wishing to draw back had begged Father Varin to consult on the subject of his vocation his own director Father Thomas, whose decision he promised to regard as final. The result was, as we have said, that not only M. Sellier, but Father Thomas himself, was recruited to the Fathers of the Faith, and hence to the Society of Jesus. But Father Varin had another work to do for God at Bettencourt. His gift of discernment in spiritual things, and his long experience were not slow to discover "the treasures of grace hidden in Julie's simple and generous soul." * Nor did he hesitate in the face of her helpless condition to tell her that she was called to labour for God's glory in a wider field than she had hitherto done. And Julie, though she answered humbly, as Mary to the angel, "How shall this thing be?" like Mary added, "Ecce ancilla Domini." This was not Father Varin's only visit; and each interview, as it made him more intimately acquainted with her lively faith and unshaken trust in God, confirmed him more and more in his belief in her mission, and he ended by giving her a formal order, in the name of God, to undertake the work of the education of youth. And so, as Father Sellier has remarked, he who was at this very time founding with Mme. Barat the Congregation of the Ladies of the Sacred Heart,

* Life of Father Varin, by Father A. Guidée, S.J.

was also chosen by God to be the promoter of the Institute of Notre-Dame. Father Varin himself always looked back with pleasure to the memory of his first meeting with Julie Billiart. Writing in his old age to Mother Blin de Bourdon on the occasion of the death of Father Thomas in 1833, he says, "Oh, how many memories dear to my heart are connected with the time when I first made acquaintance with good Father Thomas! It was at Bettencourt . . . and the good Julie, and her faithful companion, and all the results of that holy friendship formed and blessed by the Lord! Ah no! these things will never be blotted out of my mind, for they belong to the memory of the heart."* Father Thomas, though admitted into the Society of the Fathers of the Faith, was authorised still to direct the little spiritual family which owed him so much; and when, on the re-opening of the churches, private chapels were closed, the new Bishop of Amiens, Mgr. de Villaret, made an exception in Julie's favour. He had stayed at the château when he came to administer Confirmation in the Canton of Picquigny and been touched by her infirm condition.

In the month of February 1803, the little colony once more turned their steps towards Amiens. The villagers wept to see them go, but the seed had been cast in good ground and it has borne its fruit.

* Letter from Laval, dated April 8, 1833. Archives of the Mother House.

Since those days the parish has remained thoroughly Christian, and the people continue to attach to the religious education of their children an importance which, alas! is but too rare in these days. Nor have they forgotten those to whom they owed these sentiments of faith. The memory of Mère Julie and her companion is still held by them in benediction. One of the Witnesses in the Process of Canonization had been parish priest at Bettencourt from 1832 to 1860. He tells us that he had constantly heard Julie spoken of as a saint by those who had known her; and that old men would raise their hats, and fold their hands as if in prayer, when speaking of "Mademoiselle Julie."

The two friends took up temporary quarters in a small and inconvenient house without a garden in the rue du Puits-à-Brandil. Here Julie's parlysed condition gave her much to suffer, but she never left off gathering the children about her for catechism. "That," says Mother Blin de Bourdon, "was her very life." Félicité Degouy, who had been with her aunt since the age of seven, now left to be married; * her place was taken by Constance Blondel, a relation of Father Thomas.

The Fathers of the Faith were giving up the house of the Oratory which was close to the Hôtel de Bourdon, and Julie and Françoise had their eye upon it; but Father Varin destined it for the Ladies of the Sacred Heart and settled the matter by

* She married the schoolmaster at St.-Ouen, M. Thérasse.

writing to Mme. Barat, "Go and see our good
Julie, and tell her from me that the work to which
Our Lord calls her deserves to be bought by some
sacrifices." At last a house was found in the Rue
Neuve, not large, but healthy and more convenient
than the other—fitted moreover by its religious
antecedents for its pious destination. It went by
the name of the *Blue Children's Home* from the
uniform of the orphan boys who had formerly
inhabited it. Behind the high altar of Amiens
Cathedral may be seen the celebrated *Enfant
Pleureur*, a masterpiece of sculpture by Blasses,
which stands over the mausoleum of the founder of
the Orphanage, Canon Lucas. Mary seemed to
throw her mantle over her daughters from the very
outset; it was on the feast of Our Lady ad Nives,
August 5, 1803, that the removal was made to this
house which the Institute looks upon as its cradle.
Mgr. de Villaret's permission still held good, so
that, as Mère Blin affectionately notes, "the chapel
existed before the Community;" and it was thus
rather Our Lord who welcomed His Spouses to their
home than they who offered a new home to Him.
The traditions of the house were renewed, for the
first children confided by Father Varin to Mère
Julie were eight poor little orphans. Three of
these paid a small pension, the others were entirely
supported by the house. The man of God now
urged her to gather round her persons of sound
judgment and of good will, without regard to rank

or fortune. "God," he said, "will bless your apostolic spirit." Mgr. de Villaret took the warmest interest in the work, and Françoise de Bourdon offered to defray the immediate expenses. Once convinced of the Will of God, Julie did not hesitate; and the two foundresses, with those of their old friends the Carmelites who still survived, forthwith began a novena to Our Lady to obtain postulants. The first who presented herself was Catherine Duchâtel of Rheims. She had already been received among the Ladies of the Sacred Heart, but, believing herself called to evangelize the poor, asked for a trial with Mère Julie. Father Varin often sent Mme. Barat to visit Julie in these early days. "Go and see our good Julie and Mlle. Blin for me," he writes on one occasion. "Oh how their patience too is tried! For my part I rejoice in the Lord over their little difficulties. All ground for hope must be taken away from them, that they may hope against hope."

The 2nd day of February 1804 is a day for ever memorable in the Annals of the Institute of Notre-Dame. On that day Father Varin came to say Mass in the chapel of the Rue Neuve. Julie Billiart, Françoise Blin de Bourdon and Catherine Duchâtel received holy Communion at his hands, and in presence of the Blessed Sacrament made or renewed the vow of chastity, to which they added that of devoting themselves to the Christian education of girls. A remarkable note in Mère Blin's memoirs adds another purpose, the importance of which is trebly brought home to us in our own days and in the light of the present work of the Congregation. "They further proposed to train religious teachers who should go wherever their services were asked for; the future extension of the Institute is contained in this resolution formulated by the foundresses at the foot of the altar." Those who trace the workings of the finger of God in human events, will not deem it a mere coincidence that, when half a century later the Sisters of Notre-Dame undertook the direction of the first Catholic Training College for schoolmistresses in England, it was opened on this same feast of Purification.

There is one more incident connected with Candlemas, though of later date than the period of which we are writing, which makes the feast especially dear to Notre-Dame. It was in 1806. The community was, according to custom, gathered round their Mother in the work-room for the evening "Instruction" in Christian Doctrine. Julie spoke in burning words of the mystery of the day and then all at once entoned with extraordinary joy of spirit the Canticle of Simeon, which was taken up by her daughters. "Lumen ad revelationem gentium," sang the Sisters, when suddenly Julie's voice broke, her eyes fixed themselves on the crucifix in a rapt gaze of love, her countenance glowed with light. The whole community saw her thus in ecstasy, raised above the ground, motionless, inundated with the very beatitude of heaven. It is a constant tradition in the Institute that in that rapture God had shown His servant that her children should one day cross the seas and oceans to carry the light of revelation to nations sitting in darkness and in the shadow of death. The vision has seen its fulfilment.

From that first consecration on the feast of the Purification dates the name of "Sisters of Notre-Dame."

The little community received from Father Varin's hands a provisional rule by way of trial, and Julie and Françoise put the seal on their dedication by renewing their consecration to the Sacred Heart of Jesus and the Immaculate Heart of Mary. Catherine Duchâtel, whose health had given way, asked soon after to return to the Ladies of the Sacred Heart and died in their House some eighteen months later, leaving to Mère Julie's orphans some furniture and articles of clothing. Her place was not long empty. A saintly priest, the Abbé Louis Leleu, a native of Chépy near Abbeville, had just entered the Society of the Fathers of the Faith. He had left at home a dearly loved sister, twenty-four years of age, who earnestly desired to follow her brother's example. Victoire Leleu possessed all the excellent qualities which distinguished her brother—angelic sweetness of disposition, rare prudence and sound common sense. * Father Leleu presented her to Mère Julie

* Victoire Leleu, in religion Sister Anastasia, was born on July 29, 1779. She became successively Mistress of Novices at Amiens, Superior of the house of Jumet and Assistant to the Superior-General at the death

and with her one of her friends, Justine Garson, somewhat younger but not less gifted in mind and heart. Geneviève Gosselin, from Bettencourt, entered a few days later.

The Fathers of the Faith had been charged by the Bishop of Amiens with the catechetical instructions in the Cathedral. The girls of the parish were confided to the Sisters of Notre-Dame to the great satisfaction of M. Duminy, the Curé, who held them in very high esteem. One of these pupils of the Venerable Mother, Louise Lesage, became a Carmelite under the name of Mother Marie-Térèse, and in her extreme old age loved to go back on her Amiens memories—how she had sat at Mère Julie's feet in the little schoolroom, where, unable to move from paralysis, she gave her Catechism lessons—and how people always spoke of her as a saint and believed that she worked miracles. Mother Mary Teresa was one of the witnesses who testified to the sanctity of the Servant of God in the process held in 1882. "Every Sunday and four or five times in the week," she related, "Mère Julie would get together the young

---

of Venerable Mère Julie. She died on February 9, 1823. Mother Blin de Bourdon, who was already advanced in age when God took from her her devoted Assistant, wrote these touching words in announcing her death to the Sisters: "We have so often thanked God for having given her to us, but alas! He had only lent her to us for a short time. Did our heavenly Father fear that, like the weak ivy, we might attach ourselves too closely to the support which He had given us? Or did He not rather long to take to Himself that snow-white dove which has just flown into His Bosom? The peace of her soul during her illness was wonderful. A little before her death she sang quite clearly this refrain of a hymn: *Jésus est mon amour et la nuit et le jour.* Then she fell asleep sweetly in our Lord."

girls of the town, give them religious instruction, read to them and practise them in singing hymns. These meetings were very popular, for good Mère Julie had the art of mingling the agreeable with the useful. Sometimes Father Varin himself presided." Another recent testimony to the efficiency of Julie's teaching has reached us. In 1875 in the town of Northampton a priest, making his rounds among the poor, came across a very infirm old woman. A native of France, she had entered service in England, had married there, and had been reduced to extreme poverty and want. Before giving her the last rites the priest questioned her on her religion. She told him she had been instructed when young by Mère Julie Billiart at a school in the Rue Neuve, Amiens, and that she owed it to her to have preserved her faith and virtue in the midst of the greatest dangers.

Julie's rare moments of leisure were occupied in completing the religious education of her sisters, in training them to good methods of teaching, and stimulating their zeal for the salvation of souls. Contemporary witnesses tell us that she drew tears from their eyes when with burning accents she would exclaim, "My dear good daughters, we are but poor little women [*femmelettes*], and yet God vouchsafes to entrust to us souls to be put in the way of salvation. Ah! labour to render yourselves fit for the great work to which God calls you. Lean upon Him who is the strength of the weak; have so strong a confidence in Him that all the demons in hell cannot shake it. Say to Him : My God, I am but a child who can do nothing and can say nothing : do all Thyself, Lord ; Thy own glory is at stake." Julie indeed leant on Him with that trust which has never been confounded ; and for her He was about to do what His glory required, " because no word shall be impossible with God."

CHAPTER VII.

THE GREAT MISSIONS.

In 1804 Pope Pius VII. published a Jubilee to celebrate the restoration of religion in France, and the Fathers of the Faith gave a great mission in Amiens, which was carried on simultaneously in the five parishes of the city from April 29 to May 24. Father Thomas was among the missioners; two others, Fathers Lambert and Enfantin, were lodged at the Rue Neuve. The mission was a complete success; in the cathedral alone the audience usually numbered some 10,000 persons, and no less than 600 marriages were revalidated. Mère Julie's little community was assiduous in its attendance at the exercises of the mission; she herself was constantly carried to them in a sedan chair. The Fathers, moreover, found in the Sisters valuable co-operators in their labour for souls, and entrusted them with the entire instruction and preparation for the sacraments of the women and girls of the masses.

"In this apostolical work," says Father Sellier, who was on the spot, "Julie displayed all the activity at her command, and filled the office of a veritable missionary." *

* Life of Father Varin.

Françoise Blin de Bourdon was busy from morning to night teaching the Catechism; and neither of the two friends ever wearied of making the people repeat their morning and night prayers and explaining to them the duties of their state. The other Sisters took charge of the school-children.

We have mentioned the name of Father Enfantin. This extraordinary man was to play an important part in Julie's history. Born in the neighbourhood of Valence, ordained priest in a barn in the very height of the Reign of Terror by the Archbishop of Vienne, Mgr. d'Aviau-du-Bois-de-Sanzay, he was regarded by that eminent prelate as one of the band of apostolic men raised up by God at the beginning of the century to bring back erring souls to the way of truth.* His faith was profound, his zeal ardent, his life austere, his piety remarkable, his character full of energy, and his eloquence of extraordinary vehemence and vigour. In a mission given at Tours, which was on the point of failing, a single sermon of his was enough to assure its success. In his direction of souls Father Enfantin aimed chiefly at humility, the touchstone of true virtue. He soon saw that Julie's was no ordinary soul, but one that could stand being put into the crucible; and into the crucible he accordingly put her. With an unsparing hand he subjected her to every kind of mortification and humiliation, crucified

---

* See *Vie de Mgr. d'Aviau* and *Vie de Mme. de Franssu.*

nature in its every fibre, and with a view to counterbalancing the favours she had received from heaven—all of which her new director obliged her to discover to him—put her through a course of spiritual treatment which it is difficult to realise, but which was designed by the Father to make her advance with giant strides in the path of perfection.

Father Enfantin was not a man to stop at difficulties. He had made up his mind that Julie would do much more for God's glory if she recovered her health, and indeed the happy results of the experiment made during the Amiens missions rendered the Fathers of the Faith keenly desirous of associating her in a wider measure in their Apostolic labours.

It was the day after the close of the great mission—Monday, May 28. Father Enfantin came to Mère Julie and said with his usual abruptness, " I am beginning a novena to-day to the Sacred Heart for a person in whom I am interested. Will you join me?" Without asking further explanation Julie promised, and prayed with great fervour for the unknown intention. On the fifth day of the novena the Fathers solemnly opened the month of the Sacred Heart and erected with great pomp the Mission Cross in the cemetery of the church of St. James, in presence of M. Clausel de Coussergues the Vicar-General, all the clergy, and an immense concourse of people. Father Enfantin preached one of his famous popular sermons. In the evening of the busy day Mère Julie was sitting alone in her little garden, when her confessor came up, and without further preamble addressed her. "Mother, if you have any faith, take one step in honour of the Sacred Heart of Jesus." Julie rose—felt at once that a sudden cure had been worked in her—and the feet which for twenty-two years had refused to support her at the word of obedience took the required step.

"Take another."

She did so.

"A third."

She obeyed.

"That will do; sit down."

And Julie, with the simplicity of a child, sat down again, declaring at the same time that she was quite capable of walking further. But the Father would not allow it, and went off, forbidding her to tell the Sisters what had happened.

It was Friday—the first Friday of the month of June.

The long preparation was over; but who shall say that those years of waiting and of pain had been time lost? For "we know that to them that love God all things work together unto good, to such as according to his purpose are called to be saints."* Julie was assuredly so called; and she had found strength in infirmity, confidence in trial, humility in powerlessness; the instrument was

* Romans viii. 28.

ready for the hand of that God who loves to choose "the weak things of the world to confound the strong." *

When she found herself alone, Julie poured out her loving thanksgivings to the Sacred Heart, promising to devote to His glory alone the health just restored to her. Then, in order not to betray her secret, she returned to her own room—which was on the ground floor—in her accustomed manner, that is to say, by moving first one leg of her chair and then the other.

The Sisters had already retired for the night and noticed nothing, for, in spite of her infirmities, Julie was accustomed to get to bed without assistance, slipping on to her low couch from a chair of the same height. Next morning she mounted the staircase which led to the little chapel by her usual method, sitting down and raising herself from step to step by the aid of her hands. On the landing a low chair was always ready to help her to enter the chapel; but this time she took up the chair and carried it to her place. At the moment of Communion, instead of dragging herself on her knees, as she had hitherto been obliged to do, she stood up and walked to the rails. Her place being close to the sanctuary, she had but a few steps to take, and the thing passed unnoticed, thanks to the recollection of the Sisters and to the fact that in the chapel they were accustomed to wear a sort of

* I. Corinthians i. 27.

black hood which made it difficult to see what passed around them; the pupils, too, wore white veils. After mass, Mère Julie, according to the permission given her, confided the favour bestowed upon her to Father Thomas, who shed tears of joy. But in accordance with Father Enfantin's injunction, she contrived during the rest of that day, and the two following, to keep her cure still a secret, even carrying her self-control so far as to remain sitting on her chair when, on Sunday, the feast of the Sacred Heart, the procession of the Blessed Sacrament passed her door.

The end of the novena came, and Julie was at length authorised to make the matter known. On the last day she had prolonged her thanksgiving after Holy Communion, the Sisters had gone down to breakfast, and the orphans with their teachers were in an adjoining room, the glass door of which looked on to the staircase. Suddenly one of the youngest children, little Michaëlie, gave a scream, "Look! Ma Mère is walking down stairs!" "I know not," relates Mère Blin in her Memoirs, "what sort of stupor seized us—not one of us stirred to go and meet her. Erect, and with firm step, Mère Julie entered the room and saluted us with *Te Deum laudamus!* The general emotion is easy to imagine. In a first transport of gratitude the Sisters threw themselves on their knees, and then followed their Mother back to the chapel to finish, amid many happy tears, the hymn of thanksgiving.

This cure made a deep impression on all who heard of it, not in Amiens alone, but in many other towns of the Empire; and it gave a fresh impulse to the devotion to the Sacred Heart. A pious priest of Amiens, passing once through Soissons, told the story in a school kept by a nun of the Infant Jesus, whose community, like so many others, had been suppressed. So great was the emotion enkindled both in mistress and pupils that they began, there and then, a novena of thanksgiving, reciting the *Memorare* from a copy of the prayer which had belonged to Mère Julie. The narrator's niece, a child of twelve, had been the most eager among the listeners, and throughout the whole of the novena felt in her soul such powerful attractions of grace that they seemed tokens of the vocation which led her later into the Institute of Notre-Dame. "I thought," she said, "that a person in whose regard God powerfully moved another, must surely be very dear to Him."

The popular voice attributed the miracle to Mère Julie's faith and simple obedience; the Fathers of the Faith saw in it an index of God's will to use her as an instrument for the extension of His glory. "This thought of God's greater glory," says Father Sellier, "was, so to say, the soul of Julie's actions."

"Lord," she would repeat in her unselfish love, "Lord, if Thou dost not will to employ me to gain souls to Thee, give me back my old infirmities."

The fire that burned in her soul was fed by a prayer that was sometimes so rapt as to seem almost ecstatic. During the Process of Information held at Amiens in 1882, a M. Le Sellyer, Doctor of Law, who in an advanced old age kept full possession of all his faculties, gave the following testimony:

"My parents had in their service a woman named Sophie Lachambre, between thirty and forty years of age, a person of uncommon good sense and solid piety. She told me, and others in my presence, that having heard people speak of Mère Julie's frequent ecstasies after Holy Communion, she had expressed a desire to witness the same. One of her friends got her admitted into the Convent chapel while the Servant of God was making her thanksgiving; she was on her knees, with her arms extended in the form of a cross and her eyes raised to Heaven. The sight made such an impression on Sophie that she withdrew overcome with awe. "I can certify on my own account," added the witness, "that Mère Julie enjoyed in Amiens an established reputation for sanctity, and was spoken of in terms of veneration." Whether Father Enfantin feared for the Servant of God some temptation to human complacency in the extraordinary favours bestowed upon her, or whether he merely indulged in her regard his own somewhat rough and very impetuous character, it is impossible to say; but he now began to treat her humble and sensitive soul with renewed, and it would seem excessive, vigour.

Although the paralysis was cured, her stomach remained weak, and unable to bear certain kinds of food ; nor could she, without pain, drink cold water. Her director ordered her to make her meals of the dishes in question, and put her on ice-cold water, mixed, on occasion, with ashes. Often, in the refectory, he obliged her to eat on her knees. He loaded her in the presence of her own community with reproaches, couched in terms of the most stinging contempt, and the poor Sisters absolutely trembled at the severity of his looks and words.

Immediately after her cure Julie entered upon a ten days' retreat, both to thank God for his mercy and to prepare herself for the work before her. The opportunity was not lost by Father Enfantin. He made her pass the time in a garret, overwhelmed her with penances enough to have exhausted her newly-acquired strength, and doubled the vehemence of his contemptuous expressions towards her. His zeal was ingenious in discovering ways of mortifying his willing penitent. Mère Blin tells us of one of these. "For twelve or fifteen years Mère Julie had kept with her a cat which her good curé of Cuvilly, M. Dangicourt, had given her. Often and often during her long infirmity the creature had warmed her feet, and been to her a useful and legitimate distraction. Her director, whether he suspected in Julie some too natural attachment, or whether he merely wished to push his experiments on her further, determined to deprive her of it. This in itself was nothing; but as the cat fell sick he took it into his head to order our Mother to kill it herself. He was well aware that she had a perfect horror of anything of this sort; she could never even bring herself to order the cook to kill any animal, and it is not too much to say that he was, in this, requiring of Julie what was above her natural strength. But obedience carried her through. She fetched the poor animal from her garret, and, setting it down in the little courtyard struck it a heavy blow on the head with a stick." The terrible director himself was satisfied; and he lost no opportunity, in her absence, of expressing to the Sisters his deep veneration for the Foundress, and of explaining to them that all his conduct in her regard was merely a trial of her virtue and designed for her own profit. More than once he told Mère Blin de Bourdon that to speak to Julie as he did, he was obliged to make an effort over himself that caused him to tremble. He assured her further that Julie had received from God very great and very rare graces—a testimony doubly valuable in the mouth of a man who had the direction of several souls extraordinarily favoured by grace, and who himself was raised to a high degree of perfection and of prayer. Whatever we may think of this method, Julie's womanly soul came forth from the trial braced with a fresh energy which seemed to re-act upon her very body. She was now ready to fulfil the mission of the holy women in the Gospel, who followed our Lord and His Apostles and ministered to them. In those famous missions which renewed the face of the land of France at the beginning of our century, who shall say how much of the harvest was due to the humble labourer, whose work was none the less efficacious because it was hidden from the eyes of the world?

The Fathers had been so well pleased with Mère Julie's work during the successful mission at Amiens, that when, immediately after it, they were summoned to St. Valery-sur-Somme, and thence to Abbeville, they pressed her to follow them and again second their zeal in the same way. As soon therefore as her retreat was over, leaving the little community to the care of Mère Blin de Bourdon, she set out with Sister Anastasie (Leleu) as her companion. And now begins the series of Julie's letters to her daughters, which unconsciously reveal so much of her own character, and are so charming in their mixture of naïveté and strength, of maternal tenderness and authority, and whose every page breathes her love for souls and her simple trust in God.

J.M.J. Deo gratias! June 15, 1804.

May the name of the Lord be for ever blessed for all His mercies! At last we reached St. Valerie, at midnight

Rather late, as you see!—everyone had gone to bed. But the good God took care of us, and we found some charitable people willing to take us in. The weather was terribly warm, but as both the heat and the cold come from our good God, blessed be His holy name! To-day I had a happiness I have been deprived of for twenty-three years, that of assisting at Mass in the Parish Church. You must thank God for me. Then, too, I had the happiness of going to Communion in the Church: what favours our blessed Saviour is bestowing on me! . . . For my Catechism lessons I have at my disposal a little garden and a large room. May the name of the Lord be praised and blessed for all!

The mission at St. Valérie is doing well she writes again on June 23. It is quite certain that the devil has been doing his best to spoil the work, but our good Fathers are satisfied and so is the Curé. People who had not been to confession for thirty or forty years have publicly returned to God.

I feel sure you are all keeping your little rule as well as you can; I ask our good God earnestly to lead you by His holy spirit. Courage! my dear daughters; it is courage that we need in the times in which we live—great souls, who take to heart the interests of the greater glory of God. Ask this grace for me. . . . .
I must finish my letter to go to a good man whom I am teaching to say the Credo. He is nearly seventy and has not yet made his first Communion. He has the best will in the world. A thousand kind messages to my dear good little Mme. Barat; I am so glad that she goes to see you and to take the air in our garden.

One likes to note this little witness to the friendship between two servants of God whom the Church has just proclaimed Venerable almost simultaneously.

Mère Julie's compassion for sinners drew tears

from her eyes in speaking of them. "Ah! Souls, poor souls!" she would say; "the good God wants to save them, and they blindly precipitate themselves into Hell!" She had, in fact, just witnessed a terrible calamity. With a view to hindering the success of the mission, a number of young men had organised a boating party on the Somme. The sky was unclouded when a sudden gust of wind made the sailing vessel capsize, and one hundred giddy pleasure-seekers perished in the water. The hand of God was too visible not to be recognised, and to many in the town the fear of the Lord became the beginning of wisdom.*

During her stay at St. Valery, it pleased God to put His servant's faith to a new trial. She was perfectly cured of her paralysis, but so long an inaction of the feet had, naturally, left them excessively weak. One day, as she was walking in the street, some horses near her gave a sudden start, and Julie, in moving quickly aside to avoid them, sprained her foot severely. It swelled so much and was so painful that a return to Amiens was thought of, and the missionaries, seeing her hardly able to walk, began to call in question the reality of her cure. But Julie knew what Physician to seek. Dragging herself to a church, she passed several hours on her knees before the Blessed Sacrament, "exposing her needs," says Mère St.-

Vie du Père Varin, p. 157.

Joseph, "to the eyes of our Lord." She came out cured.

On July 9 Julie, on the point of leaving St. Valery for Abbeville, writes to her community:

I think I hear all my dear daughters saying: Our mother has given us up, she gives us no more news. Ah! do not say that, my dear good children. Here I am stealing the dinner-hour to write you a few lines—dinner takes no longer here than during the Amiens mission. May the name of the Lord be praised and blessed in everything! What is certain, my dear daughters, is that the good God is always very good. You will have heard of my visit to good Father Varin at Abbeville. I am glad to have made this journey, though I was well shaken in a little conveyance, and the rain came down upon us. All that was very good for us. I saw some Nuns there who were much astonished at seeing me able to trot about in this fashion. May God's holy Name be praised for all things. Let us love Him, let us love Him, and all will go well. I hope I shall find everyone in our house loving and serving God. Pray for me, my dear daughters. I think I shall be going to Abbeville this day week; I do not know how long I shall stay there. Pray that my going may be for the greater glory of God, and that I may remain as long as He sees fit. I let myself be led by the hand, which is the right thing for me. M. Clausel de Coussergues told me to go to Abbeville; he did not say how long I was to stop.

On July 18 she writes again:

We left St. Valery at ten in the morning amid the tears of the whole town. Everyone was lamenting the departure of our good Fathers; it was really touching to see that vast crowd in such a state of grief. Let us thank God for that mission—how many souls would have remained dead in sin but for its help! I beg of you to offer for me, with your Confessor's permission, the first Communion you make after the reception of this letter, for I know not how to thank our good God sufficiently for all the blessings He daily bestows upon me. Victoire [Leleu] sends love to all; she is well, and we are very happy; she always does her very best. . . Let good Father Leblanc read my letter, so that he may see once again what a poor ignorant woman the Mother is. Everything affectionate to Mme. de Franssu;* how surprised she would be to see the way in which I go about the streets of Abbeville.

Here, as everywhere, Mère Julie spent herself for souls.

ABBEVILLE, August 2, 1804.

MY DEAR DAUGHTERS,—However much I may wish to tell you the day of my return, I cannot do so, because the good God, as you know, likes me to grope my way along. Ah, blessed and praised be His holy Name for all! With this grace I am ready for anything which shall turn to His greater glory. I put off writing to you for some days so that I might be able to tell you something certain; but I do not yet see my way clearly. *Deo gratias* always! Although I am but a very useless little servant, I may tell you that the days pass with astonishing rapidity. The good people of Abbeville leave me no time to be dull—I do not know which to listen to first. . . I bless God that all is prospering in the community; the one thing I ask of Him is that you may love Him with all your hearts. See—when we love our good God, we do everything well, well; but when we do not love Him, ah! talents and intellect go for nothing.

I can find nothing to say to you, my dear daughters, but what the beloved disciple said: Love one another for the

---

* Jeanne, widow of the Marquis de Saint-Alyre-de-Franssu, put herself under Father Enfantin's direction at Amiens, and by his advice founded a congregation at Crest for the education of girls. The Mother-House of this Institute was later on transferred to Valence.

love of God, and love God, oh! love Him above all things. It is a great comfort to me to learn that you are all in the peace of the Lord. Ah! it cannot be bought too dearly—that peace which we procure at the cost of a few little sacrifices. Yes! you will all taste of it, if you are filled with charity for each other, for everybody; if you are very faithful to your meditation, as I believe each one of you is; if you ask earnestly of our Lord the spirit of simplicity, of meekness, of mutual forbearance. The good God is expecting me at my meditation; so you will not be vexed if

leave you to go with Him, with my blessed Master. Oh, what a happy thing it is to love and serve Him, and how much He deserves our love! My God! why are not our hearts simply on fire with love for so good a Father? He knows how dearly I love you in Him—so pray to Him for your poor worthless mother; she needs your prayers so much! Above all, ask Him for humility.

Julie returned to Amiens a few days before the feast of Assumption, rejoicing in the work accomplished and ready for fresh labours. But the enemy of souls, furious to see his empire so successfully attacked, did his utmost to undermine the work of the missions. The civil authorities, always jealous and despotic, and hostile to the missions from the first, published an order enjoining on the Fathers of the Faith to leave the Department of the Somme within the next twenty-four hours, under penalty of arrest. The greater number of them, therefore, left for the time being; a few, amongst whom were Fathers Thomas and Enfantin, braved the danger, and kept themselves in hiding.

It is but fair to state that this petty persecution by the administrative power, the remains of the

Revolutionary spirit, found no echo in the public voice. France was instinctively turning back to the Faith of her Fathers, and this revulsion of feeling was strikingly witnessed to by the enthusiastic reception given to Pope Pius in 1804—a reception which made the august pontiff exclaim with emotion, " We passed through France in the midst of a kneeling population."

Finding her external works of zeal thus interrupted, Mère Julie profited by this leisure time to give to her rising Institute, under the direction of Father Varin, a regular religious shape.

CHAPTER VIII.

RELIGIOUS TRAINING.

For ten years Father Thomas had been the friend and father of the little family. He had supported it in the days of tribulation, and when these were past had constantly busied himself with its interests; both he and Father Enfantin used to spend their rare moments of leisure in giving lessons to the young sisters so as to prepare them to become mistresses no less capable than zealous. For "the Institute of the Sisters of Notre-Dame," says Father Baesten in his Life of the Servant of God, "was established in order to propagate, to raise, to sanctify instruction, especially among the people," whom the Revolution, with all its boasted enlightenment, had plunged into the darkness of the profoundest ignorance. But on the 10th of September, 1805, Father Thomas left Amiens to take part in the missions organised for the West and South, * and the full responsibility of providing for these vital interests devolved upon Father Varin, a man to whom, as has been said, the Institute owes much. His first care was its internal organisation.

* Memoirs by Mother St. Joseph. For Father Thomas, see *Histoire du P. de Clorivière*, by P. J. Terrien, p. 499.

Together with the founders he now traced a more extended draft of the rule. Though not yet regarded as final, this fresh attempt was blessed by God, for its chief points are embodied in the Constitutions approved by Pope Gregory XVI. On July 2, the Feast of the Visitation, 1805, Father Varin himself presented this rule to the community. It was settled that everyone should conform to it with all possible perfection during three months, so that any needful changes might be suggested by experience. It was thus found that the rules were wise, practicable and conformable to the end and to the spirit of the little Society. They were approved by Mgr. Jean-François Demandolx, who, on the translation of Mgr. de Villaret to the see of Casale at the end of 1804, had been named Bishop of Amiens. On the feast of St. Teresa, October 15, Mère Julie, Françoise Blin de Bourdon, Victoire Leleu and Justine Garson bound themselves by vow to their observance.* To the other vows already pronounced by Julie and Françoise, more than a year

---

* Acts of the Informatory Process, Vitæ Synopsis, § 2 p. 8. These constitutions or fundamental rules, the observance of which brought down on the Venerable Foundress so many persecutions, were added to, but never changed.

The following is the Formula of the Vows pronounced by the first Mothers:—"I............, promise unto God Almighty, before the Blessed Virgin, His Mother, and the whole court of heaven, and in presence of you, Father, holding the place of God, perpetual poverty, chastity, and obedience, and, conformably to this obedience, an especial care of the instruction of children, understanding the whole according to the constitutions, the conditions, and the dispositions which have been

back, they all added those of poverty and obedience, which are essential to the religious state. Moreover, to mark more completely their separation from their former life, they now changed their names : Julie took that of " Sœur Saint-Ignace," thus showing clearly whose spirit she was obeying and making her own ; but, for prudence sake, the name was never publicly adopted, and even in community it was used only after the restoration of the Society of Jesus in 1814. Mère Blin de Bourdon was known from this time forward as " Sœur Saint-Joseph," Victoire Leleu became " Sœur Anastasie," and Justine Garson " Sœur Saint-Jean." In view of the future extension of the Institute, Father Varin would have it governed by a Superior General, charged with visiting the houses, nominating the local Superiors, corresponding with the subjects dispersed in the different Convents, and assessing the revenues of the Society. This fundamental article was one of those which the first professed Sisters bound themselves to observe. By unanimous consent the first Mother General was at once the most humble and the most worthy, and by her example was a living rule. When leaving Amiens, Father Varin, in virtue of the powers conferred on him by the Bishop of the Diocese, laid on Father Leblanc, Superior of the Fathers of the

---

manifested to me, at Amiens, in the Chapel of the House of Orphans, October 15, 1805."

The formula is in the handwriting of Sister Anastasie Leleu.

Faith at Amiens, the care of directing the affairs of the new congregation.* This was an excellent choice, but the same cannot be said with regard to that of the confessor. The priest named for this office was Father de Sambucy de Saint-Estève, professor at the College of the Faubourg-Noyon, already confessor at Mme. Barat's house, "a priest still young, enterprising and absolute in his notions, a man of letters and gifted with a brilliant imagination, but whose character was restless and changeable."† Father Varin relied upon the firm hand of Father Leblanc, who, like himself, was an old soldier, to keep the Abbé's impetuous disposition within bounds. We shall see that, wise as he was, his anticipations were entirely frustrated.

Mère Julie exercised the authority with which she was invested in a wholly maternal manner. She loved liberty of spirit; she would have people serve God from love and not from compulsion, and walk with gladness in the way of sacrifice. "The first sisters of the Institute," writes Mère Blin de Bourdon, "would be able to bear witness that our mother led us at the outset with great gentleness, like the children of a family, beginning with little, imposing on us only two or three hours of silence a day, and not strictly requiring

---

* The College of the Fathers of the Faith, transferred from the Oratory to the Faubourg-Noyon, and later on to Montdidier, had as its first Superior, Father Jennessaux, succeeded by Father Bruson, who, in his turn, was replaced in 1803 by Father Leblanc.

† *Vie de la Mère Barat*, by Mgr. Baunard.

that things should always be done at the same hour." But what, before all things, she desired was to form interior souls, closely united to God. "If you do not become *souls of prayer*," she would say, "our Institute will be lost." It is true that from the time of her miraculous cure, which allowed her to devote herself to active works of zeal, she notably shortened her hours of prayer. Nevertheless she assembled the Community in the oratory twice a day for meditation. This holy exercise, lasting an hour in the morning and half-an-hour in the evening, has always been in vigour among the Sisters of Notre-Dame. Visits to the Blessed Sacrament, spiritual reading, the retreat on the first Friday of the month in honour of the Sacred Heart, preceded by the "Holy Hour" or night adoration, the daily Act of Reparation, the examination of conscience twice a day, the Rosary, the chanting of the Little Office of Our Lady on Sundays and festivals, different practices of devotion and penance in use among the old communities,—all these things were established by the Venerable foundress from the beginning. To the very end of her life she herself kept to daily Communion and almost daily confession. The sisters approached the Holy Table two or three times a week, according to the advice of their confessor.

Mère Julie attached great importance to the formation of the Sisters destined for the schools, especially in all that concerned the teaching of religion. In their case she did not scruple to shorten the time allotted to prayer that they might have more to devote to this essential study. In her presence and under her supervision they became, by turns, teachers or pupils, repeating to each other her own inimitable lessons in Christian Doctrine, or Scripture History, or even her earnest conferences on religious life. It is a noteworthy fact that all the early Sisters thus formed immediately in the school of Mère Julie were remarkable for the fruits they obtained by their religious instructions. Manual labour was apportioned according to the strength and aptitude of each, but the distinction between choir-sister and lay-sister has never existed in the Institute of Notre-Dame. This perfect equality of rank did not in any way prevent Mère Julie from putting each sister to the work for which her capacity and education fitted her; and by mutual contact some gained in humility, some in politeness, all in charity. The greater number of Monastic Orders at least from the close of the eleventh century, established a hierarchical distinction between those who devote themselves to psalmody and study, and the lay brothers destined for manual labour, and in this distinction they have been followed by almost all Congregations of women. The Sisters of Notre-Dame are an exception, and try to revive the perfect equality which reigned in the ancient monasteries among the Paulas, the Marcellas and their companions, of whom St. Jerome said: "Here patrician ladies are put on the same level with those who were once their servants, give them the name of 'Sister,' and treat them like themselves. The daughters of the Scipios and the Gracchi share in the toils of those who have been shepherdesses, clean the lamps, cook, weave cloth, serve in the refectory, and experience, in the exercise of these lowly employments done for the love of God, ineffable delights."

Novices soon flocked in, drawn by Mère Julie's reputation for sanctity. In 1806 the little family numbered eighteen Sisters, and it became necessary to establish themselves in a more spacious house. Mme. de Franssu, a friend of Mère Blin de Bourdon's childhood, obtained the privilege of occupying rooms in it, in company with a certain Sister Martha, whom the Revolution had turned out of the convent of her own Order. On the other hand, the number of orphans diminished. Situations had been found for those already trained, so that only four remained. Experience proved that the work of the schools was, under the conditions of the times, much more productive of fruit, and so in the new house of the Faubourg-Noyon a greater extension was given to this form of apostolate. Free classes were now thrown open to poor children; up to this time the Sisters had confined themselves to instructing them in the catechism. To fill the new schools the Venerable Mother adopted St. Francis Xavier's expedient: she sent out into the surrounding streets a novice with a postulant, Adelaide Pelletier, who had begged this favour. The two went in different directions, each ringing a little bell, and making aloud this delightfully simple proclamation: "We let you know that the Sisters of Notre-Dame have just opened free schools for little girls. Go and tell your parents the news." The appeal was responded to; on the first day more than sixty children presented themselves, and the influx continued. The poor little things found in their adopted mothers an inexhaustible fund of kindness and devotedness, for all the Sisters drew their inspiration from the teaching and the example of the foundress. Mère Julie perpetually brought them back to that spirit of faith which sees nothing but the immortal soul bought with the Blood of God; she infused into them that sweetness, that benignity, that calm firmness which triumphs in the long run even over the most rebellious wills. "My daughters," she would say to them, "if you want your children to respect you, speak to them yourselves with respect. I beg this of you very earnestly—no sort of good can be done otherwise." And again: "We must go step by step in dealing with souls. We must follow the spirit of the good God—a spirit of patience, of long, long, patience. Have we not experienced this in our own case?"

Although she was Superior, Mère Julie took an active part in the teaching, reserving to herself, as far as possible, the explanation of the Catechism.

Even the other religious establishments in the town would send their pupils to attend her lessons. Mother Mary Teresa, the Carmelite already quoted, gives us the impression left on their minds. "Mère Julie's special *attrait*," she says, "was the religious instruction of poor children. The good Mother's face wore an expression of affability which never left it. She was always even-tempered, always sincerely humble. She used often to talk to us about vanity, about dress, etc. . . . She never scolded, never reproached us. . . . She used to say: 'In the matter of prayer nothing is small, nothing.' And in order to fix our attention better, when we were saying the Our Father, she would make a pause after each petition. So complete had been her cure that she never sat down while she taught." *

The foundress constantly reminded her daughters that in the work of Christian education Our Blessed Lady was their patron, that is, not only their protectress but the model which they themselves were to copy and set up before their little scholars. On this point her Rule is explicit: "To obtain this end [the formation of children to Christian virtues] all the members of this Institute shall choose the august Queen of Heaven for their Mother, their advocate, and their protectress with God; wherefore they must not only respect, love and honour her, but with filial confidence they must have recourse

* Letter of Rev. Mother Boistel de Belloy. Process de fama.

to her in all their needs. Having the happiness of bearing the name of Sisters of Our Lady, they must strive to imitate the virtues of their august Mother." *

In the community fervour and self-abnegation grew apace. Extreme poverty reigned in the house —that poverty which their Rule taught them to love and cherish as a mother, and to look upon as the very wall and rampart of religious life. The food was that of the poorest; for breakfast dry bread and water; for dinner, soup and a dish of vegetables, except on Sundays when there was a little meat. Even so, it was necessary to keep an eye on the more fervent, who were only too ready to deprive themselves of what was really necessary. The dormitories consisted of garrets divided by partitions; the beds were simple palliasses laid upon the floor. Mère Julie made herself the servant of the servants of Jesus Christ, and Mère Blin, reared in opulence, reckoned it a favour to be the last and least in God's House. Those same streets of Amiens which she had so often traversed in her brilliant equipage now saw her in the costume of a poor peasant, often too short for her, trudging back from the market laden with the provisions for the day's meal. Such a life was beautiful in the eyes of God, and He blessed it abundantly.

By the end of the year 1606, the community

* Rules of Institute, Chap. I. Art. 2.

reckoned thirty members. On June 19 the Congregation of the Sisters of Notre-Dame was approved by imperial decree, signed at St.-Cloud and confirmed on March 10, 1807, at the camp of Osterode. This approbation was provisional only, but was enough to shield the community from administrative annoyances. The storm, however, was brewing in another quarter.

In the meantime the Institute sent out its first labourers into the field where so many were to follow.

CHAPTER IX.

FIRST FOUNDATION IN BELGIUM.

It was by a sort of inspiration that when Father Leblanc was sent to inspect the College of the Fathers of the Faith at Roulers he asked Mère Julie to accompany him to Flanders. The hope of doing some good there made her at once agree to his proposal. Mgr. Fallot de Beaumont, Bishop of Ghent, to whom she was introduced, expressed a great desire to have in his diocese a convent of Sisters of Notre-Dame. The prudent Superior replied that she was ready to second his designs provided she could obtain subjects who spoke Flemish, and might form them to the religious life and the methods of teaching. The Bishop recognised the wisdom of the proposed condition and himself undertook to find postulants. The month of August, 1806, saw Mère Julie once again in Flanders. Several postulants were waiting her arrival. The first, Marie Steenhaut, was presented to her at the episcopal palace by Mgr. de Beaumont himself. The introduction over, Marie hastened home to present her new mother to her parents. Julie found herself in the midst of a thoroughly Christian family, whose faith and virtue the Revolution had left intact. Mme. Steenhaut was deeply moved by the appearance of the venerable

foundress, in whom she seemed to see a second St. Teresa, and not only did she joyfully confide to her her eldest daughter, but said eagerly : " I have so much confidence in you, my dear Mother, that I give you not merely my eldest but also the three younger ones, if God be pleased to call them to religious life."*
She then had two of her children brought in. To one of these Julie had already foretold her vocation. That morning, in fact, on her way from the Bishop's palace to the home of the Steenhauts, she had entered the parish church. " One of my sisters," relates Sister Marie Steenhaut, " whom she did not know at all, was praying there, and our Mother knelt behind her. She came out with us, and made acquaintance on the way. Mère Julie told her that she also would one day be her daughter, and when I was alone with her she said to me that God had given her special lights on the future of this child." We shall meet with both Ciska and Marie more than once in the course of this narrative.

No other postulants from Ghent being ready, Mère Julie, accompanied by Marie Steenhaut, went on to Courtrai, where she was hospitably received by the families of Vercruysse and Goethals, both devoted then, as now, to the promotion of every kind of good work. Thérèse Goethals, a child of six, was the pet of the family. Did Julie foresee when she embraced and blessed her that this child was destined as Mère Ignace to be the third Superior General of the

* Memoirs of Sister Marie Steenhaut.

Institute, and the first to send its Sisters across the seas to distant and uncivilized lands? Thérèse Goethals, at least, always attributed her vocation to this early blessing of Mère Julie.*

The foundress began at once to exercise her new daughter in obedience and opposition to the spirit of the world, and Sister Marie tells one or two amusing incidents of the Courtrai visit. When Julie went into the house of her hostess, " she made me sit down at the stall of a woman who was selling fruit, and bought from her some pears, which she told me to eat with the bread which she took out of her bag. To eat thus in the street was my first humiliation. I kept fancying that among the passers-by were persons come from Ghent to the fair then going on at Courtrai. Next day our Mother took me to High Mass, and on the way she was more than once insulted by the boys on account of her somewhat singular travelling costume; they greeted her as 'witch,' 'black sorceress,' &c. She made me translate these titles into French for her, and laughed heartily over them. Not so I; indeed so humbled did I feel, that when we entered the church I let her go on in front, and knelt at a distance from her. She did not notice this till we were leaving the church, when she asked me the reason. I confessed my pride, and she was pleased with my sincerity; but she spoke to me about humility in a way which deepened my esteem

---

* Postulatory letter of Mgr. Goethals, S.J., Archbishop of Calcutta, and nephew of the Reverend Mère Ignace.

for her, and I was stronger in the subsequent tests to which she put me." *

The indefatigable servant of God went next to Roulers to meet two other postulants. At Saint-Genois she took up a fourth, and a fifth joined her from the neighbourhood of Liège. In their company she set out for Amiens. During the long journey their noviciate began. They prayed, talked together about the object of the congregation, and the happiness of labouring for the salvation of souls. "We felt," they used to say in later years, "like the Apostles with our Lord." During the three weeks of their absence Julie wrote from time to time to the Amiens community.

GHENT, September 1, 1807.

I assure you, my dear good daughters, that all your hearts are always quite close to my own. Oh, what am I saying? No, no, I only want them all to place them continually in the Divine and Adorable Heart of our sweet and loving Jesus. See, my dear Jesus, here are all the hearts of my sisters. Oh, yes; they are much better than mine, sweet Saviour; but Thou wilt let mine slip in amongst them, wilt Thou not? How happy we are to belong to God with all our hearts. Even as I write I cannot keep back my tears, when I see my God so little known, so little loved. Ah! my dear children, let the good God fashion your hearts as He wills by His grace; show your greatness of soul by forgetting yourselves, to think only of the interests of God alone. Let us do our best to put our hearts into that state which shall procure Him all the glory which He looks for from us. Let us think of nothing but gaining souls for our Jesus: what do not the lovers of the world daily do to get followers? and we, shall

* Memoirs of Sister Marie.

we do nothing for our Blessed Master and Lord ? . . . .
There! you shall have no details of my journey; I look
upon all that as trifles compared with speaking of the dear
Master whom we have the honour to serve. . . . I do
not know when I shall get back to you. My God wills that
I should always go along like a little blind woman : He likes
that ; well then ! so must I.

Mère Julie made but a short stay at Amiens on her return ; she set out again, by the desire of Mgr. de Beaumont, to make arrangements with the authorities of the little town of Saint-Nicolas, between Ghent and Antwerp ; they wished to establish a school for girls. As she passed by Ghent she received the young Francesca, or "Ciska" Steenhaut, who afterwards became Sister Gertrude. The Bishop sent his own carriage for the postulant, and, while Julie and Ciska knelt for his blessing, he placed one hand on the head of the venerable superior, the other on that of the girl, saying: "Mother, behold your child—child, behold your Mother." They embraced each other as they rose, " and from that moment," says Ciska, " I felt for our Mother an affection so strong that nothing in the world could have separated me from her."

Mère Julie was obliged to wait some days for the person who was to introduce her to the clergy and authorities of Saint-Nicolas ; she profited by the delay in her own way. " I must tell my daughters a little secret," she writes ; " it is that this time of waiting gains me happy moments with my good God. As much as I can, I remain in the Bishop's chapel. I am there with the good God and all my dear daughters.

I give them all to Him one after another, and I hope that they in their turn see in God's presence their poor little mother in the adorable Heart of her good Jesus. Ah! yes, the Heart of Jesus: how sweet it is to make our dwelling there; for the love of God let us never leave It; let us live there by love, let us die there of love, each and all of us."

The house of Saint-Nicolas, offered to Mère Julie, had formerly been the School of St. Joseph, popularly called *den Berkenboom*. Two old religious of the congregation of St. Philip Neri still taught there, their pupils consisting of a couple of boarders and about fifty day scholars; but the task was too heavy for their failing strength. The premises were large, but the building out of repair, and the walls crumbling with damp. Promises to remedy this were made, and all being satisfactorily settled, Mère Julie returned to Amiens, choosing as the new community to take possession of Berkenboom, Sister St.-Jean (Justine Garson), Superior, Sister Xavier (Josephine Evrard), and Sister Marie (Steenhaut), who was to have special charge of the Flemish class. Two Belgian novices were to join them a little later. The last farewells were very touching. Full of anxiety that, though dispersed in different houses, the Sisters should yet have but one heart and soul, Mère Julie began by reciting aloud the words of our Lord in His prayer for His Apostles: "'Holy Father, keep them in Thy Name whom Thou hast given Me, that they may be one, as We also are one,' and that they may remain ever one with the common centre." Then all the community kissed the feet of those whose mission it was to make God known and loved by the children of Flanders. The little colony set out on December 9, 1806, and the journey was marked by two accidents: first the axletree and then the brace of the coach snapped short like so much glass. But Julie lost nothing of her gay serenity.

At Amiens, in order to render themselves less conspicuous, the Sisters wore no particular costume, but it seemed advisable that those sent to the new foundations should be clothed as religious. The dress adopted was that seen by Julie in her vision at Compiègne—a black habit of common woollen stuff, a coif composed of white linen under a stiff black bonnet, and a white linen wimple. The black veil, which completes the dress, was at first only worn in chapel; out of doors was added a long black hooded mantle almost touching the ground. This habit the Bishop of Ghent blessed at the request of Mère Julie, and it was in a room of his episcopal palace that the Sisters first joyfully clothed themselves in the livery of holy poverty. The same simplicity, both of the costume and of the ceremony of clothing, has always been maintained by the Sisters of Notre-Dame.

The foundress remained two months at Saint-Nicolas in order to set the new establishment on a proper footing. She would have liked all the day schools to be free, but yielding to representations made to her on this head, she agreed that those children whose families were in easy circumstances should pay a fee proportioned to their means. "Why can we not publish to all the world how good the good God is?" she writes on December 16. "Our Sisters look charming in their little costume; every one is pleased with it. They are well received everywhere. The school will open to-morrow with the *Veni Creator* and the Mass of the Holy Ghost. I have earnestly begged that it might be publicly announced in the church that the Poor School was free. I am very firm on this point. I must tell you," she writes on the following day, "that we have had a great feast in our school to-day. Ninety children sat down to table. We gave them tea with milk in it, and little penny cakes, and the children had a play day. The Dean and the administrators were delighted to see this large family. If there were no crosses in the midst of all this, I should not hope for much good from it. The cross is the sign which marks all works which tend to the greater glory of God, and He never leaves His dear children without it. May Jesus live in all our hearts at Saint-Nicolas and everywhere. Beg of Him that I may make Him loved by His creatures, and that I myself may love Him so much as to die of love." Replying to the New Year's greeting which reached her from Amiens, she writes, "I wish you all those things which will best please the Heart of our good Jesus: that you may all become faithful servants of that Lord to whom we are consecrated—our body, our soul, our mind, everything in us ought to be Jesus. O my daughters, how sweet it is to die every moment to our own life so as to let only the spirit of our loving Jesus live in us. But the life of Jesus in us requires that we should all become like Him—gentle, patient, charitable, forbearing. He desires to live alone in the hearts of my dear daughter. O yes, love Him, my good Sister Sophie; love Him my good Sister Frances, and with a generous love which breaks through all obstacles; love Him, my good Sister Geneviève, set yourself to work in earnest. Courage, my good little Eulalie, courage; you will see how good the good God is. As for Sister Teresa she appears to make only material bread; but she knows better—in making it she is feeding her soul with another food. Sister Firmine is going this year to acquire a simplicity which will be the delight of the Adorable Heart of our dear and good Jesus. My good Sister Angélique will now always be with the angels at the foot of the altar. My little Sister Scholastica will grow quite childlike in our Lord in the company of her little pupils: let her remember to offer them every day to Jesus, Mary and Joseph. And our good Sister Catherine with all her family, she has a work to do to form Jesus in those young hearts. She must form Him first in herself by a great courage, so as to become a manly soul. As for the others, Sisters Clotilde, Marianne, Séraphine, all that have come, all that are to come, may my Jesus live ever in their hearts."

The diocese of Namur was at this time governed

by an eminent and saintly prelate. Charles Francis Joseph Pisani, Baron de la Gaude, was the last of an illustrious family, which had given to Venice two of its Doges. He was possessed of a large fortune, and was Councillor of the Parliament of Provence, when at thirty years of age he entered Holy Orders, and became successively Bishop of St. Paul-Trois-Châteaux and of Vence. Cited before the revolutionary tribunal, he sought refuge in Rome, where he published his celebrated *Pastoral Letter of the Bishop of Vence on Obedience to the Sovereign Pontiff*. After the Concordat, he was appointed to the See of Namur, where he won the esteem and love of his flock.* Having heard of Mère Julie from the Fathers of the Faith, and probably from Mgr. de Beaumont, he sent for her while she was at Ghent in order to treat with her about the establishment of the Sisters of Notre-Dame in his episcopal city. It was the month of January, and the weather was very severe; the roads were bad, and there were few conveniences for travelling. After a fatiguing journey of two or three days Mère Julie arrived at Namur at night-fall in a storm of rain and snow, wet through, and shivering with cold. In this pitiable condition she presented herself at the Bishop's house, where a man-servant, judging her by appearances, received her with very ill grace, and bade her seek a lodging elsewhere. She was humbly going away

---

* Notice on Mgr. Pisani, by Canon de Beauregard; Histoire du Père de Clorivière.

when the Bishop himself appeared on the scene, and welcomed her with the utmost hospitality and benevolence. She stayed three days in the palace, and it was arranged that the projected foundation should be made in the following summer. The foundress was back at Amiens on February 4, 1807. Meanwhile a university had been founded by imperial decree, and a college was talked of for the city of Amiens. The Fathers of the Faith, to avoid sending their pupils to the government classes, had in 1806 transferred them to Montdidier, installing themselves in what had once been a Benedictine Priory. The direction of this establishment was in the hands of Father Leblanc, assisted by Father Sellier. Among their fellow labourers was M. Trouvelot, whose name has already appeared in this narrative. He was a trusted adviser of Mère Julie in all her difficulties, and always professed the greatest esteem for her.* From the time when the daughters of St. Vincent of Paul were driven from Montdidier by the Revolutionists in 1792, the poor of the town had been crying out in vain for Christian education for their children. In 1807, thanks to the advice of the Fathers of the Faith, and the generous cooperation of the Mayor, it was decided to appeal to the Sisters of Notre-Dame. Mère Julie accepted the

* After the death of the Servant of God he went to Cuvilly to gather together the souvenirs of her contemporaries. His nephew the Abbé Trouvelot, Curé of Morsain, says in a letter dated Sep. 26, 1882 :— "I know for a fact that my dear uncle had a profound veneration for the Rev. Mère Julie Billiart, and never spoke of her but with marked respect."

conditions proposed, and on February 21 took with her to Montdidier Sister Catherine Daullée and Sister Angélique Bicheron.* The Sisters at once won the confidence of the inhabitants; the classes opened with sixty pupils, and the numbers increased so rapidly that the premises were soon too small. A generous benefactor, M. de la Viefville d'Orvillers, whose name often appears in Mère Julie's letters, placed at their disposal a larger house.

The prudent foundress took advantage of her stay at Montdidier to obtain from Father Leblanc, with regard to the government and direction of the Institute, counsels which were soon to stand her in good stead. Foreseeing the difficulties and perplexities with which she would have to struggle, she wrote to Mère Blin de Bourdon: "All for the greater glory of God! Let us desire nothing but that. Leave alone, leave alone all the rest, all sensible support. God alone more than ever! He is our only helper when all others abandon us. Never have I understood better how frail is the support of creatures. Oh how good a thing it is to lean upon Him who alone is unchangeable! Let us cast all our care upon Him: confidence, love, total abandonment into the hands of so good a Father. The good God—He is our strength, our support."

It was with a soul thus armed that Julie entered upon the most painful combat of her life.

* Her uncle, Canon Bicheron, had with M. Louis Sellier founded the college at Amiens, which, as we have seen, was ceded to the Fathers of the Faith.

CHAPTER X.

THE BEGINNING OF SORROWS.

SUFFERING is the law of sanctity. "The souls dearest to my Father," said our Lord one day to St. Teresa, "are those He tries most;" and Benedict XIV. has laid it down as a principle "that the saints of God have often suffered calumny, notably those whose sanctity has been most eminent, and whose labours have been most useful to the Church." * On the other hand, as the same learned Pontiff remarks,† it may very well be that those who reprehend, and even unjustly condemn an innocent person, often do so without themselves incurring the guilt of injustice. It is so easy for a man—even a good man—to make a mistake, and to let his passion and imagination get the better of his reason.

This was probably the case with the Abbé de Sambucy de St.-Estève. He was, as we have said, a man of superior intelligence and attainments, but he lacked one important quality—common sense. Those who have read the Life of the Venerable Mère Barat, will remember how his enterprising and meddlesome spirit tried her

* De Canonisatione servorum Dei, lib. ii. c. 141.
† Ibid. lib ii. c. 30.

gentleness and patience, and the disorder into which he was so near throwing her infant congregation; his conduct towards Mère Julie was still more harassing and unaccountable.

Her biographer would gladly throw a veil over the painful events we are going to record, but we owe it to truth and justice to speak. We owe it too to the honour of the Servant of God; for men are but instruments in His Hands, and the Cross is the chisel wherewith He fashions His elect to the likeness of His Son. " n writing Mère Julie's life," said M. Trouvelot,* who was an eyewitness of all that passed, " I do not see how anyone could pass over in silence the wrongs done to her by the Bishop of Amiens at the instigation of M. de Sambucy."

Being well versed in canon law, M. de Sambucy thought it his duty to improve upon the little code of rules which, under the wise administration of the foundress, had succeeded so happily with the infant community. His ruling idea was to bring the new Congregation into harmony with the ancient monastic institutions, and he therefore proposed to do away with some of its most fundamental constitutions. He would have no Superior General, no connection between the different houses, and even no extension of the Institute beyond the single diocese of Amiens. As simple confessor he had of course no authority to modify

* Letter to the Abbé Belfroy of Namur.

rules which had received episcopal sanction; and he was moreover fully aware that his notions were in direct contradiction to those of Fathers Varin and Leblanc. In fact he never succeeded in prejudicing her first superior against Julie. "Mother," Father Varin often said to her, "since God has put you in the position you occupy, you have grace to act; do not subject yourself to asking so many permissions from M. de Sambucy; if you consult him, let it be as a friend, no more. Whatever confidence I may have in him for other things, it is not to him that I look to give your daughters the spirit they should have in order to enter into the designs of our Lord, and if he is not to give the spirit, neither is he to preserve or perfect it. No, this is to be done by the good Mother whom our Lord has chosen for this end." He speaks in the same strain in many of his letters quoted by Mère St.-Joseph in her Memoirs. "I am going to write this to good M. de Sambucy, to let him know in a friendly way what I think about the line of conduct he should pursue, and to put him on his guard against the love of change even under pretext of improvement. I have given him several bits of advice as to his treatment of your sisters, which were not very flattering to him, but which were intended to establish the rights of the Mother over her daughters."* After this it is somewhat surprising that Father Varin did not remove the root of the

---

* Memoirs of Mère Blin de Bourdon, vol. i. p. 95.

evil by appointing another confessor; but the Abbé enjoyed the Bishop's confidence, and his removal was doubtless a difficult matter.

On her side the foundress could not in conscience yield to requirements which were nothing short of the ruin of the primitive spirit, scope and organisation of her Institute. But firm as she was in resisting innovations which were contrary both to the Divine inspiration and to the instructions of Father Varin, the contradictions she had to endure planted in her heart no root of bitterness, wrung from her lips no complaining word; and she required the same charity of her daughters. "His intentions are good," she used to say; "leave all to God. M. de Sambucy is full of merit, but he is not the right man in the right place *(il n'est pas l'homme de la chose)*. Let us humble ourselves and wait. God holds all the events of life in His hands, and can make those which to us seem the most vexatious turn to His greater glory." And M. de Lamarche, who knew her thoroughly, wrote later the following testimony to her virtue during this period: "She set her daughters the example of every virtue, giving out wherever she went the good odour of Christ. It was enough to see her and to speak with her to be convinced that the spirit of God ruled her thoughts, her sentiments, her whole conduct. God made her pass through great trials; her projects were thwarted and opposed. But though she mourned over all the cavilling of which she was the object, she never lost the peace of her soul; she was always watchful over herself, and never spoke to her ecclesiastical superiors but with the most profound respect."

The displeasure of the confessor first broke forth on the occasion of the visit of the foundress to Flanders. Obliged to yield to the authority of his own Superior, Father Leblanc, he could not hinder the foundation of Saint-Nicolas, nor the steps taken by Mère Julie towards establishing and visiting the new houses. But he managed to prejudice against her the ecclesiastical authorities at Amiens, and on her return she was met with undeserved rebukes, which she accepted in silence. Mgr. Demandolx was a man of warm heart and real virtue. When left to himself he showed Julie the greatest kindness, but, unfortunately, M. de Sambucy had completely won his confidence, and the Bishop was ready to adopt his ideas without examination. Worn out with the difficulties he had met with in the organisation of his vast diocese, already suffering from the disease which was to prove fatal to him, he passed quickly from one impression to another, was influenced in the most contrary directions, and when his nerves were unstrung, gave way to uncontrolled movements of passion or indignation. It need not, therefore, astonish us to hear of his behaving towards the foundress one day with severity and another with kindness.* But

---

* Notice on the Bishops of Amiens by the Abbé Roze. Mgr. Demandolx died of softening of the brain.

when once he was delivered from his prejudices, we shall find him bearing striking witness to the heroic virtue which he had put to so severe a test. M. de Sambucy was also fully aware of Mère Julie's merit, but he considered her an obstacle to his projects of reform, and when he found he could neither change her ideas nor alienate Mère Blin from her, he resolved to separate them, in order to give himself a free hand. An opportunity soon offered. Mère Julie had not forgotten the promise made to Mgr. Pisani to found a house at Namur. The imperial authorisation had been granted, and the Mother General submitted to Mgr. Demandolx the arrangements made and the names of the Sisters destined for the new foundation. The Bishop of Amiens had approved of everything, when, at the last moment, M. de Sambucy persuaded him to change his decision. Two days before the departure he came to tell Mère Julie that she was to send to Namur as Superior, not the Sister who had been named, but Mère Blin de Bourdon. This was to deprive the Mother General of her chief support and counsel. Nevertheless, the two foundresses, trusting all to God, prepared to obey, and Mère Blin did not even give herself time to take leave of her family. M. de Sambucy's next step was to obtain control of the temporal resources. The Marquise de Franssu had given to Julie a sum of money to be employed in good works. This small capital, together with the proceeds of the sale of some property belonging to Mère Blin de Bourdon, was destined to go towards the purchase of a larger house. Now it happened that just at this time the Ladies of the Sacred Heart were anxious to acquire possession of the "Maison de l'Oratoire," which they had so far only rented; and M. de Sambucy did not hesitate to ask Julie for the loan of the money she had just put by. It was lent to him with no other security than a written receipt, and with no stipulation as regards the payment of interest. Madame Barat was thus enabled to acquire the property she desired. Moreover, the Abbé obliged Mère Blin to empower him to act for her in gathering her rents and apportioning her revenues; these he decided should be settled on the house of the Faubourg-Noyon alone. The two Mothers, thus deprived of all control over their property, were without the means necessary for the foundation at Namur. Mgr. Demandolx, who was really but a nominal agent in the matter, now ordered Mère Julie to accompany Mère Blin to Namur, and thence to proceed to Bordeaux, where a community of Sisters of Notre-Dame was asked for by Mgr. d'Aviau. Performing a heroic act of obedience, they left their convent on June 30, 1807. M. de Sambucy walked a few steps with them; his farewell was significant : " Mère Julie, you have finished your business here, you may now go and do it elsewhere." He did not venture to dismiss Mère Blin de Bourdon in direct terms, deterred, probably, by some regard for her position as temporal foundress of the Institute.

"The foundation at Namur," writes Father

Terwecoren in the Précis Historique of 1857, "was the most important of all . . . . therefore it was not to be made without many difficulties and obstacles; such is the ordinary course with the works of God." For God in all this was working out His own designs by means of the petty passions of men. He had decreed that the frail plant thus violently torn up from its native soil should take root at Namur and become a great tree, "and shoot out great branches, so that the birds of the air might dwell under the shadows thereof." The two travellers passed through Saint-Nicolas, where they took up Sister Xavier for the new community, and a little later Sister Elizabeth joined them from Amiens. On July 7 Julie and Françoise took possession of their convent, which the parental care of the Bishop had so thoughtfully provided with everything necessary for a beginning that, as Mère Blin said, "not even a match was wanting." *

The day after her arrival Julie wrote a long letter to Sister Anastasie (Leleu) and her companions at Amiens.

J. M. J.

NAMUR, July 8, 1807.

May our good Jesus and His Holy Mother live in all our hearts!

MY DEAR SISTERS AND GOOD DAUGHTERS IN OUR LORD,—It is only half-past three in the morning, but I cannot put off giving you some tidings of our arrival, so that we may all unite in blessing the merciful goodness of the good God towards us.

---

* This house, now occupied by the students of the Grand Séminaire, stands at the corner of the Rue du Séminaire and the Rue de l'Évêché.

We were received by the Bishop with every mark of kindness. He made us take our supper in his palace, and honoured us with his presence during it. How good the good God is, my dear daughters; and what thanks we owe Him for vouchsafing to be mindful of His poor servants! "Leave all and you shall find all," says the Following of Christ. Our Sisters are very happy, and bless God with all their hearts. They thought the house very nice, if anything too nice. How good God is! Now, then, courage! a manly sort of courage, my daughters, which no difficulty can alarm : if God is for us, who shall be against us?—a profound humility, an obedience without a thought of self, a confidence so strong that not all the demons in hell can trouble or shake it. . . . . Remember always, I beg of you, that virtue is made strong in infirmity; the more faults we see in ourselves, the more eagerly we ought to take them to the Adorable Heart of our Saviour Jesus.

The letter added an injunction to send an answer to it as soon as it should be received; but the answer never came. A visit which Father Leblanc paid to Julie on July 23 explained this silence. Mgr. Demandolx had taken from him the office of Superior of the community of the Faubourg-Noyon, and had replaced him by M. de Sambucy the very day after the departure of the foundresses. The correspondence was, no doubt, intercepted. "My good Mother," concluded the holy religious, "you have at this moment no more authority than myself in your house at Amiens." They agreed upon the course to be followed—to be silent, to pray, to leave all in the hands of God.

At Namur, happily, things were on a very different footing. The Bishop had named as confessor to the community M. Minsart, a former Bernardine of the Abbey of Boneffe, who had, therefore, personal experience of religious life, and who was, moreover, prudent, zealous and charitable in no ordinary degree.* This good priest took a warm interest in the work entrusted to him, and became to the Sisters of Notre-Dame a faithful friend, a wise counsellor and a true father. The schools were opened and gave promise of the happiest results. The religious spirit of the people, the intelligence and confiding character of the children, the affection they showed their teachers, all contributed to endear to the Sisters the city which was about to become a second cradle for their Institute. Mère Julie, as has been said, had orders from the Bishop of Amiens to proceed from Namur to Bordeaux. Mère St. Joseph was not without anxiety concerning this long journey, and in her humility, fearing the responsibilities of superiority, was for some days very unhappy about the approaching separation. But on the eve of Julie's departure, casting her eyes on a picture of the Descent of the Holy Ghost, she was filled with sudden consolation and joy. Embracing Mère Julie she said: "Adieu, ma Mère, you will come back to die at Namur." † The Archbishop of Bordeaux had formed a project of uniting to

---

* He was Vicar at the Church of St. John the Evangelist, and afterwards Curé of St.-Loup, a model priest and a father to the poor. He founded several schools, built and restored churches, established some religious congregations. He died at Namur in 1837 at the age of sixty-eight.
† Memoirs of Mère Blin de Bourdon.

the congregation of Notre-Dame a pious association in his diocese which was working on the same lines. Mère Julie, after a fatiguing journey of over nine hundred miles, arrived at Bordeaux on August 5. She was received with marked esteem by Mgr. d'Aviau, who at once put her in communication with Mme. Vincent, the Superior of Ste-Eulalie. The union of the two societies was quickly decided on, and Mère Julie hastened to relate all that had passed to Mère St.-Joseph.

> May our good Jesus ever live in our hearts and in all hearts.

MY DEAR GOOD FRIEND,—At last I am in this famous Bordeaux of which we have spoken so often. The Sisters here received me with the greatest charity. There are eighteen or twenty of them, all in excellent dispositions, wishing to serve our Lord as perfectly as they can in the person of His poor children. These children are very numerous; it was warm work going from class to class embracing them all. There are altogether three hundred, Mme. Vincent tells me. She is a woman of great merit and strong good sense. I hope our union will bring much glory to the good Master. I am longing for news from you. Have you any more children in your poor school? Now that I see so many at Bordeaux, I should like to go all round the world to snatch these poor little creatures from Satan's grasp and to teach them what their souls are worth. The little girls here are very quiet; not a word is to be heard in their large crowded schoolrooms. The mistresses speak little and in a low tone, and they all use *signals*, as we do at Amiens. My dear daughters, I beg of you, do not get into the habit of speaking too loud. I cannot say more to-day; I am obliged to call on the Prefect and on the Mayor; all this takes up time. This is my penance—we must each do our share. Pray that my sins, my innumerable infidelities, may not hinder the work of God. When I think that all founders of Orders have been Saints, and I am nothing but an infamous sinner. . . . Oh! my God, have pity on me in Thy great mercy. Oh! I shall fly back to you as soon as my good God allows me. No news yet from Amiens. You will understood what a sacrifice this is for my heart.*

Mère St.-Joseph answered:

The long wished for letter from Bordeaux was received with much consolation. It tells us you have arrived safely and that you have eighteen grown-up daughters and three hundred children. That looks like a full-fledged brood, which will not long need its mother. She must hasten back to her chicks that are still without feathers . . . . God in His infinite goodness has allowed me to feel persuaded that you will return here for a very long stay. Whether it be so or no, my weakness needed the comfort which this hope gives me.

Meantime weeks went by, and nothing was heard of Amiens, either at Bordeaux or Namur. "Our path has been marked out for us," wrote Julie; "let us walk in it with courage, through the brambles and thorns, remembering that Jesus, our good Master, goes before us. Let it be said that He has at least some little servants on earth who are entirely devoted, entirely consecrated to Him. . . . My heart is intensely tried just now. I have not heard a word from Amiens. I have written them four letters and nothing comes. I offer this in the best way I can to our Lord."

* This letter is addressed to "Mme. St.-Joseph, Schoolmistress, near the Episcopal Palace at Namur."

On September 8 the Archbishop of Bordeaux gave the habit to eighteen new subjects, and soon after a second convent was founded in the district of Les Chartrons. Mère Julie left behind her in the two schools at Bordeaux seven hundred poor children.

In the meantime letters from *M. Joseph* [*] pressed her to return; Father Leblanc urged the same thing. And when Mgr. Demandolx himself, "our good and holy Prelate," as she calls him, wrote paternally, "Return, return, my daughter, as soon as obedience allows you," it seemed that the wind had turned, and Mère Julie set out on November 12, 1807.

We must now go back to Amiens to explain what had happened during her absence. No sooner had Julie and Françoise left, than M. de Sambucy went straight to the Convent, assembled the community, and in the Bishop's name appointed as Superior Sister Thérèse Boutrainghan, to be called henceforth "Mère Victoire." He changed the names and offices of the other Sisters, made new regulations, established new customs, and gave it to be understood that the absence of the foundresses would be indefinitely prolonged. All letters to or from the Convent passed through his hands and were intercepted at his discretion.

The poor sisters in a spirit of obedience accepted

---

[*] The name by which Julie's letters at this time designate Father Varin, who was under the secret surveillance of the imperial police.

all without remonstrance; the one who felt these measures most deeply was the mistress of novices, Sister Leleu, whom Mère Julie playfully named her *petit conseil*, the *grand conseil* being Mère Blin.

Elizabeth Victoire Boutrainghan, thus suddenly installed as Superior at the age of twenty-one, was not without good qualities,—qualities which had indeed induced Mère Julie to make an exception in her case to her first prescription of excluding from the congregation those who had been in service. To an attractive exterior Victoire united insinuating manners, good taste and a certain *savoir-faire*, which is not uncommon in persons of her class; she had, moreover, a good heart and some strength of character. But she had received no education, and the religious training which goes so far to supply its want was still very incomplete, for she had only passed nineteen months in religion. Further, her former position was well-known in the town. Mère Julie had employed her in household work, for which she was fitted, and which supplied the exercise required by her active and sanguine temperament. But Sister Thérèse had somehow or other contrived to win the good graces of M. de Sambucy, who had allowed her to make annual vows after only one year's noviciate. He had proposed her to the foundress as temporary superior during her absence, and had seen in the objections raised a proof of jealousy towards his protégée. It is but just to say that the young person herself opposed a measure of which she had the sense to see the dangers. No sooner was Sister Thérèse transformed into Mère Victoire than she thought to win for herself prestige by adopting an extraordinary course of life. She ate scarcely anything, performed indiscreet austerities, and spent daily three or four hours in meditation. "I know not," writes Mère Blin de Bourdon, "what spirit was then abroad, but certain it is that praises fell upon Victoire like rain. M. de Sambucy consulted her, and sent persons from outside to seek her direction. People of the town, even Superiors of convents, praised her to her face. Young ladies, finding her respond to their expansive affection, became inordinately attached to her; they kissed her habit, they cut off locks of her hair for relics, they called her 'the Saint,' 'the holy penitent,' they vied with each other in exalting her virtues. In the Convent, some of the young sisters, seeing their Superior going without food, thought it their duty to deprive themselves of the nourishment they needed, and several were on the point of ruining their health." * On the other hand, the reserve and religious modesty to which Julie had formed her daughters suffered, and in a short time the whole tone of the house was altered. Unfortunately for herself Mère Victoire had undertaken, in imitation of Mère Julie, to give the daily instruction in Christian doctrine to the

* Memoirs, vol. i. p. 98.

younger Religious. The attempt proved a signal failure; tales of her incapacity reached the ears of the Bishop, and several of his clergy pointed out to him besides that Victoire's former social position was not a recommendation for a house of education. The prelate, who was sincerely desirous of doing the right thing, first made an abortive attempt to impose on the community as Superior a former Ursuline, and finally, as we have seen, joined with Father Varin in pressing Julie to return as quickly as possible. The Sisters, on their side, were beginning to call out loudly for the restoration of the two foundresses.

But M. de Sambucy again managed to change the face of affairs. He multiplied letters and negotiations to prevent Mère Julie's return, and spread against the servant of God suspicions which travelled, as such things will, and took hold even of those who best knew her and should most completely have trusted her. Her journey was but one series of disappointments and rejections. At Poitiers, where she stayed at the newly-founded house of the Ladies of the Sacred Heart, she found Mme. Barat and her daughters about to enter into retreat. On the invitation of Fathers Lambert and Enfantin, who were to give the exercises, she began the retreat with them, but "felt herself," say the Memoirs, "so strangely troubled that she understood she was called elsewhere." Father Lambert agreed with her, and she decided to proceed on her journey. It was probably on this occasion that Father Enfantin predicted to her "that persecution on the part of the good which was to burst upon her, and of which she had already felt the first effects."* Mme. Barat herself, with whom she had hitherto been on such affectionate terms, now showed herself somewhat distant and cold. At Paris, which she reached on November 23, a freezing reception awaited her from many an old friend,—from Mme. Leclercq at the Abbaye-au-Bois, and from the Superior General of the Sisters of Charity, who had once received her hospitality at Amiens. The latter indeed had been commissioned to deliver to Mère Julie a crushing letter from Mgr. Demandolx, which, in direct contradiction with his former one, forbade her to return to the Convent of Notre-Dame, or even to enter the diocese of Amiens; she might go to Namur if she pleased. Absolutely ignorant as to the cause of his displeasure, and in deep sorrow of heart, Julie sought that Friend "who, when all forsake, will not leave His own nor suffer them to perish."† In the chapel of the Visitation she passed two hours prostrate in prayer before the altar, and then went to seek counsel of Father Varin, who happened to be in Paris. The moment was an unlucky one. She found the Father on the one hand overwhelmed by the decree which Napoleon had just fulminated against the Fathers of the

* Memoirs.　　† Imit. ii. c. 7.

Faith, ordering their dispersion and the dissolution of their colleges; on the other, under the unfavourable impression produced by a lengthy memorial from M. de Sambucy detailing his complaints against Julie. So he, too, only received her with hard words. But let it not be supposed that the sentiments of the Father towards his humble penitent ever underwent any real change. After her death, seeking to express in a word her spiritual character, he called her "one who while on earth lived upon love."

Meanwhile Mme. Leclercq, disabused of her first impressions, had written to M. Duminy, Curé of the Cathedral of Amiens, to beg of him to obtain from the Bishop permission for Julie at least to enter the diocese. While waiting for the answer the servant of God went to St.-Sulpice to get counsel and help from the venerable M. Montaigne, to whom, from this time forward, she continued to apply for advice. After eleven days of suspense a letter came, authorising Mère Julie to go to Plessier-sur-St.-Just, to M. de Lamarche. But here again disappointment was her portion—her old friend and confessor was absent. After much prayer and deliberation she decided that, since she was no longer banished from the diocese, she might venture as far as Amiens, provided she did not show herself at the Convent. She sought refuge therefore with one of her friends, Mme. de Rumigny. A somewhat singular incident belongs to her stay here. We give it in the words of the memoirs. "At the dispersion of the Fathers of the Faith, one of the brothers, named Leonard, had attached himself to the service of the Abbé Louis [de Sambucy]. This man happened to come to the house of Mme. Rumigny, and there saw Mère Julie, who was at the time in the company of this good lady, M. Bicheron, and several other ecclesiastics. Our Mother has since told me that it was impossible to conceive the hideousness of Leonard's expression of countenance; when he perceived her, he merely said, in an extraordinary tone of voice, 'You did very wrong to come back!' M. Bicheron, a strong and robust man, cast one glance at Leonard's face and, a moment later, was taken so ill that he could not even go down to his own room, and the doctor was sent for. When he was a little better, Mère Julie said to him: 'How did this happen? What was the matter with you?' 'It was Leonard's face,' he replied; 'did you not see Leonard's face?'"

The foundress now wrote to the Bishop of Amiens in the humblest terms, begging pardon for whatever had displeased him, and was at last admitted to the episcopal palace. She obtained permission, though not without difficulty, to go and recruit her shattered health at the Faubourg, but was given to understand that as soon as she was better she must go back to Namur. And so, on December 3, the Venerable Mother re-entered her convent stealthily, like a criminal, and went up by a back staircase to her own room, where, worn out with fatigues and emotions, she fell ill, and was obliged for some time to keep her bed. It was soon whispered in the community that the foundress had returned, and the Sisters went in little groups to see her. Mère Victoire was one of the first; she threw herself into her arms with the strongest protestations of attachment, and even offered her the keys of the house, which Julie, however, prudently declined. But neither her unalterable patience, nor the gentleness and kindness with which she treated Victoire could overcome the prejudices of the Abbé, who was still doing his utmost to maintain the now damaged prestige of his favourite. By his orders, pupils and externs addressed her as *Madame*; her very dreams, which were narrated to him, he invested with deep and mystical significance; while, under his influence, a cabal was formed which, not content with criticising and misinterpreting all that Julie said or did, reproached her to her face in the strongest terms. Victoire was an angel—Julie behaved to her like a cruel wild beast,—and so forth. In the midst of all this storm of calumnies and insults, the servant of God felt "no more resentment," says the friend who, to borrow Julie's words, had the key of her heart, "than a new-born infant." And she adds somewhere these simple but touching words: "In all the trying circumstances she met with, she felt every blow, offered her pain to God, and kept her soul in peace." * How beautiful in its reticence and unshaken confidence is the letter she writes on December 8 to Namur! " God is so good that He helps us through everything like a tender Father. Let us put our whole trust in Him, always, always. I have not been well since I came, but God will mend all that in time. Let us love Him with all our heart, let us serve Him as well as we can, let us put our trust in Him alone. I repeat this twice over, because this God of all goodness likes to hear it said to Him often." And to Mère St.-Joseph : " I know that the good God will come to our help. I cast myself into His merciful arms and into His adorable Heart; put me deep into It, my dear friend. This is my one prayer : ' My Jesus, fasten me tight to Thy blessed Cross, and hold me there, for I am nothing but misery.' . . My heart and my soul rest in God, in spite of all the fogs of the Somme. God alone!" And up and down the page comes that song of her heart, " How good the good God is! Ah! how good He is!" The naïve pleonasm has passed into a kind of motto for Notre-Dame, and was familiar to all who knew the Servant of God. " Tell my good Julie," Father Varin once wrote to Mère Barat, " that I constantly think of her, for I like to remind myself often that *the good God is good.*"

All of a sudden the Bishop who, as we have said, passed rapidly from one impression to another,

* Memoirs, vol. i. p. 121.

deposed Victoire to the post of assistant, reinstating the foundress as Superior. But such half-measures produced no real difference in the situation. Neither did the seemingly radical change of substituting M. Cottu, his Vicar-General, as spiritual superior to the community in place of M. de Sambucy, who was restricted to his functions as confessor. The Abbé was still the moving power. He lived with M. Cottu who did nothing but by his advice. As to "Mme. Victoire," he informed the Sisters that, her name having gone up to Government as Superior for three years, she must continue in office conjointly with Mère Julie.

This arrangement brought the confusion to a climax, and it needed all the courage of the servant of God to support the trial; but she drew her heroism, as the memoirs remark, straight from its source in the Sacred Heart.

Dec. 23, 1807. How much we shall have to say to each other, my dear friend, when it pleases the Divine Goodness to let us meet! Ah, yes! much that I have laid down in the sweet and loving Heart of Jesus—otherwise I could not have borne the burden. It was heavy enough to kill ten poor Julies like me. I am worth nothing at all for heaven yet. Do pray that the various trials it pleases our Lord to send me may serve to sanctify me. I am so clumsy, I make a mess of everything. You know how much I need to cleave to God alone. Oh! yes, may He alone be my strength and my support. . . . . . Courage! let us not ask for rest yet. No, no, time presses, and the day is far spent. Let us set no bounds to our generosity towards the good God, and He will be lavish towards us.

A few weeks later she is writing kind words about Victoire—who would seem to have resigned her post of her own accord—giving her credit for a right will and a good intention, and asking prayers for her perseverance ; noting gratefully that the interior spirit among the younger members is resuming its former vigour. "They needed an older person to guide them," she says delicately, " grey hairs are good for something after all." A word at the end of the letter lets us know that the temporal interests, no less than the spiritual, had been compromised, and that she is troubled by the heavy debts which have been contracted, but "the good God takes care of us like a good Father."

Meanwhile the reputation of the new Institute and of its teachers was spreading in Belgium ; and Jumet, a busy and populous town not far from Charleroi, applied, through Mgr. Pisani, for an establishment of the Sisters of Notre-Dame. Mère Julie submitted the proposal to the Bishop of Amiens, and gave him the names of the Sisters she had fixed upon for the new foundation ; amongst them was that of Mère Victoire, whom she thus hoped to free from her present false position. Everything had been approved by his Lordship, when the storm burst afresh. The old charge of jealousy was revived, and the permission to go to Jumet withdrawn. "Man proposes and God disposes," she writes quietly to Mère Blin de Bourdon. " Everything is changed—I cannot give you details; all I can do is to ask you to try and gain time for this little foundation at Jumet, if indeed it is to be. . . Ah! my daughter, we must pass through the fire if we are to be purified, and if we are to do anything of worth for the greater glory of God. The devil rages, but God shall prove the stronger."

She had other serious anxieties. Napoleon was contemplating the fusion of all religious congregations of women into two bodies only, the *hospitalières* and the *enseignantes*, and Mère Julie's letters of this period make frequent allusion to this proposed amalgamation, which threatened the life and spirit of her Society in a different manner. She consulted, prayed, took such wise precautions against the contingency as lay within her reach, and then fell back on her old rule, "Leave things to the good God." Of a truth she could do little else in the incessant fluctuations of her life. "Things change from one moment to another," she writes again. "I am now kept prisoner, as it were, in our own house. I must not move an inch in your direction for fear I should stay with you, and the Amiens house should fall"—that house, be it remarked, whose existence not three months before had been supposed to depend upon her absence! "God has spared you in not letting you be here when we fell into other hands.* My God, my God, how good Thou art! support my weak-

* In allusion to the departure of the Fathers of the Faith.

ness. . . . Did I not tell you, my dear friend, that if you stayed with me I should get you plenty of crosses? Come! let us share between us these treasures of the good God, these precious pledges of His love. All that I ask of our Lord is that I may enter into His adorable plans, since He wills to lead me by this road. I am still so far from the end, from the measure that I need in order to fill up all that God requires of me."

Verily, Julie's was the charity which "thinketh no evil, believeth all things, hopeth all things, endureth all things;"* a charity which to Mgr. Pisani, who had watched all the circumstances, seemed so heroic that he did not fear to say after her death: "Mère Julie will be canonised some day *because during all her long trials at Amiens she never once failed in charity.*"†

* 1 Cor. xiii.
† Informatory Process de heroica charitate; Apostolical Process de fama sanctitatis.

CHAPTER XI.

EXPULSION FROM AMIENS.

MÈRE JULIE's tribulations were far from being at an end. But gleams of consolation came to her from time to time, sent by God that she might not be utterly crushed. The news from Namur was excellent. Under the wise direction of Mère St. Joseph, assisted by five or six Sisters, all was going on prosperously; a boarding-school had been opened, the poor-schools overflowed with children, a work-room for lace-making had been established. Mlle. Anne Leroy, who taught the lace-work school, had begged to enter the noviciate; but six months afterwards an obstinate attack of quinsy reduced her to the last extremity. She made her vows on her deathbed and gave up her soul into the hands of her Spouse on February 18, 1808. Thus it was from Namur that the first of Julie's daughters went to her reward. "A very beautiful soul," said Mère St.-Joseph, "who had gone through extraordinary suffering. I trust she now intercedes for us before the throne of God."

Mgr. Pisani, who took the deepest interest in his daughters at Notre-Dame, omitted no opportunity of showing them kindness and encouragement. Every evening during Lent he invited them to the

MONSEIGNEUR PISANI DE LA GAUDE,
Bishop of Namur 1804-1826.
From an Oil Painting in possession of the Sisters of Notre-Dame, Namur.

To face p. 150.

meditation on the Passion which he gave to his household in his domestic chapel. The other Belgian foundation, Saint-Nicolas, notwithstanding its unhealthy situation, gave promise of excellent results, and the little community at Montdidier, under the paternal direction of the holy M. de Lamarche, was equally blessed by God. At this last place the only difficulty of the Sisters was to keep away from their schools children who could pay fees, Mère Julie having, out of consideration for a neighbouring convent, forbidden any of this class to be admitted. Yielding, however, to pressure from the parents, the Sisters had received a few well-to-do pupils. The concession brought them a letter from their mother, once more exhorting them to admit none but "very poor children who cannot pay anything at all." Of these they were to gather as many as possible, for they were at Montdidier absolutely and only for the poor. It was against her express wish that payment had been taken from any one, and if any such scholars were still with them they were to be at once sent away. "Let us not trouble ourselves, my dear Sister Catherine,* about who will feed us; our good Father is in heaven. Suppose you find after a while that what you have is only enough for two of you, the good God will feed the third, or He will put her somewhere else." They had life and raiment—what more could daughters of hers desire? She indeed had but one desire and

* Sister Catherine Daullée, Superior.

prayer for them—that they should daily grow in the spirit of their holy vocation by a thorough detachment from the things of earth. There is the usual joyous exultation over that grand vocation which made war on the devil by snatching souls from his grasp; and the usual exhortation to the "masculine courage" needed for the task; there is a practical counsel to do all their work in an orderly spirit because "the Lord loves order and has Himself done all things in order and measure;" and a maternal recommendation to take great care of their health, "without softness of course, in God and for God."

Meanwhile the Jumet foundation was still in abeyance, for as we have seen Mère Julie was forbidden to leave Amiens. She abandoned herself unreservedly to the Divine Will. "Although our Mother," say the Memoirs, "was, so to speak, identified with the Institute and full of zeal for all that could procure its advantage, she was perfectly ready to accept all that might happen to it by God's permission. I believe that what St. Ignatius said of himself could have been said of her, that a quarter of an hour's prayer would have been enough to console her for the destruction of all our houses. At these critical moments she used to repeat, "The good God can destroy what He has set up. We must keep very quiet in the hands of the Lord. Is He not the Master to do and to undo?'" As far as *undoing* went, M. de Sambucy took it in hand. It will be remembered that umbrage had been taken

at the appointment of "Mme. Victoire" to the Jumet mission. A counter arrangement followed, destined to remove from Mère Julie's side one of her most warmly attached daughters. "Do you know," she writes to Mère Blin on March 4, 1808, "who are now named by the Bishop for Jumet? Sister Leleu, Sister Agnes and Sister Madeleine. Little Agnes is a dear, good child, but she needs another year of formation. . . . Our Sisters are much distressed at having to go without me. Pray that God may give them grace to make their sacrifice. Mine too is a great one." And some days later:—
"The situation remains the same. They think I want to leave the Amiens house to go and settle at Namur. But I have no intention of leaving. It was the first which God, in His mercy, and through many tribulations, established."

Again the plans were changed. Sister Leleu and Françoise Belin were to set off for Jumet alone, with an understanding that others would follow. So the foundress had lost her *petit conseil* as well as her *grand conseil*. But the brave heart was too firmly anchored in God to be shaken by the removal of any human support. "All who consider the guidance of God in our affairs are inclined to think that He wants something very special of us. When and how? That is what I must adore. And yet," she continued, "to be tied here without having the right of saying or doing anything for the good of the Institute, to be wholly inactive,—I do not know if God asks that of me, after having in His great mercy restored to me the use of my limbs."

There was a rumour that M. de Sambucy was to be named Visitor; Julie "by God's grace blesses the good God for all;" she is not sorry that he should go and see them at Namur, her only grief would be that she herself, as seems likely, should be forbidden to visit her dear sisters. The good father, she knows, means well—only "in his own way and acting of himself." But "if such is the holy Will of God all will go well; if He wishes differently He will know how to direct all for the best."

Sister Leleu arrived at Jumet to find the house just left by the Sisters of the Visitation, without beds, fuel, or bread. Thanks to some charitable friends the poor nuns were enabled to procure what was absolutely necessary, and Mère Blin de Bourdon soon arrived from Namur bringing help and consolation. It was then only that she learned the full details of Julie's painful position at Amiens, and she wrote to her on the spot: "My good Mother, I arrived here the day before yesterday, and I go away again to-morrow. I have seen all, read all, understood all. Ah! my poor mother, what can be the meaning of all this? And yet nothing surprises me. Rejoice with a great joy; for it is thus that God treats His friends. Be convinced that all will come right in the end, and that a path will open out before you. I own that at this moment all is darkness;

one does not know which way to turn, nor what steps to take. One thing only appears tolerably clear to me—and Sister Anastasie (Leleu) is of my opinion,—and that is that I should acquaint M. Minsart with the state of affairs before M. Sambucy comes to make his visitation at Namur and Jumet. M. Minsart is so good and so well disposed towards us and our work, that this can do no harm. Let us pray that God may grant us always to do His holy Will: that is all I desire, nothing else is worth striving after."

A few days afterwards, to Julie's great surprise, Mgr. Demandolx sent for her and asked her if she was satisfied with the establishment at Jumet. "Not too much so," she replied. "Nor I either" rejoined the Bishop; "Mère Julie, you must go there, and if our sisters have not all they need, bring them back to me, and those of Saint-Nicolas too. I will not have them killed. It was a mortal sin," he added, smiling, "to put them in such a damp house." Julie did not wait to be told twice; she set off the very next day, the more eagerly as news had come that Mère Blin de Bourdon was ill at Namur. Her unexpected arrival was a joyful surprise to the sisters at Jumet. With her accustomed energy and decision she soon acquainted herself with all the difficulties, and in a few days had provided for the needs of the house and regulated the schools. At Namur, she was relieved to find Mère St. Joseph convalescent. They hastened to confer with M. Minsart, and it was decided to explain to the Bishop the nature of the opposition made at Amiens to the progress of the Institute. Mgr. Pisani was also consulted on the delicate question of the power to dispose of her income, which M. de Sambucy had obliged Mère Blin to give him before she left Amiens. In this way the Bishop learned for the first time the family name and social position of Mère St. Joseph. He advised her to go back with Mère Julie in order to arrange this business with all due circumspection. The two holy friends set off from Namur together, leaving Sister Xavier as temporary Superior of the house. They took Saint-Nicolas on their way. Here they found the Superior, Sister St. Jean (Garson), seriously ill through the humidity of the situation. As the Committee did not come forward, Mère Julie undertook to remedy things herself. Within two days she had taken another house for a year, and removed the sisters and boarders into it. She was just leaving Saint-Nicolas when she received a crushing letter from the Bishop of Amiens, which contrasted strangely with the kindness of his words and manner at her last interview with him. He reproached her in severe terms for her want of obedience and simplicity, he revived the charge of secret jealousy of Mère Victoire, " a subject whom you dislike because she is worth more than yourself, and on whom God will take pleasure in showering His graces in proportion as you seek to humble her," and wound up with the stern admonition to cultivate sentiments of true humility, " without which you can do no real work for souls." The motive of this grave reprimand was the following : Sister Jeanne Godelle had succeeded Sister Leleu as Mistress of Novices. She had entered the congregation when thirty years old, and joined to a very careful education an excellent judgment, a lively spirit of faith and considerable prudence ripened by her experience of the world. Just as Mère Julie was leaving Amiens, some of the sisters who had little confidence in the Assistant, asked their Mother to whom they should address themselves if they needed some spiritual advice in her absence. It seemed quite natural to suggest the Mistress of Novices, and Mère Julie named her without hesitation. This simple action was represented to Mgr. Demandolx as an attempt to rebel against authority.

The travellers arrived at Amiens on May 5, and Mère Blin de Bourdon sent at once to present her respects to the Bishop and to ask an audience. His Lordship's answer was that he was going away in a day or two for a two months' journey and would see the Mothers on his return. Mère St.-Joseph wrote, therefore, to Mgr. Pisauni to excuse her prolonged absence, and on June 7, 1808, the benevolent prelate replied gracefully : " Accustomed as I am to sacrifices, my dear daughter, I submit to that of being deprived, for some time longer, of your presence here, and of the example of your virtues and works of charity." And he added : " The propositions you are submitting to Mgr. Demandolx could not be wiser or more reasonable. Do not doubt that this worthy prelate, who is a true father of his flock, will grant with kindness as well as justice the request you are making. I am convinced that my opinion is his, and I should not offer the least opposition to your wishes. I console myself with the belief that the salubrity of our city, the religious spirit which reigns there, and the proofs I have given you of my pastoral affection, will all induce you to return to your daughters at Namur, who indeed are sighing to have you back amongst them. Their conduct continues to be beyond praise ; the number of pupils increases, but the house cannot be enlarged, which I am very sorry for. Take care of your health, come back to us as soon as you are able, and bring with you, if possible, your good Mother, whom I salute and love in the Lord. I entertain the same sentiments towards yourself, my dear daughter in Jesus Christ, and in them I leave you at His Feet, pierced, as was His Heart, by His love for us."

While awaiting the return of the Bishop of Amiens, Julie was not idle. She visited the little convent at Montdidier, and installed there as Superior Sister Marie-Caroline Cardon, while she transferred Sister Catherine Daullée to Saint-Nicolas. This holy religious carried away with her from Montdidier the regret of all the inhabitants, and her virtues soon won for her the same esteem and affection in Flanders. Good Sister St.-Jean, whose robust constitution had been ruined by the two winters passed in the unhealthy house at Saint-Nicolas, was thus set free from her duties. Mère Julie offered her the alternative of returning to Amiens or going to one of the other houses, but the invalid protested against being allowed any choice in the matter.

> My dear and good Mother (she wrote),—We received your letter of May 25 with the greatest pleasure. The happiness that I experienced on learning that you were about to give me a substitute made such an impression on me that I at once began to get better. But your letter of to-day has a very different effect. Never has any letter of yours caused me so much pain, because you tell me to do as I like. It is only naughty children who are told to do as they like. I have deserved this, no doubt, by paying too much attention to a little suffering, and giving you so much trouble. But, my good Mother, you could not give me a greater punishment than to tell me to do as I like. Oh! a nice mess I shall make of things if I do as I like. . . .
>
> My dear Mother, do not say so to me any more, but reckon me among your true daughters, and tell me what you wish me to do.

The young religious formed in Mère Julie's school was obedient unto death. She went back to Amiens, but, as her health did not improve, her native air was, by the advice of the doctors, tried for her, but without effect. She only lived till January, 1809.

Authorised by the Vicar-General, the foundress also paid a visit to Paris to try and get the assistance of a government grant which might enable the community of Saint-Nicholas to establish themselves in a more healthy locality. Nothing discourages her. She is obliged, she writes word to her daughters, to run from one end of the town to the other, but after having done all in her power to bring matters to a successful issue she shall leave everything in God's hands. She sees, indeed, that He had His own merciful designs in allowing her to take this little journey—she will tell them all about His goodness to her on her return.

The special grace in question seems to have been some new cross, for she exclaims : " Let us look at our daily trials with the eye of faith—the cross is the most excellent present, the most precious gift that God can give to His children. I have read somewhere that the more crosses God prepares for a soul the more light and grace He also prepares for it. So let us try to help one another to carry the cross He means for us." To Mère Blin, who had communicated some fresh complaints against her, she is more explicit, and more unreserved in that " joy of the spirit " which the author of the " Imitation of Christ " says the cross brings to its lovers. " All that you tell me in your letter I had already heard, and also something better still. Tell me, then, whether the good God is good enough, and whether He is not able to find me at Paris as at Amiens and Saint-Nicolas. An abundance of good things does no harm for a happy eternity. Remember what you used to say to me—that it was unlucky to be with me, because there was nothing to expect but crosses. Indeed, we have our share. But take courage, my dear friend, you know where all this is to land us. Heaven, yes, heaven, shall be the reward of our constancy."

As the year before, the return journey to Amiens was for her a way of the cross; now, as then, those whom she most revered met her with altered mien and manner, thus helping her, as Mère Blin de Bourdon reflects, to a total detachment from all that is human by teaching her through personal experience that God alone changes not. And she adds that without this discipline her affectionate and grateful nature might have clung to those who had shown her kindness.

In the meanwhile Mère Blin had had an audience with His Lordship, had answered with perfect frankness the questions put to her on the subject of the foundress, and had plainly expressed her opinion that things would go on better without M. de Sambucy. The sequel proved that she had made little or no impression, and Mère Julie arrived to find that matters had culminated—the Rule was to undergo revision. The Bishop himself informed the two Mothers of some of the projected changes—the suppression of the office of Superior General, of the visitation of the secondary houses, and other no less radical departures from the primitive plan of the Institute. Just at this juncture the presence of the foundress was requested at Bordeaux by Mgr. d'Aviau, and she embraced

the opportunity of extricating herself from the
labyrinth in which she was. The Bishop of Amiens
gave his consent, withdrew it on the morrow, and
finally authorised her to go: she was to pass
through Paris. While in the capital she sought
out "her good Father Varin," to whom she delivered
a packet of letters entrusted to her by M. de
Sambucy. Whatever accusations against herself
they contained must have been serious enough,
for the Father fairly overwhelmed her by his
severity. She and Mère Blin were two mad
women; all the bishops were against them: new
Rules must be drawn up, and by no one else but
M. de Sambucy. He forbade her to go on to
Bordeaux; she was to return at once to Amiens,
and herself petition the Abbé to frame the constitutions in accordance with his own inspirations. It
is from Father Sellier that we learn that Mère
Julie on this occasion "was the victim of an odious
scheme:" she had, in fact, been sent to Paris,
not *en route* for Bordeaux, but to hear her
sentence pronounced by Father Varin. In reality,
the Father had no authority to command her, as
since the dissolution of the Fathers of the Faith the
ties of obedience to the members of that Society had,
by his own desire, ceased to exist. But, to use her
own words, she "had never found obedience to be an
insupportable, or even a heavy, yoke," and with a
simple submission which, under the circumstances,
Mère Blin fitly characterises as heroic, she turned her

face towards Amiens instead of Bordeaux. Though she arrived both tired out and ill, she went direct to M. de Sambucy, and with the generosity and openness which were part of her great character, and the perfect trustfulness which came of seeing God's will in all, begged him with the best grace in the world to draw up the new rules. On his side he accepted the offer which he had himself provoked, and promised to treat this grave affair with herself and Mère St.-Joseph. But no sooner was she back in her community than she learned that the seeming cordiality of the Abbé cloaked a very real vexation. The occurrence that had awakened it in her few days' absence was almost childishly trivial—the involuntary laughter of some novices in the refectory, misinterpreted by Mère Victoire as a personal affront, and by her reported as such to the too willing ear of the Abbé. The Assistant did not appear in the Refectory again that day, and Mère Blin judged it a matter of wisdom and duty to explain in a few words the situation of affairs to the Sisters, who must indeed already have been aware that there was something in the air. "If," she said in conclusion, "we cannot stay here, we will go elsewhere; let those who love us follow us!" The response was unanimous: cries of "I will," "And I," rang out on all sides. This scene, like the preceding one, was severely judged in high quarters, and the whole community was for a time punished by the deprivation of Holy Communion. But it must at least have convinced the authorities of the genuine attachment of the community to the Superior whom, among other things, they accused of harshness and inflexibility.

In the midst of these trials consolation and encouragement came from other quarters — from Bordeaux, whence Mgr. d'Aviau wrote in terms of paternal esteem to the Superior General — and from Namur.

Mgr. Pisani de la Gaude, while still hoping that his colleague of Amiens will yield to "the wise reasons of the Superior General," regards these contradictions as "trials that shall pass," and assures both Julie and Mère Blin, in separate letters, of the devotedness of his own diocese to their Institute, and of the joy he shall feel in welcoming "the whole swarm," if it be God's will that it leave the hive.

M. Minsart, too, wrote on August 14, 1808, in the same strain to Mère St.-Joseph:

> I am not surprised at the sufferings your Mother has to endure from her Superiors. It can hardly be otherwise when they are attempting to infuse into a society like yours a spirit opposed to that which gathered you together and which is engraven on your hearts; and when, again, they are giving their support to a young Superior, who may be virtuous, but who lacks the experience necessary for directing souls. The accounts I have had from Sœur Anastasie, who co-operates so worthily in the work of God, and fills so capably the post entrusted to her at Jumet, convince me that you ought not to tie yourselves to one place more than another. You must examine whether the rule they wish to impose on you is contrary to the spirit of the original one, and to the work of God which Mère Julie has so well begun, and which could not

have made such rapid progress without His special protection.

I should assuredly never be against your receiving, in all humility, the crosses, tribulations, and sufferings sent by God; but if the work of God and His glory are diminished thereby, I think it is good to seek them *in the place whither a road is pointed out to you by God.*

Father Varin, on his side, had been deeply edified by the humility with which the servant of God had borne his hard reproaches, and the obedience with which she had fulfilled his orders; further enquiry had completely disabused him of his momentary impression, and he had written an indignant letter to M. de Sambucy. "If the whole universe had been against her," he says, "you, at least, should have taken her part; yet it was you, as I know, who have injured her cause with the Bishops."

And he adds that if the Abbé's intentions were good, their consequences had, unfortunately, not been so. This reproof from his former Superior seems to have made an impression on M. de Sambucy, and to have been recognised by him as deserved. He wrote to the Bishops of Ghent and Tournay, as well as to the Vicar General of the Bishop of Bordeaux, retracting the unfavourable statements he had made to them concerning the foundress.

She, meanwhile, following the counsel of the wise man, "Make not haste in the time of clouds," neglected nothing that might bring about an amicable settlement of affairs. Moreover, bound to France and to Picardy by so many ties, the two Mothers ardently desired to carry out their work in their own country. It depended only on the Bishop and his delegates to retain the services of the Sisters who had been so warmly encouraged by his predecessor, Mgr. de Villaret. Julie, therefore, lent herself cheerfully to long conversations on the rules with M. de Sambucy; met his proposed restrictions and innovations by pointing out to him the liberty enjoyed by the congregation at Namur; and even carried her trust in him so far as to show him Mgr. Pisani's letters, "to let him know," says Mère Blin de Bourdon, "that we were not staying at Amiens for want of another resting-place, but from fear of not following the Divine will, which had not as yet been clearly manifested to us." These discussions, as may be supposed, resulted in nothing, and soon prejudice and persecution were again the order of the day. The allusion to the paternal government of the Bishop of Namur was censured as the sign of a spirit of independence, the communication of his letters as an indiscretion; Julie was forbidden to show herself at the Bishop's house without an express summons. One day, however, she was sent for, and Mère Blin accompanied her to the door, and then went to wait for her in a neighbouring house. The precaution was not a needless one, for the Venerable Mother came out weeping—the first tears she had shed in the course of these long and painful trials. She owned to her friend that the stormy scene had been too much for her; and though, thanks to the witness of her conscience, the depths of her soul remained unruffled, the vehemence of the Bishop's tone, gestures and language had been such that her nervous system received a shock from which she did not recover for days.* "How," asks Mère Blin de Bourdon, in relating the incident, "how could a prelate, otherwise so estimable and virtuous, treat with such rigour a person whose only desire was to do good in his diocese?" Faith found an answer to the question; as the Servant of God used to say, "she discerned something which came from God" *(elle découvrait quelquechose de Dieu)* through it all. And so she prayed and waited. "The good God will do something that will astonish us," she would repeat to her companion in her simple but almost prophetic language. "He will manage it all. We must not worry; there will come *a stroke of His Hand*, I look upon it as already done. Light will appear: we shall see a road open up before us. I think that God will take us to Namur." She had declared long before to Mère St.-Joseph that she had felt an extraordinary attraction for this city the first time she had seen it.†

Notwithstanding all the external difficulties, the

* Mme. Barat had the sorrow of seeing her old friend, Mère Julie Billiart, misunderstood and persecuted, the Bishop's mind poisoned against her, and herself and her Congregation on the point of being driven out of a town and diocese which teemed with their good works. *Vie de la Mère Barat*, by Mgr. Baunard, vol. i. p. 223.

† Memoirs of Mère Blin de Bourdon, vol. ii. p. 10.

community of the Faubourg-Noyon had, since the foundress's return, resumed its former religious tone, and its earnest work for God and souls. Postulants presented themselves; children filled the schools; fervour, zeal and regularity reigned in the house. The blessing and protection of God were felt in countless delicate attentions of His Providence, some of which seemed almost miraculous. One day the Venerable Mother was about to give the habit to a postulant, and sent to Sister Gertrude (Ciska Steenhaut) for the bonnet to which the veil is fastened. The Sister replied that she had not got one, and that there was no stuff in the house to make one of. Mère Julie ordered her to go to the chapel and lay her difficulty before our Lord, after which she was to go back to the habit-room and would find there the article required. Sister Gertrude obeyed, but sought in vain for the bonnet. "Child of little faith," said Julie, when she came to tell her, "go back to the chapel." Ciska went, and in language as earnest as it was naïve begged of Jesus to come to her assistance, "because *ma Mère* wishes it." This time her prayer was heard; on returning to the room she found the bonnet she wanted carefully laid on a chair. She carried it to the Servant of God, who immediately placed it on the head of the novice; "and never," said the old Sisters, "did bonnet fit so well."

"Some time afterwards," relates Sister Louis de Gonzague, "our Mother sent for Sister Gertrude again, and told her to make a new habit for the next day. The Sister objected that she had no stuff but a piece of white serge. "Reasoning as usual!" rejoined her Superior; "go back to your office, and you will find black stuff there." Great indeed was the surprise of Sister Gertrude to find the piece of white cloth which she had left in the room changed to black; but the foundress showed no astonishment at the news, "for," say the contemporary witnesses, "she knew the goodness of Him in Whom she placed her trust." *

Meanwhile, the colony at Namur was becoming uneasy at the prolonged absence of Mère St.-Joseph, and, supported by Mgr. Pisani and M. Minsart, was earnestly petitioning for a visit from their Superior General. Jumet and St.-Nicolas urged their own claims, and M. Cottu, in spite of his theories, was forced to admit that it was sometimes desirable to visit the houses. Accordingly Mère Julie was authorised to go to Belgium, and on her way to make a new foundation at the little village of Rubempré, near Amiens. Here she placed, with two other Sisters, Sister Scholastique Pelletier, a niece of M. Bicheron, the Curé of St.-Remi at Amiens, whom we

* See Notices on the First Sisters of the Institute, by Sr. Louis de Gonzague, and cf. testimonies of Sisters M. Claudine Godefroid and Agnès-Marie Bochkoltz, authenticated by the Bishop of Namur. Sister Louis de Gonzague (Hortense Monseu) was Superior of the first colony of Sisters who went to America in 1840. She spent her last years at Namur, collecting details for biographies of the early Sisters from the lips of those who had been their contemporaries. These notices she wrote with the most scrupulous exactness. She died at Namur in 1866.

have already mentioned. The arrangements for this establishment brought her into frequent intercourse with the Abbé Chevalier, Curé of Rubempré, and later on Dean of Rosières, a man distinguished for his piety, learning and zeal.* Julie consulted him on her difficulties, and he encouraged her in adhering to the primitive plan of her Institute, and in withdrawing from Amiens if she could not carry it out.

She took with her for Namur and Jumet, where help was greatly needed, Sisters Eulalie de Laporte and Firmine Queste. At Namur the necessity for more extensive premises was making itself felt. The wing of the Seminary generously lent by Mgr. Pisani could only accommodate a very limited number of Sisters and children; moreover it had no garden, a drawback which was affecting the health of the inmates. M. Minsart, the devoted friend of the Institute, busied himself actively about procuring more suitable premises, and at last set his heart upon the former house of the Counts Quarré in the Rue des Fossés. With its beautiful gardens and suites of spacious rooms this property seemed exactly what was wanted. "You could house thirty boarders there and two hundred poor children," wrote the good priest in the joy of his heart to Mère St.-Joseph.† But the authorisation of the Bishop was necessary, and Mgr. Pisani, from financial reasons,

* Vie du Père Louis Sellier, by Father A. Guidée, p. 90.
† Letter dated September 26, 1808. The Convent at Namur reckoned later more than a hundred boarders and more than six hundred poor children.

hesitated. No difficulties, however, could cool M. Minsart's zeal; he secured the aid of charitable friends, and the expenses of the rent were guaranteed for the first two years. On October 23 the Servant of God writes:

This journey has been directed by the kind providence of my God. I arrived at Namur on the 21st at eight o'clock. The next day the Bishop sent for me towards evening, and the good God permitted that I should have a very kind reception. He made his observations with regard to the house in the Rue des Fossés which M. Minsart wants to take for us. I kept myself in perfect indifference, and referred the matter entirely to His Lordship's decision. In the end he told me to go and see the house, which turned out to be just what had been described to us.

Seeing that it suits us, the Bishop ended by giving his consent, and to-morrow we sign the contract. Our Sisters are much pleased with their future dwelling; they will go into it at Christmas. I think that our good God has some hidden purpose in all this. . . . I speak quite openly to His Lordship. He thinks our reasons sound and good, and approves of our waiting a little longer.

She then reminds "all her good daughters at Amiens" that simplicity and straightforwardness are the true way to find the Lord and win His divine help. She hopes to see these virtues in her "dear, good Sisters, whose sole ambition ought to be to procure the glory of God," and she ends her letter with her loving cry in sunshine or in storm, "How good the good God is! Blessed be our dear Jesus!"

During this journey the Mother General found many things to regulate and amend. She exchanged

Sisters between Namur and Jumet; she dismissed a novice who proved to have no vocation. "She is guided by nothing but her own scrupulous head," said Mère Julie; "we should have an inexhaustible fund of trouble with her." At Ghent, where we find her on All Saints Day, she has an interview with the newly-appointed Bishop, Mgr. de Broglie, and his Vicar General, M. Le Surre, to discuss the affairs of the Congregation; at Saint-Nicolas she makes a fresh effort to obtain healthier premises for her Sisters, and, failing that, rents another house for the overcrowded Poor School. And in the midst of it all she finds time to send words of encouragement and exhortation to her children at Amiens. "Courage," she writes to them from Ghent, "let us keep our eyes on heaven. Let us go out of ourselves by the little sacrifices God asks of us moment by moment, one at a time. So we shall complete our crowns; so shall we reach our happy eternity."

Namur, too, had its own difficulties. She had found the provisional Superior, Sister Xavier, very ill, and, moreover, somewhat deficient in the tact and gentleness required by her post. Mère de Bourdon was sadly wanted back, but in the critical condition of affairs at Amiens the welfare of the Institute rendered her return impossible for the present. Mère Julie did the best she could by substituting for Sister Xavier Sister Eulalie de Laporte, a young but excellent religious, whose amiability of character and superior education conciliated all parties.

While the servant of God was meeting in Belgium with nothing but benevolence and sympathy from Bishops and clergy, clouds were thickening over the horizon in Picardy. As twice before, she returned to find old troubles sprung from new causes. A malignant and highly contagious epidemic, a sort of typhoid fever, had broken out in the convent. Mère St.-Joseph, after nursing the sick, was herself attacked, and Mère Victoire then undertook the chief care of the infirmaries. Finding herself too busy to give the daily religious instruction to the community, and perhaps not sorry to avail herself of a plausible motive for dispensing herself from the task, she begged Mère St.-Joseph to fulfil it in her place, a request which the latter acceded to without difficulty as soon as she was sufficiently recovered. Once more the Bishop saw in the occurrence an interference with the rights of Mère Victoire, and a message brought by M. Cottu informed the community that when the Assistant was hindered from giving the Catechism lesson, there would be none at all.

Mère Julie found twenty-three Sisters still in bed with fever, with no signs of improvement in their state. She went at once to visit the infirmaries, and exclaimed as she entered: "My children, if you have faith, rise." All got up at her bidding, perfectly cured, except four whose convalescence was very slow, and who all, after their recovery, were found to have no vocation and left the convent. This striking miracle, reported by contemporaries,* and quoted several times in the Informatory Process, as well as in the Apostolic Process *de fama sanctitatis*, contributed in no small degree to confirm Julie's daughters in their opinion of her sanctity. It seemed as though the more men opposed her the more God delighted to invest her with His power. And not only with His power, but still more with His mercy and goodness: her life abounds in touching instances of her motherly care and love. What more charming, for example, than the following letter written to console the young Eulalie de Laporte, who had felt very keenly the separation from her Superior General? The delightful dialogue, with its overflowing kindness, its simplicity, its playful allusion to the "five tears" which Julie had given her daughter leave to shed every day in honour of our Lord's five Sacred Wounds, might almost be a page out of the letters of St. Francis of Sales.

Well, my dear daughter, what is your little heart saying just at this moment? Have you not gone beyond your five tears a day? "Ah! my Mother, what are you saying? Five tears every day? As soon as ever I made my sacrifice, my soul got strong. No more tears, my Mother, but souls, souls which have cost the Blood of our good Jesus! No, no, I will no longer be a child; I can behave as a grown-up person now. What! my Mother, do you then no longer remember the charge you laid on my weak shoulders, the charge of watching over the whole house? The courage of

---

* Testimony of Sister M. Bernard Bochkoltz, Superior at Gembloux, authenticated by Cardinal Goossens; and of Sister Geneviève Charlier, authenticated by Mgr. Belin, Bishop of Namur.

a man has taken possession of me." You see, my dear child, how I make you talk; we are having a little conversation together in God. Ah! my dear daughter, you know what a place you have in my heart; but, as for you, never leave our good Jesus or His blessed Mother. Think only of pleasing God in all things.

When installing Sister Eulalie at Namur the Venerable Mother had desired her to keep her fully informed of all that passed in the community and schools. The young religious was somewhat forgetful of the recommendation, and her Superior General wrote to remind her of it a long letter dated December 6. With that practical wisdom which characterised her administration, she enters into the minutest details, and tells the new superior all she wishes her to say—about the health of Sister Xavier, the pupils, the relations with outsiders, the new house, &c. She knows well, she says, that Sister Eulalie's time is filled to a minute, but when an order has been received everything must give way to obedience. She—Mère Julie—likes to be present in all her houses by the continual letters she receives from them—to know everything just as if she were there in her room. Sister Eulalie must remember that she will have to answer to God for any harm that comes through her not having told things. "You see that you have been in fault, my child," says the Venerable Mother tenderly; "well, now you are going to repair it by giving me full details of everything." She repeats once again the assurance that she knows the good will is there, and that it is rather time which is wanting. But the required account must be given, and if Sister Eulalie really has no other leisure, she must take the hour of meditation, and the act of obedience will be her prayer. It will be a good plan for the future to set down in a memorandum book all the little incidents which are to furnish matter for her letters. Very likely all sorts of objections will suggest themselves to her repugnance or her self-love—as that ma Mère will not be able to read her handwriting, or that she composes badly, writes at too great length or too meagrely, and so forth. All these reasonings are "rubbish which comes from the devil."

This letter [she says in conclusion] will be of use to you for all your life; it will tell you how you ought to make to your superiors the reports they ask of you. You know that they hold to you the place of God. Even should they require difficult things of you, this God of goodness will always be with you to help you; but in the present case the thing is not difficult.

Thus did Mère Julie govern her houses from afar. The reader will bear in mind that she was presiding over an institute yet in its infancy, in which everything had to be settled and regulated, in which the rule was still unstable, the subjects unformed, and few of her companions were old enough or experienced enough to help her. Like all founders, she had to lead the way and to clear it, to set up sign-posts which should point out to her daughters that special path which, for them, was to lead to evangelical perfection.

During Christmas week M. Cottu preached the Spiritual Exercises to the community at Amiens. Mère Julie did not make the retreat, and in order to leave her Sisters free for it, took upon herself all the work of the house, even to the office of cook. At the same time she was occupied, together with Mère Blin, in examining the new rules, a first draft of which the Superior had brought with him ; for M. de Sambucy, too busy to see the matter through himself, had transferred the task to him. These rules had been largely drawn from those of former religious of Notre-Dame, founded in the seventeenth century by Mère Jeanne de Lestonnac. It was putting new wine into old bottles, and the first glance made it evident to the two Mothers that no understanding between the parties would be possible. Yet a peace which they could not explain to themselves filled their souls, with an increased attachment to the first rules, to which they had bound themselves by vow, and a deep conviction that no others would ever bring them grace or blessing.*

It seemed, however, prudent to give no decisive answer off-hand, but try and gain time without displeasing authorities. So, in returning the manuscript to the Vicar General, they asked him to give them a year to consider the matter. But delay did not

* Memoirs, vol. ii. p. 13.

chime in with the Bishop's plans; they were told that the new rules must be accepted forthwith, and that the vows would be taken in accordance with them on the feast of the Annunciation.* The announcement presaged severer measures; the two servants of God held their peace.

Early in January, 1801, at the desire of their Superior, M. Cottu, they went to the Bishop's house to present their wishes for the New Year. His lordship refused to see them. They returned, offering to God this fresh humiliation, and, abandoning themselves entirely to His holy Will, betook themselves to prayer as the only resource left them in a position which was fast becoming untenable. On January 5, as the servant of God was pouring forth her soul before the Blessed Sacrament, she felt a strong inspiration to begin a novena for their deliverance to the Infant Jesus. The six oldest Sisters—the only ones apparently who knew what was going on—were asked to join in this novena, which consisted of penances, prayers and other pious practices. On the fifth day Mère Julie experienced wonderful spiritual consolation, and said to Mère Blin, "I have no shadow of anxiety left, I am in perfect peace. The Child Jesus has taken us under His protection; He will deliver us."

In the mother house at Namur is still shown a picture of the Infant Jesus which hung for a long

* Ibid., vol. ii. p. 31.

time in the room of the servant of God. The memory of that novena has been perpetuated in the Institute; the devotion to the Sacred Infancy flourishes in its houses, and the 25th of each month is honoured with special devotions in its schools. And every year, on Christmas Day, the Sisters of Notre-Dame begin a novena around the crib of the little King who, nearly a century ago, made for them the crooked way straight and the rough places plain.

Next day, January 10, in answering the New Year's wishes of her Sisters of Montdidier, Julie made a discreet allusion to the difficult circumstances in which she found herself: "Our Lord's wish is that our work should be founded on the Cross; it is His gift to us at the present moment. We are praying much to God to know His holy Will. Whatever happens, I will not forsake you."

On January 11, the seventh day of the novena, M. Cottu paid an early visit to Mère Julie. He accosted her with these words: "We must come to an agreement, ladies. His lordship says that Mme. Blin may at any moment take it into her head to carry off her property and leave him alone to support the community; that he cannot afford to do this; and that he will take away your chaplain and establish no rules unless she settles her income on the Amiens convent." "Father," answered Julie quietly, "this is a question which concerns Mère Blin. I will fetch her, and you can repeat to her, if you wish, what you have just said to me." Sister St.-Joseph, who was in the adjoining room, came at once, and M. Cottu reiterated, though in calmer tones, the Bishop's message. The Mothers asked time to reflect before giving a decisive answer to so serious a proposition. The question at issue was whether, in the interests of the single house at Amiens, where so many difficulties beset them and where their work was opposed in every possible way, they were to forsake the other foundations which might require their help. Was this indeed God's will? Was it for His greater glory?

To these two, weighing things in the balance of the sanctuary, and looking back over the long chain of circumstance which had bound them to those first rules, it did not seem so. Nor did it to the prudent and enlightened persons whose counsels they eagerly sought. Even M. de Sambucy was not in favour of an unmodified affirmative; he thought that part of the income of Mère Blin should be sufficient for Amiens. But Julie's clear good sense refused to compromise; she saw the futility of half-measures, and cut the matter short with an energetic " All or nothing, Father."

Other troubles weighed upon her heart. Alarming news came from Namur: the class-mistresses were no longer able to cope with the increase of work consequent on the sudden influx of new pupils since their removal to the Rue des Fossés, and were breaking down; Sister Xavier was rapidly approaching her end; the Sisters, most of them young and inexperienced, and separated by so great a distance from their first Superior, were becoming universally discouraged, and doing each other harm by giving way to their feelings; worst of all, many of them were assaulted by cruel interior doubts and troubles, and violent temptations. "Mère Julie," says the writer of the Memoirs, "set all down to her own sins; I think we ought rather to attribute it to the terrific rage of Satan against the new Congregation."*

M. Cottu, it might be thought, was hardly likely to prove an unprejudiced adviser; but Julie only saw in the good priest her appointed Superior, and consulted him without hesitation, representing to him the necessity of another journey to Namur. The Vicar General decided that, considering the circumstances, there would be no want of respect or obedience to the Bishop in setting off even without his permission; he considered it no longer possible for the foundresses to remain in Amiens; he acknowledged that they were bound by no engagement to stay in the diocese, and went so far as to suggest that Mère Blin should go first to Namur, and thence write to invite the Superior General and the Sisters to follow her. Such a plan, however, was hardly in accordance with the transparent straightforwardness of Julie's dealings; she redoubled, therefore, her prayers and austerities, and, as she writes on January 11 to Sister Eulalie, "waited for *the moment*

---

* Memoirs, vol. ii. p. 45.

of the Lord." "My dear child," she says in this letter, "our Institute must be built on the foundation of the Cross. Oh! yes, there must be great crosses for rising Congregations destined to further God's greater glory. Let us accept the sorrows which come to us from the hand of our good Father. Let us rest quietly in His blessed Will, submitting for love of Him to all manner of privations." And speaking of the impending necessity of leaving Amiens, she adds: "We are trying to act in the utmost spirit of moderation, so as to make no noise about it. But when once God wills it, nothing shall keep us back." That same day, after mature consideration, Mère Blin gave in her final answer to the Bishop, formally declining his proposal. On the morrow the Vicar General read to the foundresses by his Lordship's order an episcopal document to the effect that "having leased to Mère Julie Billiart the house in the Faubourg Noyon for a community of Sisters of Notre-Dame, and seeing that she was leading the Sisters by a different spirit, he left her free to withdraw into whatever diocese she pleased; that as for himself he would take back the house and form in it true Sisters of Notre-Dame." M. Cottu added by word of mouth that she was to take all her daughters with her.* The "moment of the Lord had come." Those who read the simple facts of the history and the original documents, and still

---

* Memoirs, vol. ii. p. 46; Positio super dubio; vitæ synopsis.

more those who will follow the course of the Informatory Process and of the Process *de fama sanctitatis*, cannot fail to be struck with the heroism with which, throughout these long and painful oppositions, the servant of God practised the virtues of prudence, humility, patience, obedience, faith, charity and fortitude. She had made no effort to quit the diocese of Amiens, and now its gates are opened to her by other hands, and she is to pass out of the city she had loved under the shadow of the Cross.

Mère St.-Joseph confesses in her Memoirs that, for her own part, she wished the servant of God to set off at once, in the very natural fear of a counter-order; but that Julie, on her guard against any too natural eagerness, and wishing, so to speak, to leave Providence time to confirm or annul its indications, delayed yet a few days.* After the mid-day meal on that 12th of January which had brought her the episcopal sentence, she laid the whole state of affairs before the assembled community, and, having done so, told the Sisters that she left them absolutely free to go or stay. Then came a repetition of the enthusiastic outburst of some weeks back: every Sister cried that she would follow her Mother, not the least ardent in her protestations of attachment being Victoire. "If I remain," she said vehemently, "it will be because they have im-

---

* Memoirs, vol. ii. p. 48.

prisoned me. I will follow our Mother wherever she goes."

But obstacles were now put to the departure. We have said that the foundress was told to take all her daughters with her. Objections, however, were raised in regard of Sister Gertrude (Ciska Steenhaut), of whom M. de Sambucy had a high opinion and on whom he founded his hopes for the future, and Mère Julie finally consented that she should remain, promising at the same time that every Sister should be left absolutely free. Later in the day Ciska was summoned to the Vicar General's house. "My child," said Mère Julie to her affectionately as she was going out, "I leave you mistress of your choice. Reflect carefully, that you may know what you ought to do." "Ah! ma Mère," cried the young religious eagerly, "my resolution is taken, nothing shall make me change it. I am yours for life." "Go then, God will be with you. Speak little." And so in M. Cottu's room the following conversation took place. "You are doubtless aware that your Mother is leaving: what is your opinion about it?" "I shall go with her, Father." "But, my child, you will lose your soul. You are in the wrong path; Mère Julie is labouring under a delusion." "I belong to my Mother, I shall follow her." "Do you know that you are disobeying his Lordship? He will not have you leave." "I shall follow my Mother."

M. de Sambucy was next called in. He spoke to her at much length of the judgments of God, and of the terrors which would assail her at the hour of death if she disobeyed; he warned her that, in case of her leaving Amiens, Mgr. Demandolx would get his friend the Bishop of Ghent to send her back to him. To all Ciska only reiterated modestly but firmly, " I shall follow my Mother." " But, my child, you are listening to nature, mere nature. Mère Julie is deluded. I have light to guide you—I have grace to direct your soul. Were you at confession, I should speak much more strongly." But Ciska showed no wish to go to confession, and when a compromise was finally suggested in the shape of a four days' delay, burst out with all her Flemish energy, " No, no! If I stayed, you would give me another Mother." Finally, the interposition of the Bishop was deemed necessary for the conquest of this child of seventeen whom neither threats nor persuasion could move. " Sister Ciska," began M. Cottu, as soon as they were introduced into Mgr. Demandolx's room, " has some doubts on the subject of her departure with Mère Julie." " I have no doubt at all," muttered Ciska between her teeth, and when questioned by the Bishop as to her intentions, gave the old answer, " I belong to my Mother; I will never leave her." The Bishop told her she was an ignorant girl who did not know her catechism, which enjoined submission to her pastors, and at last, getting angry, dismissed her with humiliating words and without his blessing. M. de Sambucy next wrote to threaten Julie with the anger of the Bishop of

Ghent, whose friendship he boasted of. Finally, on Saturday, January 14, he brought to the convent a letter, unsealed and unaddressed, which he declared to have been written to the foundress by the Bishop, but which, nevertheless, instead of putting into her hands, he chose to read aloud himself. It conveyed a double order: first, that she should oblige Sisters Ciska and Clotilde and Mère Victoire to remain at Amiens, whether they wished or not; secondly, that she should take with her nothing either from the house or the chapel.

As the greater part of the furniture, and almost everything which the chapel contained, had either been brought with her by Mlle. Blin or purchased by her, the measure was an injustice, and the foundress therefore defended the rights of her Congregation; but she did so with the utmost moderation, gentleness and charity, even consenting to leave behind her the ciborium and valuable tabernacle, which had been personal and unconditional gifts from Madame de Franssu to her friend Mère Blin de Bourdon.

In the meantime Mgr. Pisani had been made acquainted with what was going on at Amiens, and on January 14 M. Minsart wrote to say that he would receive the whole community with the greatest pleasure for the glory of God and the good of souls. When this answer came, Mère Julie had left Amiens. Her energy had only needed a few days to complete all her preparations, and so thoroughly did she possess her soul in peace that no one would have thought there was question of anything but an ordinary journey. She went round the classes and distributed rewards to the children as she was accustomed to do every month, and nothing in her words or manner gave the slightest hint that she was leaving them for ever.

CHAPTER XII.

INTO EXILE.

It was the 15th of January, 1809. One o'clock had just chimed from the tower of the beautiful cathedral when, for the last time, Mère Julie stood in the midst of the assembled community in that city of Amiens where she had suffered so many tribulations, received so many graces. In a voice broken by her tears she addressed to them a few words of farewell, gave them her blessing, and then, while all her daughters wept around her, got into the coach with five Sisters, and took the road to Belgium.

The journey, which lasted a whole week, was painful enough, for the cold was intense. She writes on the evening of the same day to Mère St.-Joseph :—
" Here we are, thanks be to God, at Doullens, very cold but very courageous, in great peace and union with our Lord Jesus Christ. May the divine love of our dear Jesus set all hearts on fire ! My little travellers are brimful of the spirit of God. How glad one is to be cold when one's heart is warmed by the charity of Jesus Christ ! "

The severe frost had rendered the roads dangerously slippery, and the horses could hardly move a step without falling, so that the poor exiles were forced to trudge on foot through snow and ice for five or six hours. But Mère Julie led the way, and her bright courage communicated itself to the little party as they trod in her footsteps. They cheated the length of the journey by saying the Rosary aloud, and by singing, with voices whose freshness and enthusiasm lent to the lines a poetry which of themselves they could hardly boast, the verse of a quaint old hymn in honour of the Apostles:—

> Let us hasten, let us run
> To every clime beneath the sun;
> Let us brave the frost and snow,
> And praise the God Who loves us so.*

The time allotted to silence and spiritual exercises was religiously observed, and when an amelioration in the road allowed of getting back into the coach, a spiritual book was read aloud. Except for north wind and ice one might have fancied it was St. Teresa and her daughters on their way to some new Carmelite foundation. Like the Carmelites too, our Lady's Sisters had their little adventures. Mère Julie had placed the journey under the protection of the holy Angels. She experienced their loving assistance in an extraordinary manner in an incident which occurred on the frontier, and which she herself related to Father Sellier.

> * Allons, courons porter nos pas
> Dans tous les lieux où l'on respire;
> Affrontons glaces et verglas,
> Louons ce Dieu qui nous inspire.
> —*Cantique sur les Apôtres assemblés.*

One evening the coachman, whom the delays consequent on the severe weather had put into a very bad temper, drew up before a wretched looking little inn, standing by itself. On entering, Mère Julie saw sitting at table with the master of the house some men of sinister appearance, who looked at the Sisters, and then left the inn saying that they would return shortly. It flashed upon her immediately that she had fallen into a den of thieves. Not to awaken suspicion, however, she accepted the frugal supper which was set before her in plates of very questionable cleanliness, and then went a little way along the high road to explore the surroundings. As she walked on, lifting her heart to God in earnest prayer, she suddenly saw before her a youth of dignified and modest bearing, who accosted her with these words: "Ah! this is not the place for you! go further on. Fly from this house!" She wished to question her kind friend further, but he had disappeared. She was retracing her steps, full of what had occurred, when two of her Sisters ran to meet her, saying: "Ma Mère, we have just seen a kind and venerable old woman who said to us, 'Ah! Sisters, this is not the place for you, go further on. Fly from this house.' We wanted to bring her to you, but she disappeared."

Evidently this was a warning from heaven; but how were they to get away? It was late, the horses had been taken out, the luggage removed from the coach, the rooms and beds—such as they were—prepared, and all the travellers were overcome with fatigue. No matter: they must leave there and then. Mère Julie went to rouse the driver, and, by means of kind words and a little present of money, persuaded him to push on further. She then asked to see the bedrooms, and when the host pointed to the two wretched couches in the single apartment of which the would-be inn consisted, telling her that he and his family would pass the night in the loft, she said that she could not consent to such an arrangement, and would seek a more comfortable lodging elsewhere. "At the same instant," she related afterwards to Father Sellier, "and without our being able to explain it otherwise than by the intervention of the blessed Angels, my daughters with all their packages were somehow or other in their places in the coach, the horses, moreover, put to, and only waiting for the signal to start. We pursued our way rapidly in spite of loud opposition from the innkeeper, and in a short time we reached a village where we were able to pass the night without mishap. When I considered all the circumstances of this event, and above all the very rapid manner in which we had got off from that inn, I could not help seeing in it the Hand of Divine Providence, who by means of His Angels had delivered us from a great danger." *

When the people of the neighbouring village learnt what had happened, they congratulated the

* Father Sellier's notice.

Sisters on having escaped from a regular nest of brigands, and a house of such ill repute that for some time past the eyes of the police had been upon it. Sister Bernardine (Adelaide Pelletier), the last survivor of Mère Julie's companions on this journey, used to love to tell the story to a younger generation; she was one of the two whom the old woman had bid to fly.*

On another day the coach stuck in deep ruts full of half-melted ice, and the travellers had to get out of the cumbersome vehicle, and walk on in front. Worn out by fatigue and hunger, they reached a small hamlet; but Mère Julie was not going to let her daughters choose their quarters at random; rest was not rest to her if she was not in the company of the friends of her God. And so Sister Bernardine draws a charming picture for us of how she went down the village street with fixed gaze and thoughtful air, her footsteps guided, we may well believe, by those Angels who had once already so well borne her up in their hands—passing by this door with "Not here," and that other with "No! God is not there," until at last she stopped before a poor-looking house saying, "This is the place. Let us knock." The door was opened at once, and the good village woman, at the sight of the large black cloaks, cried out joyfully,

---

* See Father Baesten's Life, and cf. testimony of Sister M.-Bernard Bochkoltz, p. 9.

"Nuns! Oh, what a joy to see nuns once more! I thought there were none left on earth. Joseph," she called to her husband, "come and see the nuns;" and then to her little son "Kneel down, Nicholas, to get their blessing." Delighted to offer them hospitality, these good and simple folk spread the table with milk and bread, and Julie sat talking to them, as she so well knew how to do, of God and the happiness of knowing and loving Him. Nicholas had volunteered to watch in the meantime on the high-road for the coach, and stop it. "But our Mother," adds the narrator, "knew the ways of children, and did not trust too much to Nicholas. Well for her that she did not, for just as she herself went to the door she beheld our equipage rolling away beyond the house," and the faithless little sentinel, ashamed of his neglect, had to run after it.

Charity and joy go hand in hand, and the party kept its peace and gaiety throughout all the little adventures of the way. To some of the young French Sisters a journey to Belgium seemed a journey into an almost savage country, and Ciska must have laughed heartily when, on reaching Courtrai, one of them gravely said to her Superior: "Please show me a Fleming, ma Mère." She herself, who had gone through so valiant a struggle not to leave her Mother, was overjoyed at seeing once again the fertile plains and the old belfry-towers of her native land,

and proud to point out its beauties to her companions.

At last, on the evening of St. Agnes's feast, the white walls and grassy ramparts of Namur came in sight. Next morning the party was joined by the second caravan, composed of the more delicate Sisters under the leadership of Sister Jeanne Godelle, the Mistress of Novices. Their coach had left Amiens three days after the first, but having had a more intelligent driver, had taken a shorter route.

But Mère Julie's cup was seldom one of unmixed sweetness. The Bishop of Amiens, anxious to justify his measures towards the foundress, had lost no time in drawing up a detailed list of his grievances in her regard, and "the packet," says Mère Blin, "arrived before she did." And so, when she presented herself at the Bishop's house, Mgr. Pisani received her coldly, reproached her with moving a whole community in the depth of winter, and told her that she had come uninvited and without informing him of her plans. "Take care, Sister," said the prelate sternly; "there have been persons who have had revelations, and who have lost their souls."

Fortunately, Mère Blin's letter of the 14th was found annulling the second charge, while the formal dismissal by Mgr. Demandolx and the letter bearing the signature of his Vicar-General sufficiently explained the precipitate departure from Amiens in so rigorous a season.

But the good Bishop naturally hesitated to annoy his colleague, and moreover the grave complaints of the latter did not admit of being so easily disposed of. Two whole hours were spent in examining them; but at the end of the interrogatory Mgr. Pisani was not only convinced of the innocence of the Servant of God, but deeply impressed by her humility and charity, her patience and courage.

Mère Julie's account of the incident to her intimate friend betrays no trace of rancour or complaint.

> His Lordship showed me all the letters that had been written to him. It did one good to hear them! I kissed the Hand of my God. These details are for yourself alone. After a rather long conversation with him the Bishop had the kindness to invite me to dine with him. I am lost in astonishment at the mercies of God towards me.

Still less is there any tone of triumph at the issue of the affair.

> If you could have heard the letters written about me to the Bishop of Namur! There was enough in them to send me to prison for, then and there. His Lordship is not the least surprised at all this, and he was good enough to read me his own letter to the Bishop of Amiens. Tell our *bonne dame* * that if she could hear him it would be balm to her heart. A Bishop of twenty-five years' standing would not let himself be imposed upon by a poor little Mère Julie. Oh, no. Besides, I make no effort to convince him at all; he gets his information from the letters that have been

---

* Mme. de Franssu.

written to him, and not *one* only. It was the good God Himself Who took our cause in hand. . . . Oh! yes, He would rather have sent an Angel to us from Heaven than have allowed us to fall into delusion, for we only wished, you and I, to do His blessed Will. We knew that He is faithful to His promises, and in Him we placed all our trust.

His Lordship bids me tell you to do as I did; leave free those who wish to remain, but if all wish to come, bring all. The house is large enough to contain them; and if God increases our numbers, He will extend our walls. O holy and adorable Will of God, be thou for ever accomplished!

She renews the counsel to act very gently in the matter of the Amiens property, and sends special messages of affection to Mère Victoire. As for her "eldest daughter" herself, she hopes that God will make her strong with His strength through the Heart of Jesus. Everything has happened by his permission. Blessed be His Holy Name!

Courage, my dear friend! God is very good thus to make us pass through the furnace of tribulation. Is it possible that God should forsake those who have been, so to say, forced to quit their beloved solitude in order to go to the assistance of poor little souls plunged in darkness, deprived of the knowledge of our Lord Jesus Christ? Let us ask Mary our Mother to get us a great love of humiliations; what a happiness it would be for us to follow her Son Jesus!

Mère Blin de Bourdon stood in need of this language of faith and hope. Every effort was being made at Amiens to persuade her that Mère Julie was in error, that she would fail in her attempt, and would return to ask pardon; and the necessity in which she found herself of differing from her ecclesiastical superiors was torture to her delicate conscience. "One is very free," she writes bravely but sadly, "when one has no wish but to do God's Will. At heart I am really at peace, and I believe that all this is meant to purify the work. I cannot regard these vexations as an evil, since sin is the only evil. Yet I suffer exteriorly. I should like to be able to hurry matters, so as to be soon with you again. . . . I hope that things will go more smoothly elsewhere for the glory of God, which must be our only aim. Pray that I may not make any blunders, as I am quite capable of doing. Best love to all the dear Sisters. How I long to see them again!"

A last assault was attempted by a good missionary, named M. Dalainville, whose herculean figure, stentorian voice and vehement gestures ministered to an ardent zeal, not always tempered by equal prudence. In one of his visits to the episcopal palace he had been informed of all the supposed delinquencies of the Sisters of Notre-Dame. Without further inquiry, he went straight to the half-empty house, and apostrophising Mère Blin de Bourdon with the utmost energy, sought to shake her confidence in the foundress. He himself felt no doubt whatsoever: Mère Julie was the victim of a delusion; the Sisters were on the wrong road; they would not be blessed by God; they would fail in all they undertook. But the torrent of eloquence was lost upon the Sisters, who merely thanked the missionary for the interest he took in them. He next betook himself to Mme. Franssu, who, suffering as she was from a nervous affection, and rendered more sensitive by her grief at the loss of those with whom she had hoped to end her days, was terrified by the loud tones of the vehement orator, who forbade her to show the least sign of approval for those "refractory nuns, the victims of deplorable delusions, suspected of heresy, and already fallen into the abyss."

On hearing of this incident Mère Julie wrote gravely:

> Before speaking of illusion, people ought to have ground for what they say. Courage, courage! Like St. Paul, let us only glory in crosses and humiliations. My dear child, the thought strikes me that we are beginning to be really *Sisters of Notre-Dame*. Crosses are pouring in upon us on all sides. "It is only now," said St. Ignatius the Martyr when he was found worthy to suffer for Christ's sake, "it is only now that I begin to be a Christian." Ah, my dear friend, how happy we are! What a joy it is to have something to suffer for God during the little space of this short life!

Mère Blin de Bourdon had some difficulty in disembarrassing herself of the lease for the house in the Faubourg-Noyon, or in getting permission at least to sublet it, as this was not mentioned in the terms of the contract. The difficulty was placed in the hands of Our Lady by the communities of Namur and Amiens, and Mgr. Demandolx at last came to understand that, as he had himself sent away the Sisters, they could not be expected to pay for a house which they were no longer allowed to inhabit.

On January 31 six more Sisters set out for Flanders, and Julie writes word of their joy at being united to the Namur community, and of the Bishop's kind reception of them. She hopes that Mère St.-Joseph will soon follow, in spite of all the obstacles that are being put in her way. As for all that is being said against herself at Amiens, she cannot help laughing at it.

But Mgr. Pisani did not laugh. He wrote a letter of eight pages to M. de Sambucy to refute the charges against the foundress, and finally cut matters short by sending a formal order to Mère Blin de Bourdon to return immediately to Namur. She was not slow to obey, and on March 1, 1809, left France with one Sister and a postulant.

And so there remained at Amiens only two—Mère Victoire and a certain Sister Clotilde.

We can look back now over the long storm which transplanted the tree of the Institute, without bitterness or regret; and no words can more fitly close the record of it than the wise and charitable judgment of Mère Blin de Bourdon herself:

> In all this affair there was a tissue of errors and misunderstandings on the part of persons full of zeal and piety. In occurrences of this sort we have to adore God's permission, not to judge the persons concerned. Moreover, the mistakes, the inconsistencies, the precipitations, of which God makes use for the fulfilment of His designs, are easily pardoned by Him afterwards, when they do not proceed—and we know that these did not proceed—from an evil intention.

CHAPTER XIII.

THE MOTHER-HOUSE AT NAMUR.

READERS of Macaulay's history will remember his description of the picturesque town, whose impregnable citadel crowns the steep rock which, jutting out at the apex of the triangle formed by the junction of the Sambre and Meuse, "looks down on a boundless expanse of cornfields, woods, and meadows," with the clean and cheerful-looking little city in their midst. The view from the hill-fort is very beautiful. To the north the glittering waters of the Meuse extend till they are lost beneath the grey rocks of Marche-les-Dames; to the west lie the fertile plains of Brabant; to the east the Condroz—the granary of Belgium and the frontier of the Ardennes; while to the south the view ranges over the district of "Entre Sambre et Meuse," covered with waving forests till it is closed by the high promontories of the upper valley. To the visitor who sails down the Meuse from Dinant the fortress is still a conspicuous object, but the strong walls and gateways, on which the eyes of Julie's exiled daughters rested, have disappeared, demolished by William of Orange, their memory alone surviving in such names as Porte Saint-Nicolas, where now no gate is to be seen.

The taking of the town and its maiden fortress by

NAMUR
At the Junction of the Sambre and Meuse.
From the Western Ramparts.

[To face p. 200.

Louis XIV., and its retaking by William III. in 1695 are probably the only claims to interest which Namur possesses for most Englishmen. But for Christian hearts it has other and nobler associations than the great siege and the neighbourhood of Soignies and Waterloo. In the Church of St.-Aubain, now the cathedral, a slab of white marble marks the last resting-place of Don Juan of Austria, the hero of Lepanto. Beneath the shadow of the same church the Saint of Corpus Christi, Julienne, Prioress of Mont-Cornillon at Liége, found a shelter when, driven from her own convent, she took refuge at Namur. Later on she dwelt in the Cistercian abbey of Salzinnes, a suburb of Namur, whose church in 1103 was consecrated to Mary by Pope Innocent II. in the presence of one of the most devout of Mary's servants, St. Bernard himself. For Namur—and the biographer of Julie Billiart loves to note the fact—is pre-eminently Our Lady's city. In the crypt of the collegiate church of Notre-Dame, which once stood at the foot of the citadel, was preserved till 1663 a statue of the Virgin Mother, said to have been brought by St. Maternus, disciple of St. Peter, and first apostle of Namur. In the episcopal palace may still be seen a painting in which the Dominican, Antoine Havet, first bishop of Namur, who assisted at the Council of Trent, is depicted devoutly kneeling at Our Lady's feet and receiving the beads from her hands; and a confraternity of the Rosary was erected in 1571, the very year of that Rosary-victory, Lepanto.

Twice a year the townspeople honour their patroness and protectress with special and public solemnity. The processions of the feast of the Visitation date back to the twelfth century, while the festivity in honour of the Immaculate Conception, likewise celebrated in July, owes its origin to a vow made by the entire population on occasion of their preservation in the midst of a terrific storm which ceased as soon as the promise was made. The historian who relates this fact attributes the comparative rarity of storms in Namur, and the small amount of injury done by them, to the special protection of the Blessed Virgin. During the disastrous wars which desolated the country under Spanish rule the inhabitants trusted not half so much to native valour or their famous fortress as to her who is " terrible as an army set in battle array." In 1663 they once more solemnly consecrated their city to Mary Immaculate, and bearing her miraculous statue through the streets poised it on the very summit of the fortifications. " In that solitary spot," says the old author, " Mary became at once the refuge of common piety, the Mother of Mercy, the consolation of the afflicted, and the joy of hearts." Nowadays the venerable image stands in a little chapel at the foot of the citadel, but still bears the name of " Notre-Dame des Remparts." The good Namurois will suffer no opposition to their immemorial devotion. In 1789 the Emperor Joseph II., nicknamed "the Sacristan," on account of his constant meddling with Church affairs, forbade the procession of Our Lady, and caused a part of the garrison to be drawn up in arms in the Cathedral square to prevent it; but the crowd rushed through the bayonets into the church, seized the holy image and carried it in triumph through the town, ready to shed their blood, if need be, in defence of the Patroness of Namur. It was M. Minsart who, after the Revolution, restored the Chapel of Our Lady of the Ramparts, and by one of those delicate attentions of Providence, which men call coincidence, it was just then that Julie's daughters passed into the gates of Our Lady's city.

The reader will have pardoned us for thus dwelling in some detail on the town which was to be the haven of rest to the little barque so long buffeted by the storm. "Let us go to Namur; it is the usual refuge of exiles." So said Saint-Julienne of Cornillon. Five centuries later it became the refuge of another saintly exile; and Cardinal Dechamps, the holy and learned Bishop of Namur, loved to dwell on this point of resemblance between the two servants of God who were the glory of his diocese.

The Mansion of the Counts Quarré in the Rue des Fossés still stands as it stood in 1809, and the visitor to the Convent sees over the gateway which faces him as he enters the first quadrangle, a stone shield bearing the family arms with the motto *Iter para tutum.* But God has indeed fulfilled Julie's prediction, " and extended its walls." In the centre of the principal courtyard is the church with its white marble altar over which bend life-size adoring angels, and its unique collection of relics, which make so magnificent a show when exposed once a year on Relic Sunday. This collection is as ancient as it is valuable, having originally been brought over from the Holy Land in the thirteenth century by Cardinal Jacques de Vitry, whose mitre and missal form part of the treasure. At his death it passed to different communities in succession, was hidden during the great Revolution, and bequeathed by the last survivors of the Convent in whose possession it then was to the Sisters of Notre-Dame. From the clock tower of the church the view extends over the whole city. On two sides the church is flanked by the Noviciate and professed quarters; on the third by the flourishing *Pensionnat*, whose museum boasts contributions from every quarter of the globe, and whose little sodality chapel contains a singularly beautiful statue of our Blessed Lady. At the east end of the spacious garden, with its terrace walk and its fine old chestnut-trees stands a little Gothic chapel. Here rests the body of her who for seven years sanctified the Mother-House with her presence, and whose spirit still seems to linger within its walls, filling it with an indefinable atmosphere of peace and fervour and joy. We have reached the last period of her life—not indeed a decline but rather its " perfect day," an autumn rich in fruit, during which she reaped in joy the harvest which she had so long sown in tears. "She looked upon our Mother-House at Namur," say the manuscript *Annals*, "as the centre whence was to radiate that spirit which should pass to the secondary houses; every day she urged the Sisters not to content themselves with a life which fell short of the sublimity of their vocation. . . . . 'you must become *living Rules*,' she would say to them, 'for the sisters who come after you will form themselves on your example.'"

The following are the points [we translate from the Annals] which she particularly inculcated on the first Sisters.

1. Try to have your heart always filled and occupied with God, let His will be the centre and mainspring of your actions.

2. See in your Superiors the image of God; be persuaded that obedience is a guide which cannot err.

3. Make use of prayer and mortification, in order to conquer your inordinate inclinations and become instruments worthy to be employed for the salvation of souls.

4. Labour unceasingly to advance in the paths of interior perfection, without which our Institute cannot subsist. . . . . Consider your vocation well, and you will understand that in the matter of perfection what would not be little for others would be infinitely little for you. "Oh! my children," she would add, "when you thank God for the inestimable gift of your vocation, ask of Him earnestly the courage and strength to fulfil your high destiny." . . . "I conjure you," our good Mother used often to say to us, "I conjure you by the love which you owe to our Lord Jesus Christ, perfect yourselves in virtue and in learning; understand the necessity under which you lie of stretching forward to attain the end of an

Institute which does not only guide you along the way of salvation, but which obliges you to lead all the children entrusted to you to the knowledge and love of God. Ah! how unworthy of her vocation would she be whom such considerations would not urge to forget herself and her little personal interests, in order to sacrifice herself entirely to the glory of her Saviour. . . . If I had here to sustain the Institute a dozen interior souls who could understand me perfectly, how happy I should be! . . . Then learn, my dear daughters, learn to conquer yourselves, so as to obtain from the very first that *true spirit* which must guide those who shall come after you. And above all remember to abide and ever to grow in the practice of the precept, 'Love one another.' Labour unremittingly to become holy, for the holier you are the holier will be those who follow you. You ought by your good example to be the *pillars of the Institute*."

The Superior General herself was indeed this living rule, this perfect example. Distinguished from the rest of the community only by her greater regularity, mortification and fervour, she enjoyed but one privilege—that of daily Communion. Every morning, in spite of age and infirmities, break of day found her kneeling in chapel absorbed during the space of an hour in the deepest contemplation, the fire which burned in her soul betraying itself by the supernatural glow on her countenance. Numbers of eyewitnesses have deposed to her being often rapt in ecstasy, especially during her thanksgiving after Holy Communion; at such times her head was surrounded by a halo of light. For a long time the Servant of God was unconscious of this marvel; as soon as it came to her knowledge, she adopted a larger veil, so arranged that she could drop it over her face during her prayer. This peculiarity may be remarked in all her portraits, and one of these veils is still reverently preserved at Namur. But though she had the word of eminent directors of souls, such as M. Dangicourt, M. de Lamarche, and Fathers Thomas, Varin and Enfantin, that God led her by extraordinary paths, she was well aware that virtue does not consist in sublime contemplation or divine favours. And so she taught her children to walk along the safe path of humble simplicity, bidding them follow for their morning's meditation the method of St. Ignatius. As for the half hour which gathers the Sisters of Notre-Dame round the Tabernacle at the close of each day, she loved them to pass it in a childlike and familiar talk with God, in colloquies of contrition and gratitude and love. Julie had made thoroughly her own that great saying of St. Ignatius which she incorporated into the rules of her Institute * that it is from the interior dispositions of the heart that external works derive all their efficacy.†

In her conferences and exhortations she constantly came back to this true interior life—to mortification, self-conquest, self-annihilation. She held high and firm before the eyes of her daughters the standard of renunciation, of death to one's will and judgment; nor did she hide from them that these things are in the beginning difficult and painful.

* Rule, Chap. XVII. Art. 1.
† "Illa enim interiora sunt, ex quibus efficaciam ad exteriora permanare ad finem nobis propositum oportet."—*Summ. Constit. reg.* 16.

"But," she added in her vigorous and untranslatable simile, "as soon as a soul has given God leave to act with a free hand (*couper en plein drap*), He comes to her assistance. The soul is no longer disturbed by her faults; she knows none of those fears, those anxieties, which are the lot of those who are for ever calculating with God. Many of you act through fear; I cannot lead souls by that road, you know that is not my way. No, God wants generous souls, who serve Him for love. Would you like to know how you may tell really spiritual persons? In their relations with their neighbour. They speak little, they remain united to God; they *lend* themselves to exterior occupations, but *give* themselves never." * And again:

> Ours is one of the most difficult vocations because we must live an interior life in the midst of external work. If that interior life were lost, our Congregation would not last, or if it did live on, it would be only an outward life, by uniformity of customs—even that would soon come to an end. It is in the Mother-House especially that this primitive spirit must shine forth. We were saying to each other not long ago, Sister St.-Joseph and I, that if our Sisters do not penetrate themselves with this interior spirit, if in the midst of their occupations they do not keep their hearts united to our Lord Jesus Christ, all they do will be worth nothing. No man can give what he has not got.†

Once more:

My dear Sisters, be persons of prayer. It is impossible

---

* Conferences of Ven. Mère Julie, written by Sister Gertrude Steenhaut. No. 17.

† Conferences. No 21.

to pray well and not to be obedient, not to be charitable. To meditate on the maxims and teaching of our Lord and not to shape our conduct by them is, says St. James, to be like a man who looks at his face in a glass, and going away presently forgets what manner of man he is. No, no; those who do thus, do not make good meditations; prayer must bring forth fruit.*

We might multiply quotations indefinitely; every page of Mère Julie's conferences is full of this virile and solid teaching expressed in that vivid, simple, persuasive language of hers which not seldom attains true eloquence. If during the day she had been unable to assemble the Community, she would give them her instructions and counsels just before they retired to rest for the night. "Often," say the memoirs, "the fire of a holy zeal would carry her away. . . . . With that greatness of soul, that invincible courage, which were her distinctive characteristics, she longed continually to see her children filled with the same zeal. 'O my dear good daughters,' she said to us one evening, with a majesty in her look and an inspiration in her voice that went through us—'My dear daughters, we need magnanimous souls for our sublime vocation. There must be nothing little amongst us; we must have the hearts of Apostles. . . . You are the *hinges* on which all the spiritual life of our holy Institute must turn. . . . You are the first—you have the first graces; we must have saints, yes saints, if we are to do the work of God.'"

* Conferences, No. 18.

It had been impossible, owing to the repairs which the house needed, and which required both time and money, to transform the little oratory into a chapel until the arrival of Sister St.-Joseph with the vestments and other necessaries. "Ah! bring us our Divine Master," pleads Julie in her letters to her, "bring Him under our roof. Ah! with what love we long for that happy moment." On April 21 Mgr. Pisani said the first Mass in the humble sanctuary, and henceforward the holy Sacrifice was daily offered. The Bishop, however, wished the children of the boarding school to attend Mass on Sundays at the parish church, and several months passed before he allowed the Blessed Sacrament to be reserved. Mère Julie, in her humility, attributed the delay to her sins. At last the favour was granted, and from September 21, 1809, our Lord has had a permanent dwelling in the midst of His spouses.

One of the chief means for maintaining or renewing that spirit of which Mère Julie has said so much, and which was to emanate from the Mother House, is the annual retreat. In the month of September, 1810, we find Father Thomas giving the Exercises of of St. Ignatius to the Community. The foundress, as on a former occasion, sacrificed for the sake of her children the pleasure of following the general retreat, and with two or three Flemish Sisters, who did not understand French, to help her, undertook the office of Martha, that they might be free to sit with Mary at the Master's feet. When the exercises were over, the Father took the Sisters through a course of "Pedagogy," that science of which we hear so much nowadays, but which is only solid when it is built upon foundations of faith. In the archives of the Institute are preserved some precious notes of the principal discourses made by the zealous Jesuit to whom it owes so much. Speaking to the Sisters of the necessity of maintaining the primitive fervour, Father Thomas lays down the principle that a society is preserved and increased by virtue of the same causes which gave it birth. And he drew a moving picture of the fervour of the Mothers and elder Sisters in the first days of the Congregation, in the little house of the Rue Neuve at Amiens—of the humility, the mortification, the spirit of prayer, which had drawn down such blessings from on high. He insisted strongly on the obligation which lies upon a Sister of Notre-Dame of perfecting herself in her studies so as to render herself capable of discharging fitly her duties as teacher. He lifted their thoughts to the august nature of their mission.

To train up children, to form them to knowledge, and, better still, to piety and virtue, to cultivate souls, to fashion hearts—what is there nobler, what is there more divine? In whatever place obedience may fix you, my dear Sisters, you can say:—I am doing the same work as Jesus Christ and the Apostles. To help you to attain that sublime end—the Christian education of youth—more surely, God wills you to enjoy a certain consideration, a reputation for learning and virtue without which people would not entrust their children to you. Do not imagine for a moment that this is meant to make any one of you personally conspicuous. Oh! if that were what you aimed at, I would ask the Lord rather to visit you with His thunderbolts. But this shall never be. My God had in His mercy far other designs in instituting this new Order destined to procure a solid Christian education for persons of your sex, who in their turn will afterwards gain others to religion and piety . . . Jesus is, and always will be, the Resurrection and the Life; it was from His Heart that your Society came forth for the conversion and sanctification of many. Each one of you should say to herself:—My vocation is entirely heavenly and divine. Ah, what need of a whole retreat? One word sums up all for me—I am called to save the souls which Jesus Christ has bought with His Blood. That thought is enough to make me sacrifice myself wholly, incessantly to this divine work.

The zeal of the ardent religious was contagious; it thrilled through his audience and inspired the most generous resolutions. For several years in succession he renewed his ministrations, always producing marked fruits of sanctification. Under this wise direction, and animated by the example of their Mother, the community of Namur tasted the peace that comes of obedience, the joy that comes of sacrifice. A young girl who had been a boarder in the convent of Amiens and had followed the Sisters to Namur, fell into a decline which obliged her to return home. On her deathbed she never tired of praising the union and charity of those who had brought her up, to live with whom, as she said, "seemed like living in paradise." This kindness and charity very soon won the hearts of the people of

Namur, and they have ever since held the memory of the venerable servant of God in benediction. Two stories have come down to us. One day as she was returning from Mass at the parish church, she met a poor woman bathed in tears. Julie went up to comfort her, and learnt that the husband, an honest shoemaker named Massart, was out of work and the family starving; but the woman could not bring herself to beg. " Do not weep, my good friend," said Julie, full of sympathy, " the good God is so good that He is going to help you at once. Come with me to the Convent of the Dames Françaises "—the name by which the Sisters of Notre-Dame were at first known. " The Sisters' shoes are quite worn out, for they have just come a long journey. You shall take them to your husband to mend, until we can afford to order new ones of him, and I will pay you in advance." The shoes—or the hands which gave them—brought a blessing with them. Customers flocked in again, Massart's fortune was made, and some years later he was able to open a large shop and to send one of his sons to the seminary. The grateful family never forgot their benefactress and reverently kept a book on Devotion to the Sacred Heart, which she had given to the poor wife in her first grief. The venerable Mother had often noticed at the street door a little ragged boy of unprepossessing appearance and with an expression of mingled defiance and cunning, who ran away as soon as he was spoken to. One day she held out an apple to him; hunger conquered shyness, and the little arab seized it. Acquaintance was thus made, and Julie was able to question him on the subject of religion. The poor little fellow was in the most absolute ignorance—had never even heard the name of God. "Go and fetch me your mother," said Julie gently. And the woman came, told a sad and too common story of misery and want brought on by sin, and touched by the kind words of the Servant of God, was converted from her evil ways. Her husband followed her example; the child was sent to the Catechism-class and then to school, and the whole family was thus brought back by Julie to the practice of religion, and with it to peace and joy of heart. The little girls who crowded the poor school were the best beloved portion of her flock, and in their old age many of them loved to tell what joy there was when Mère Julie went round the classes with the beaming smile which always won children, questioning them on the Catechism and giving her Crucifix to kiss to those who answered well. But her visits were chiefly welcome at those Sunday gatherings in the convent held, as at Amiens, for the elder girls, and where they received not only religious instruction, but the prudent counsels and maternal guidance which their position so often called for. It was noted that Mère Julie's watchfulness over these young girls went so far as to see that each one was under the care of a trustworthy companion when they returned home in the evening. The foundress was ably seconded by the capable mistresses whom she had herself formed. Among others we may mention Sister Madeleine Goemaere, a native of Warneton in Flanders, who spoke French and Flemish equally well, and who was so successful in instructing children and preparing them for the Sacraments that Canon Théodore de Montpellier, the future Bishop of Liége, used to call her his "third curate." In 1829 her class was visited by William I., King of the Netherlands, but the good Sister was not the least disconcerted by the presence of royalty, and, at His Majesty's request, continued with perfect composure the lesson she had begun. In Sister St.-Nicolas, who had charge of the day school, the contemplative life was united to the active in a remarkable degree. "Her horror of sin was so great that the thought that, as long as she was on earth, she might still offend God made her continually long for death."* In the same supernatural spirit Sister Eulalie, whose acquaintance we have already made, directed the Pensionnat of the Rue des Fossés, forming her pupils not only to virtue but to a certain exquisite politeness and a simple distinction of manner and bearing which are the ornament of Christian womanhood. Mgr. de Pisani, the holy Bishop of Namur, was the first to praise the devotedness of the Sisters. "My dear children," he said to them on January 1, 1810, in replying to their wishes for the New Year, "I pray God to sustain your courage in the good work which

* Notice on Sister St.-Nicolas (Desirée Guerlin).

the Holy Ghost has inspired you to undertake, and which He so visibly blesses. Your two Mothers are the models of what you ought to be; as long as your eyes are fixed on them our Lord will give you the grace of perfect fidelity to your vocation." Whenever the pastoral visitation of his diocese, and his labours for its ecclesiastical re-organization left him leisure, the pious prelate delighted to visit the convent. Great were the rejoicings when he returned safely from the too-famous National Council of Paris, after having, through the intervention of his friend the Minister Portalis, escaped the fate of his brother bishops of Ghent and Tournai, a hard although glorious captivity in the dungeons of Vincennes. The full length portrait of Mgr. Pisani still to be seen at the Mother House was presented shortly afterwards by himself, and is to the Institute a perpetual memorial of one in whom at the hour of need it found a defender, a protector and a father.

CHAPTER XIV.

NOTRE-DAME AT GHENT.

IN the year 1807 Mgr. Fallot de Beaumont had been transferred from the see of Ghent to that of Piacenza. His place was filled by the Bishop of Acqui in Piedmont, Maurice-Jean de Broglie, son of Victor Francis, Duke of Broglie and Marshal of France, whose glorious military enterprises during the Seven Years' War were rewarded by Francis I. with the princedom of the Holy Roman Empire for himself and his posterity. The Prince-Bishop's career had already been a chequered one, and, as we shall see, he was reserved for fresh and greater sorrows. His younger brother had lost his life by the guillotine, and he himself had been forced to emigrate with his father to Germany. On his return to France Napoleon created him his chaplain, a post he filled till his consecration to the see of Acqui. His personality was in many ways a remarkable one. Deep learning and an austere private life were combined with keen sensibilities and great warmth of affection; while the weakness of his physical constitution was more than compensated for by a hereditary vigour of character, which his staunch devotion to the Church and her interests was to glorify into an apostolic intrepidity. He had made his theological studies at the Seminary of St.-Sulpice, where the Abbé Louis de Sambucy had been for a time his fellow-student. We have already seen that the Abbé turned this former intimacy to account in order to influence the Bishop against Mère Julie, and his first attempts in this direction had been successful. In a conversation with Sister St.-Jean, Superior of the convent at St.-Nicolas, Mgr. de Broglie had expressed himself very harshly on the subject of the foundress, calling her a *coureuse*, and affirming that her convent would perish, and that all who persisted in following her would share the same fate. He added, however, with characteristic straightforwardness that his impressions had only been formed on hearsay. They were the easier, therefore, to dispel. Sister St.-Jean refuted the calumnious accusations by a quiet statement of facts, and the prelate, thoroughly satisfied by her firm though gentle answers, was loud in his praises of her goodness. "My Lord," quickly rejoined the loyal religious, "if the Mother were bad, would the daughters be good?"

As time went on, the Bishop's eyes were still further opened, and when on her return from a journey to Namur at the close of 1808 Julie sought an audience with him, his last prejudices fell before her simplicity and frankness. "They have given me a bad name to you, have they not, Mère Julie?" were his first words, and then followed a conversation which, as she tells Mère St.-Joseph, made her once again sing that "her good God was very good."

Shortly after the emigration to Namur, the affairs of the St.-Nicolas convent, whose insanitary condition the authorities had taken no steps to remedy, again took the foundress to Ghent. She desired to lay the matter before Mgr. de Broglie, hoping that his influence might obtain some relief for the suffering community; she was also not a little anxious to learn in what light he regarded the departure from Amiens. A letter dated April 25, 1809, gives an account of this second interview.

> I reached Brussels at six in the evening. God, always infinitely good, allowed me to pass a quiet night in the *diligence*. Arriving in Ghent at half-past five in the morning, I went straight to the Church of St.-Bavon to seek my good God, and I renewed my act of abandonment for all which it should please His Divine Goodness to send me, or that I might have to suffer during this journey. I did not know where the Bishop was; I did not yet want to know; I only wanted to throw myself into the bosom of my God. This He gave me grace to do. As soon as I had received my Lord, I set out in search of good Father Bruson. He told me that Mgr. de Broglie was in Ghent, but was leaving for St.-Nicolas on the next day, and he offered to conduct me himself to the Bishop's house. His Lordship had gone out for the parochial Mass, and I waited for him in the chapel, alone with my God, putting everything into His hands.

The audience proved entirely satisfactory. "Tell me all your troubles, Mère Julie," was the Bishop's cordial greeting; "come, tell me everything." And so, as she playfully says, she had made her general confession to him, only, of course, she had passed over many things for the sake of charity. Still, he had quite understood. He had said to her: "Those who hear but one bell hear but one sound. How could they dream of making you give up all the property of your companion? For my part, I should be quite opposed to such a measure." And he had added: "The more I see good people harassed, the more I try to help them." In the course of conversation he had asked her how she stood with the Bishop of Tournay, and Julie had made him laugh heartily by her answer: "My Lord, I have been well blackened to the Bishop of Tournay, and I do not know whether I am white again." "Yes, indeed, they manage to do that well in this part of the world." One remark of the Prince had made her specially happy; he had said to her spontaneously and with great emphasis: "You are not intended to be shut up in one diocese; no, Mère Julie, *your vocation is to go all over the world.*" Mère St.-Joseph would rejoice with her at seeing how God thus arranged that their cause should be taken in hand by the very person whom they had been led to believe most ill-disposed towards them. As to the question of St.-Nicolas, the Bishop had arranged to meet her there on the morrow and try to settle the business on the spot.

The prelate was as good as his word. He convinced himself by personal inspection that *Berkenboom* was quite uninhabitable; he did his best to induce the civil authorities to remedy matters, and even carried his benevolence so far as to visit a house which he thought might suit the Sisters. But all his efforts failed, the authorities refused to bestir themselves; the people were prejudiced against religious who were Frenchwomen. "Shake the dust from off your feet," said the Bishop to the foundress as he parted from her. "If St.-Nicolas does not treat you better, come and settle yourselves in Ghent; I must keep you in my diocese." The affair pressed, for the lease of the house then occupied by the Sisters expired on May 8, and if they remained another day they would have to pay the rent for an entire quarter. Mère Julie's search for a house proved as unsuccessful as her negotiations with the burgomaster; and when, on her return to Ghent, she reported matters to Mgr. de Broglie, he sent her straight back to the inhospitable little town with orders to bring away the community without delay; he himself promised to find a lodging for them in Ghent. Mère Julie's activity made short work of the *déménagement*. In two days the boarders had been returned to their families, the day school broken up, and the household articles belonging to the Sisters packed up, together with a large provision of bread which Mère Julie caused them to bake before setting out, so that they might not have to burden any one in Ghent with supplying to them the necessaries of life. A crowd conducted the coach out of the town, hurling in Flemish a discordant volley of insults and abuse at the religious who for two years had done their utmost to serve them. Mère Julie herself arranged another humiliation for her daughters. On reaching Ghent she bade the little band deposit their bundles and packages in the courtyard of the *Hôtel du Cerf*, the coach-terminus, and sit down upon them to await her return. She herself went with Sister Catherine Daullée to the Bishop's house to make enquiries about the proffered lodging for the Sisters. Sister Marie Steenhaut, who tells the story, must have recalled her old Courtrai experiences as a crowd of little urchins trooped round to stare and laugh at the poor nuns, while the passers-by offered various conjectures as to who the new-comers were. "It was," she adds, "an exercise of patience and humility from which we may hope to have gained some merit, since the absence of our Mother was prolonged for several hours." Julie, on her side, had met with some mortification. The Bishop, who had forgotten about the expiration of the lease, and who, in any case, had not been prepared for so prompt an evacuation, was not quite pleased to have the Sisters on his hands. However, he sent Julie with his secretary, M. Van Schouwenberghe, to the Sisters of Charity with a request that they would give a temporary shelter to the Sisters of Notre-Dame. This met with a cordial assent; two rooms and a small kitchen were speedily placed at the disposal of the little community. The Sisters now understood why their Mother had kept singing during their journey: "Oh! what a pleasant dwelling is a dwelling without a house." *

* "Oh! l'agréable demeure que la demeure sans maison!"

The furniture of the convent at St.-Nicolas was the property of the town, so that they now found themselves without the most absolute necessaries; and Julie, happy both for herself and her daughters to suffer some of the effects of evangelical poverty, had hastened to assure their kind hosts that they had everything they wanted. No privations, however, damped the gaiety of the little party, and their trust in God was often wonderfully and unexpectedly answered. "There are four beds and we are seven," writes the foundress. The missing ones were improvised by spreading their clothes on the floor, some faggots found in a corner serving as pillows. The preparations for supper were equally simple—it consisted of the dry bread they had brought with them. The worst difficulty was that they had no light. Suddenly a knock comes at the door, and the director of the hospice appears with his servant, bringing them a lamp and a jug of beer. Later on the famous bread became so mouldy that it was converted into a kind of paste full of green patches; "but," says Sister Marie Steenhaut, "Mère Julie used to bless it, and it never did us any harm." "To-day I set up our kitchen with fourteen pence," writes the foundress herself; "that was not dear. We have bread, salt and butter, and we are buying potatoes. We are the happiest women in all the city of Ghent. Of the six *louis* which I brought away with me I still have five. I believe God, like a good Father, must multiply them in my purse."

One day, as the Sisters were regretting that their Mother had nothing to drink but the cold water which was so bad for her, a hamper of wine was left at the door—a present from M. Lemaire-Kinet, a good merchant of the town. A few days later another benefactor appeared in the person of M. Van Schouwenberghe, brother to the Bishop's secretary. From that time these two kind friends relieved the most pressing needs of the community, while the Vicar General, who had constituted himself its confessor till a suitable priest should be appointed to that post, spared himself no pains to find them a house in a quarter where they could be of most use to the poor. While waiting, the Sisters employed themselves, some in making lace as a means of support, some in perfecting themselves in the subjects they would be required to teach. Mère Julie had returned to Namur, but early in June we find her again in Ghent, looking for the house, which had not yet been found. Through the good offices of Father Bruson and of the Curé of St.-Pierre she was introduced to the Baron Coppens, who offered the Sisters for a few months the use of a large house and garden belonging to him. Thither Julie at once transferred her little colony, and wrote to tell the good news to Mère St.-Joseph. "After this house, please God, we shall find another. Confidence, therefore, and love, and entire abandonment into the hands of our merciful Father." The Servant of God desired that her daughters should prepare themselves for the work they were about to begin in Ghent by the exercises of a spiritual retreat. It was preached by Father Bruson, who communicated his own zeal and fervour to his hearers. The foundress herself took part in it, but was called from her solitude by Mgr. de Broglie, who had formed the project of founding and endowing an establishment of Sisters of Notre-Dame at St.-Gilles, an important country town in the Waes district. She writes on June 17 to her friend and colleague at Namur:

My good Friend,—Always something new! I have just come from the Bishop, who could not be kinder than he is. I told him I was going back to Namur with some of the Sisters. He answered that he forbade me to remove a single one; he has in view an establishment in the country. On Monday he is giving Confirmation there, and on Wednesday he will send for me to see if this foundation would suit us. I cannot write all he said; amongst other things: "I will not do like the Bishop of Amiens; I will not send you out of my diocese; I mean to keep you—yes, to keep you." "My Lord, we are at your command." "I am not afraid of having plenty of you in my diocese." I cannot tell you all the kindness he shows us. . . . . I can see his good heart: no one could be kinder than he, firm at the same time. . . .

The Curé of St.-Pierre, in whose parish we are, is bent on having the Sisters permanently established there. The Bishop, too, wishes it. May the good God direct everything to His greater glory! Write me word what you think of both these projects. . . . . I am dragged about on all sides. We must let the good God do with us as He pleases. He is so good that He can will nothing but what is very good, both for our welfare and His own greater glory. It is late; I cannot write more now. Patience! when we see each other again, we shall have all kinds of things to talk of in God and for God.

It will scarcely be credited that while the Bishop was interesting himself so warmly in the Sisters of Notre-Dame and treating their foundress with so much confidence, he was being continually importuned with letters about her from Amiens harping on the old accusations. We learn this from a severe epistle addressed by his Lordship to M. de Sambucy, which is preserved in the archives of the Bishopric of Ghent:

GHENT, June 25, 1809.

You are very young, Sir, to set yourself up, as you do, to judge, or rather to censure the actions of a Bishop. Salvien, St. Jerome and St. Bernard were called in their time the Masters of the Bishops, but between them and you there is, you will allow, some difference. I had intended to give no answer to your letters about Sister Julie, but your last to M. Le Surre prevents me from following this plan. If you have a copy of that letter, read it over again, and I hope the expressions used with regard to myself will strike you as very unbecoming. I will not follow all your diffuse remarks; I will merely observe that—

1. It is very strange you should give so much praise to the Bishop of Namur, who has done much more than the Bishop of Ghent, who has received at Namur the Superior and the religious "emigrants" from Amiens, to use your own expression, who has occupied himself with their establishment in his city, and has spent whole hours in their convent after offering the holy sacrifice there; while the Bishop of Ghent has confined himself to allowing the removal into another town of a community which existed already at St.-Nicolas under Mgr. de Beaumont. It is not I, but they who have decided not to adhere to the changes made in their Constitutions at Amiens and at Montdidier, and who have remained attached to the same Superior and the same rule as before. Notwithstanding this, you dare to

say: "The excellent Bishop of Namur has treated of this with the Bishop of Amiens and myself in so frank and loyal a manner that we have only to congratulate ourselves on our correspondence with him." This means the contrary for me, so that I am neither frank nor loyal. M. de Sambucy, I forgive you this language, but do not use it again, and remember to whom you write, and of whom you speak. Mgr. of Amiens has not written a line to me on the subject; if he had, I should have done myself the honour of writing to him in all frankness and loyalty, for I never act otherwise.

2. You add: "Mgr. of Namur approves, it is true, of a Superior General, but this point is opposed to the wishes of the majority of the Bishops." One would suppose that you were the confidant of the "majority of the Bishops." Mgr. of Amiens will not hear of a Superior General. Mgr. of Namur wishes for one. And yet, if I am to believe you, these two are in perfect harmony. And Mgr. of Ghent, who has nothing to do with all this, who has done no more than keep in his diocese the nuns established by his predecessor, is the only person in the wrong. You wanted me to take part with the Bishop of Amiens against the Bishop of Namur. You are really very strange. Could I carry moderation further than to send you word I would conform to whatever my two colleagues decided? The Bishop of Amiens and you (for you consider yourselves one) do not want a Superior General; now, if there is no Superior General, there are only local Superiors. What in that case is to prevent Sister Julie from being Superior in the house that exists in the diocese of Ghent?

3. If Mgr. of Namur is right in holding to a Superior General, Sister Julie was that Superior before the changes introduced, under your direction, into this Association. And why may I not incline towards the opinion of one of my colleagues rather than that of another?

4. The truth of all this is, that your changes have not had the success you hoped for, and yet you do not repent of having made them. As for me, I keep what Mgr. de Beaumont left me. I leave these nuns under the same rules they

came with, and as you will not have a Superior General you cannot find fault with a Convent governed by a particular Superior.

5. You say I owe nothing to Mgr. of Namur. I may tell you that both before the Revolution and since, I have been much more intimate with him than with the Bishop of Amiens, whom I scarcely know at all. I like and esteem both these respected colleagues, but why should I blame what the Bishop of Namur does, in order to please the Bishop of Amiens? And if while he received all the emigrant nuns, I had not kept them in my diocese, should I not have appeared to censure what my colleague did?

6. You tell me these nuns belong to Mgr. of Amiens; they came into my diocese under my predecessor. Besides, as neither you nor your Bishop will have a Superior General, theirs cannot be considered by you as a true congregation, but only as consisting of isolated communities. Every Bishop has equal right and jurisdiction over all such associations existing in his diocese, for, properly speaking, we have now no real religious orders, and above all we have no communities of nuns exempted from episcopal jurisdiction.

7. You maintain "that it would be very easy for me to conciliate the parties." No one has asked me to do that, and how could there be agreement on this point between one Bishop who wants changes in this Congregation, and another who receives the emigrant nuns in his diocese? Besides "these two respected Bishops have had only to congratulate themselves on their correspondence regarding this business." As they are completely in harmony, what need is there to conciliate those who agree so happily?

8. Before concluding, I cannot pass over in silence your saying now that there are thirteen nuns on your side, instead of two, according to Mgr. of Amiens, and six, according to your own note. It would have been more straightforward to say thirteen from the first, but it did not, seemingly, suit you at that time. You add, that *four of these new subjects have had a long trial with the* "*Dames de l'Instruction chréti-*

enne," * *and were formed under your supervision for the new Institute;* which means that long before this reform of yours you were preparing in another association the means of putting an end to that of Sister Julie. Is this frankness and loyalty? The interest I take in you prompts me to advise you not to judge and blame a Bishop, and not to meddle with so many matters. For my part, I have kept what I found, and I have left things as they were.

Accept, Sir, the assurance of my sincere attachment.

☩ Maurice, Bishop of Ghent.

Thus began the restoration of Mère Julie's reputation; we shall see that her rehabilitation was not long in being complete.

In October, 1809, the foundress was again in Ghent. The Coppens mansion, which had been lent for a few months, could not be retained much longer, and the Sisters longed to be settled in a more conventual dwelling, and in a quarter nearer to their dear poor. The Curé of St.-Pierre, bent on keeping the Sisters in his parish, offered to take a house for them at his own expense. He was even ready to support the community himself, as he wished to make the school an establishment of his own. Not without some hesitation did Mère Julie accept this offer, but she had no alternative at the time. The first obstacles that arose came from the Government. The imperial decree permitted new foundations only on condition of obtaining a separate authorisation each time. When the Abbé Malingié, Curé of St.-Pierre, applied for permission to open a school in

---

* Afterward called "Dames du Sacré-Cœur."

his parish, the Prefect of the Department of the Scheldt declared that *the Minister expressly forbade the Sisters of Notre-Dame to make any new foundations.* There was nothing to be done but to submit. The foundation of St.-Gilles (Waes) had to be abandoned, as well as that of St.-Pierre.* This was the first difficulty the Sisters of Notre-Dame had met with from the civil authorities. It caused considerable surprise, and Mère de Bourdon in alluding to it in her Memoirs says that both Mgr. de Broglie and Mère Julie suspected in this rigorous measure "the influence of a personage strongly opposed to the foundress."†

At this juncture the Abbé Malingié stepped in with a proposal to open a lace workroom under the care of the Sisters. This would occupy the poor girls of the parish, who could be taught their religion without the name of going to school. The Bishop, however, did not favour the project; he feared it would seem to the Prefect an indirect act of disobedience to his orders. His Lordship then said to Mère Julie : " Bring me your statutes, which have been approved by the Emperor, and I will see what can be done with the Minister at Paris." The statutes were at the Prefecture, and the foundress went immediately to obtain them. " I was just thinking of you," said one of the employés at the

---

* This foundation was made in 1866, during the Generalship of Reverend Mother Constantine.
† Memoirs of Mère de Bourdon, vol. II. p. 197.

office. "I was going to write to the Bishop about you." "Is it not a singular thing," exclaimed Mère Julie, "that we who ask nothing from any one should be refused permission to gather together a few poor children to teach them in school?"

At these words the head of the Bureau approached and said: "What is this lady asking?" "I am complaining," rejoined Mère Julie, "of our being forbidden to open a school for the poor." "Make a beginning at all events," said the official. "But if the Prefect refuses the authorisation?" "I tell you, make a beginning." "And suppose difficulties arise?" "We will shut our eyes; you need not fear, begin."

Julie left the Bureau rather puzzled how to act. The Bishop's secretary reassured her by saying that the functionary who had spoken to her was very influential and could be relied upon. Mgr. de Broglie was of the same opinion.

The Curé of St.-Pierre was of course most anxious that the Sisters should take advantage of the toleration of the authorities. Mère Julie, however, still hesitated. She feared something precarious in this parochial establishment, and possibly some restrictions on the liberty of the Sisters, and her own free hand in placing or removing them as the good of the Institute required. Nevertheless her great obligations to the kind-hearted Curé made her wish to precipitate nothing. She took her favourite course of abandoning things to Divine Providence.

While these deliberations were pending, she was

told of an ancient abbey in another part of the town, which had been suppressed by the Revolution. It had been a vast monastery of the Cistercian Order, tracing its origin back to the thirteenth century. Established at first in the Waes district at a place called Oudenbosch, or "The Old Wood," and also, as the "Memoirs of the City of Ghent" inform us, *Locus Sanctæ Mariæ*, the Cistercianesses took refuge in Ghent during the troubled times of the sixteenth century. Here they erected a new abbey, which still bears the name they gave it of *Nouveau-Bois*, though the Flemish equivalent has naturally, and not unfitly, been corrupted into "*Nonnen*-bosch," or the "Nuns' Wood." Other memories of the daughters of St. Bernard linger in the place. The church, raised in 1640, and surmounted a century later by its graceful tower, is substantially the same, and is adorned with several paintings by Roose,* which attract the admiration of connoisseurs. Many of these represent scenes from the life of the Saint of Clairvaux, while that which surmounts the High Altar, "The Sibyls in Adoration before the Infant Christ," formed the dowry of his only daughter on her entrance into religion at Nouveau-Bois. On either side of the altar are fine statues of St. Bernard and his sister, St. Humbeline. The present altar, of Carrara marble, replaced an older, and, as some think, a handsomer one, of which a bas-relief, also

---

* Nicholas de Liemacker, known as Roose, was a pupil of Otto Venius, the master of Rubens. He died in 1645.

representing an episode in the Saint's life, is preserved in the sacristy. The superb cloisters of the Abbey stand as of old, and the portrait of the last Abbess still hangs on the convent walls.

During the French Revolution these daughters of St. Bernard contrived to save their house from utter destruction by selling it for a very moderate sum to a gentleman of Ghent, M. Pycke de Peteghem, on condition of being allowed to buy it back, if they were ever able to reconstitute their scattered community. At the period of which we write their re-establishment had become impossible. Of the former community only two very aged religious remained. The buildings were in the most neglected state. The church had been turned into a barn and a powder-magazine; later on an engineer had built a chimney and set up a forge, which greatly damaged the nave. "Our Mother's heart was touched to see the temple of the Lord thus degraded," writes Sister Marie (Steenhaut) in the Annals of Nouveau-Bois; "her zeal and her love were set on fire. She longed for the time when the praises of God should again be sung there, and she seemed to hear Him say: 'That day will come; do not lose heart.'" One part of the sacred edifice was given up to workmen, but a large wing was occupied by a schoolmaster, who seemed disposed to part with his lease in favour of the Sisters of Notre-Dame. The Curé of St.-Pierre, meanwhile, in great haste to have his school opened by the Sisters, hired a house for them in the Rue des

Femmes. The foundress was absent at the time; when she returned, she accepted the acomplished fact, quitted the house of the Baron Coppens with many expressions of gratitude for his hospitality, and installed her daughters in their new premises on November 21, 1809. Her heart bounded with joy at the sight of the good to be done amongst the poor of that district, and she writes exultingly to her friend at Namur of the hundred and thirty-two children who at once poured into the school. There are as many poor in the place as there are stones; she does not know how the good Sisters will be able to get through all the work they have before them. But the good God is very good! She herself has been trotting about all the morning buying this article or that for the modest ménage of the Rue des Femmes—a stove, a saucepan, a gridiron—all sorts. Mère Blin will wonder where the money comes from. Well, for one thing, she takes care to get cheap things, though sometimes she has to hunt a long time before finding them. And then, too, somehow or other, she cannot quite understand how, she always finds a few crowns in her pocket.

The children who were crowding into the classes of Notre-Dame were ignorant beyond all conception. "I find myself in the midst of a troop of wretched little creatures," writes the Superior; "their ignorance is lamentable, and that of their parents still worse. One of the mothers has been married thirty years and does not even know her prayers!

How can the poor children be expected to know theirs?"

At the same time the hoped-for establishment at Nouveau-Bois was approaching its realisation. The same day that the Sisters took possession of the house in the parish of St.-Pierre, Mère Julie opened negotiations with M. d'Hont, the schoolmaster mentioned above. Both Mgr. de Broglie and the foundress foresaw that the foundation at St.-Pierre was not likely to be a permanent one; his Lordship considered it too near the schools of another teaching Institute. The Abbey of Nouveau-Bois pleased him exceedingly, and he gave his cordial approbation to a speedy arrangement of terms. All was finally agreed upon to the entire satisfaction of every one concerned. The two ancient Cistercianesses were pleased to have their beloved monastery once more occupied by religious; Mme. Pycke, to whose family the property belonged, also rejoiced to see it restored to its original destination. Her son, who was preparing for the priesthood, held Mère Julie in high esteem. He was studying his theology under the Fathers of the Faith, and had learnt from them a good deal about her apostolic labours in France and the sufferings she had endured. When, to his great delight, he had made acquaintance with the servant of God, he hastened to ask her whether it was true that she had been miraculously cured after a novena to the Heart of Jesus. Julie could not deny the favour which she never made known unasked, and the young cleric who had himself a very special devotion to the Sacred Heart, did all in his power to procure favourable terms for her from his mother. In after years the Abbé Pycke became honorary Vicar General of Ghent and secret chamberlain to Pope Gregory XVI.

The foundress was now free to occupy the Abbey as soon as she pleased. She had, moreover, perfect liberty to give it up at the end of that year or any other year, and even to cancel her engagement altogether, if unforeseen circumstances should prevent the opening of the schools. But Mère Julie still hesitated to close with these offers, however advantageous, fearing to tempt Providence if she opened a second house in the city without being sure of the means of subsistence. Moreover, the reply of the Government to the application of the Sisters for legal recognition had been couched in sufficiently ambiguous terms, and new laws were threatening Christian schools and colleges. She returned to Namur and laid the matter before Mgr. Pisani, who, after due deliberation, counselled delay, and Mère Julie at once communicated his decision to the Vicar General of Ghent. But the ardent and intrepid bishop of that city thought otherwise. He had long learnt to reckon on God's help for the good works which he undertook for the benefit of his diocese, and he knew that the Sisters of Notre-Dame would gladly buy the privilege of helping souls at the cost of any privations. So he merely answered the servant of God that the second foundation had to be made, and that he expected her immediately with some good Sisters to open the "Abbaye aux Bois." There was something in the Prince's bold and decisive manner of acting in harmony with Julie's own spirit. She was by nature neither slow nor timorous, and, say the Memoirs, had only waited so long in this instance for a higher authority to confirm her own interior conviction that this undertaking was willed by God. When once she had this confirmation, she went boldly forward. "Whether we are helped or not," she said to Mère St.-Joseph, "the thing must be done; we must not draw back even if we have to bear the whole cost." So indeed it happened.

The desire of a colleague for whom he entertained so deep a respect at once drew the consent of Mgr. Pisani, her own immediate superior; and it only remained to choose the subjects for the new house. Two were taken from Namur, and others were to be supplied from the Convent of St.-Pierre. On February 12, 1810, the two Mothers went together to Ghent, and while Mère Julie returned for a few days to take four postulants to the Mother-house, Mère St.-Joseph conducted the little party to the Abbey, which thus became once again the "Nonnenbosch," the "Locus Sanctæ Mariæ."

CHAPTER XV.

REHABILITATION OF THE FOUNDRESS IN FRANCE.

WE must now return to Amiens, where tribulations were not yet at an end. No sooner had the last Sisters left for Namur than M. de Sambucy set to work to re-organise a community. Mère Victoire had by this time somewhat gone down in his estimation; he sent her to Rubempré and transplanted to the Faubourg Noyon four young Sisters from the novitiate of the "Dames de l'Instruction Chrétienne," afterwards "Dames du Sacré-Cœur." One of these, Marie Elizabeth Prévost, who had entered religion only nine months previously, he named Superior, without even consulting the Venerable Mme. Barat, who was treated with just as little consideration as Mère Julie had been.*

Madame Prévost, whose excellent judgment compensated to some extent for her lack of experience, was commissioned to win over the Sisters still remaining at Montdidier, who were as determined as those of Amiens had been not to be severed from their Mother. For this purpose she visited them

---

* In the letter addressed to Mother Prévost by Mother de Baudemont, Superior of the Oratory house of the Dames de l'Instruction Chrétienne, Mère Barat, though then at Amiens, is not even mentioned. M. de Sambucy is named as founder, and the object of the document is "to establish an indissoluble union between the two associations."

several times, but all her gentleness and kindness failed of their effect. Sister Marie Caroline, the Superior, was sent for to Amiens, retained there several days, and exhorted by the Bishop and the Abbé with no better success. Forbidden to correspond with Mère Julie, the Sisters at Montdidier were consoled and encouraged by letters from Mère Blin de Bourdon and from Sister Catherine Daullée, who, it will be remembered, had been Superior of their little establishment before her transference to St.-Nicolas. The spirited appeal of the latter merits quotation.

My Sisters [she writes], "stand firm—know for certain that our good Mother carries you in her heart and will never abandon you, so long as you attach yourselves to our primitive spirit. . . . As for me, I have but one thought in the matter, to follow our Mother. Whatever she does not accept—were an angel from heaven to beg me to accept it, I would not receive. Let it be our pride to follow her wherever she is, let it be our happiness to feel that we are children of such a mother. If we share her crosses here below, we shall share the crown which awaits her in heaven. Be persuaded that God did not restore her health to no purpose. Though all the powers of hell should be let loose upon us, let us fear nothing; all new foundations have had their trials—a certain sign that they are the work of God. Far from letting them depress our courage, let them rather reanimate it: there is no victory without combat, no road to heaven but that of the Cross. The more crosses we have, the more we ought to thank our good God. Everything else indeed may be taken from us, but God we shall find everywhere. Courage, Sisters, courage! The pain is little and soon over, the joy will be eternal. Let us face all the difficulties we meet with in God's holy service; let us carry our cross joyfully; our dear Jesus Himself carries three-quarters of it, and He carries ourselves with the other quarter in His Divine Heart. In the cross virtue is purified as gold in the furnace.

Ultimately the firmness of the Sisters of Montdidier overcame the assaults to which they were subjected; they obtained permission to join their Superior General in Belgium, and went to await a favourable opportunity of doing so at Plessier-sur-St.-Just. Now it happened that just at this juncture the foundress had arrived in Picardy with a postulant whom she was returning to her family as unsuited to the Institute. She sent a note to Montdidier, refraining, however, through motives of prudence, from entering the convent herself. The Sisters had already left, but Mme. Prévost went at once to meet Julie at the hotel. She spoke to her of effecting a reunion, but in such terms that the servant of God saw clearly that the idea was out of the question. "Madame," she said simply at the close of the conversation, "you will do a good work at Amiens and we at Namur, with the help of God." From Montdidier Mère Julie passed to Plessier in order to learn news of her daughters from her old friend the Curé, M. Trouvelot; but as she was turning a street corner, she suddenly met all three of them. The joy and surprise may be imagined, and no time was lost in setting off together for Ghent, taking with them a postulant for whom Mère Julie's presence had at once and unexpectedly obtained the long-refused permission to follow her vocation.

An anecdote has come down to us from one of the travellers which reads like a page of the *Fioretti* of St. Francis. As they left Plessier, they came face to face with a mad dog which had already bitten a great number of persons. The Sister was terrified, but Julie said to her: "Do not be afraid, daughter; God is with us," and when the animal had come close up to her, she said to it very sweetly and gently: "Let us pass, my friend; we are the little Servants of the Lord, and are going to do His work." Then the dog became quiet for a little space and let them pass without doing them any harm; after which it was again rabid and dangerous as before.

This was by no means the last visit of the servant of God to her native land. It will be remembered that a considerable sum of money belonging to the Institute was still in the hands of M. de Sambucy, and no less than seven times between the years 1810 and 1811 had she to traverse that road to Picardy, which for so many years had been to her a Way of Sorrows. The interviews with Mère Victoire and the Abbé which this affair entailed were necessarily painful, and only considerations of justice and of God's glory could have induced her to pursue the matter. But the decision of Father Varin, to whom the question had been referred, and the opinion of Father Enfantin were formal. The authority of Father Thomas, as well as Mère Julie's gentleness and straightforward dealing, finally brought M. de Sambucy to the point, and the money was refunded.

Unfortunately for the poor Foundress it was all delivered to her in coin, and so, too, was the price of the sale of Mère Blin's property. Many a time at recreation did Mère Julie make the Sisters merry with the adventures of the two baskets which she had to carry back with her to Namur—the terrors that seized her when she had to entrust them to strangers' hands in lifting them in or out of the carriage, her anxiety as they drove along for the safety of the large basket under the seat and the small one on her knee, the indiscreet curiosity of the coachman and waiters at the inns as they felt the unusual weight of this luggage, and finally her joy when they stopped before the house of M. Vercruysse at Courtrai, where she was well known and always received with truly Christian hospitality. This pious family looked on her coming as a favour from heaven. Father Vercruysse, S.J., writes:

Mère Julie, the saintly Foundress of the Sisters of Notre-Dame, made a very deep impression on us children. This was at first mingled with awe, caused probably by her singular costume, but very soon fear gave place to love; she drew us by her caresses, her gifts of pious pictures, and her air of sanctity. As we did not know French, we could not talk to her; but we all understood her oft-repeated and incomparable : " *Que le Bon Dieu est bon.*" More than once, at the request of my parents, she gave me her blessing, which has profited me not a little.

Connected with these Amiens journeys are two or three little incidents, which we may place together here. On one occasion she met again in Paris M. Montaigne, then director of the Seminary of St.-

Sulpice. In giving an account of herself to this holy man, who had helped her so much in former trials, she accused herself of having shown some vivacity in replying to a reproach addressed to her by the Bishop of Ghent. The Abbé, to humble her, replied, "Mother, that is not the way to speak to a Bishop; you must repair that fault without delay." No sooner had the servant of God arrived at Ghent than she hastened to throw herself at the feet of Mgr. de Broglie and to entreat his pardon. The wise director himself related this circumstance to a young Belgian pupil of his (the Abbé Poncelet, afterwards Vicar General at Namur and Domestic Prelate to his Holiness), adding: "They tell me she was cured by a miracle; that may be, but I value that act of obedience and humility more than any miracle."

About six leagues distant from Amiens is the Château of Hénencourt, the residence of the Marchioness de Lameth, aunt of the Bishop of Ghent. Here Mère Julie once stopped in order to consult the prelate, then on a visit to his aunt. She found him just stepping into his carriage. "Mère Julie," he said kindly, "I must take my drive; go in to my aunt." The marchioness received her affably, and put a room at her disposal. As usual, Julie found the means of employing her enforced leisure in doing good to souls. The little daughter of Mme. de Lameth's maid happening to come in, the servant of God began to hear her the catechism, and then went on to explain it with so much charm and unction that the child, delighted, knelt down to pray for rain, " so that the good Mother who spoke so well of the good God might not go too soon." On the Prince's return she was invited to dinner with himself, the Marchioness and several ecclesiastics—no light mortification for her. Hénencourt was close to Rubempré, where her niece Félicité, who had married the schoolmaster, was living in very narrow circumstances. Julie sent for her, and with a tenderness mingled with gratitude for the long devotion of bygone years, encouraged her to that patience under afflictions of which she herself had once set her so beautiful an example.

During one of these absences in Picardy she writes charmingly to her daughters at Namur:

I should like very much to be with you, but "my Father's business" calls me elsewhere. He needs some little messengers to go His errands, and He has been good enough to choose me for one—it is too great a happiness. There are many circumstances which I should not at all enjoy if it were not for such a good Father. For Him we must work, suffer, die. Let us die then, my soul, die to the sweet consolation of being with those who are so dear.

It seems scarcely credible that the Abbé de Sambucy was now urgently insisting on the return of the Foundress to the convent at Amiens. But Julie had met the suggestion with a tone of decision that put an end to all arguments. "When a king exiles a subject," she said, " that subject cannot return unless recalled by his sovereign; I shall not put my foot in the house of the Faubourg until I am recalled by the Bishop." And now the convent at Amiens was dying a natural death. The author of its misfortunes, M. de Sambucy, was paying the price of his presumption. One after another his ambitious projects fell through and it may have been almost a relief to him to be carried off from Amiens by the Imperial Police on some suspicion of interference in politics. After a species of confinement in Paris he contrived to go to Rome as Secretary of the French Ambassador, Mgr. Cortois de Pressigny. He made one more vain attempt to interfere with the nuns of the Sacred Heart, but his intrigues were finally unveiled, his acts were disowned by his patrons, and he was obliged to leave Rome. He returned to France as anxious as ever to exert his zeal, but considerably lowered in public estimation. He died in 1848, titular Canon of the Church of Notre-Dame in Paris.

This unfortunate adviser once out of the way, the eyes of the episcopal and clerical authorities at Amiens were opened, and they saw clearly how completely he had misled them. Mgr. Demandolx lost no time in endeavouring to repair his error and its fatal consequences. He wrote to the Bishop of Namur to express his regret at having been so deceived, and his desire to reinstate the Foundress in her proper position as head of all the houses of her Institute in his diocese. Father Sellier was charged with making the first overtures. In a letter dated September, 1812, he informed Mère Julie that he had undertaken to speak to M. Fournier, the Vicar General, about her, and to suggest that it was now time to recall the Foundress to Amiens. "It is more than time," cried her former adversary; "we have been deceived! yes, deceived! But do you think she will be willing to return to us?" "I am sure she will." "Well, then, I shall speak to the Bishop about it." A few days later Father Sellier wrote to Mère Julie enclosing a letter from M. Fournier, worded thus:

SIR,—It is a real pleasure to me to inform you that our Bishop approves with all his heart the project of recalling Mère Julie. Her return would give us an opportunity of repairing the error which we were induced to commit with regard to this holy person. Therefore, Sir, will you let her know our wishes and persuade her to come back as soon as possible, in order to confer with his Lordship and to make all necessary arrangements. For my part I shall see her amongst us again with a real satisfaction, in which all my colleagues will share.—FOURNIER, *Vicar General*.

The servant of God was at Lille, for some temporal affairs of the Institute, when this letter reached her. Hers was not a heart to rejoice over her justification before men; neither would she act without consulting the Bishop of Namur and Mère Blin. "I shall not go quite so quickly as they seem to wish," she writes familiarly to her first companion; "we must let the good God have time to complete His work; nothing succeeds when we go precipitately before Him." Shortly afterwards the Bishop of Amiens sent her the following autograph letter:

AMIENS, October 23, 1812.

M. Sellier has undertaken, my dear daughter, to express to you the desire I have to see you back at Amiens, in order to take up again the superiority of the Sisters of Notre-Dame in my diocese, which you left in consequence of an error caused by one whom I believed I could trust. Now, more enlightened, I am not afraid to own to you that I have been deceived in your regard. I urge you then, my dear daughter, to return as soon as possible, if not to fix yourself here at once, at least to make the arrangements which the new order of things will necessitate. You may depend upon the most cordial welcome from Sister Mary [Prévost] and her companions, who will be enchanted to submit to your authority, as they have unanimously assured me. You will meet with no obstacle, and I will make every effort to second you. I can certify that every one will be anxious to manifest the satisfaction given by your return. You can undertake from here the journey you have in view * when you have made all the arrangements which you consider desirable. I flatter myself, my dear daughter, that you will concur in my wishes, and that you will not doubt my good will nor my paternal affection.

✠ J.-Fr., *Bishop of Amiens.*

As nothing was said about the mode of government which was to be adopted in future for the Sisters of Notre-Dame in the diocese of Amiens, Julie thought it well to reply in her usual straightforward manner.

My Lord,—I am exceedingly grateful for the letter I have had the honour to receive from your Lordship, in which you are good enough to favour me with your confidence by wishing to make me Superior of your house of the Sisters of Notre-Dame. I should like to be able to comply immediately with your wishes, and to carry out your views, but I have thought it right to lay before you the following explanation :

I feel myself bound by the engagements I have taken to

* Probably to Fontainebleau, where the servant of God went four months later.

have no fixed residence, having to look after several small houses just beginning in Flanders, without reckoning others which are being offered, and which are deferred on account of circumstances. It is therefore impossible for me to fix myself in one place or another; I have to come and go according to the needs of the moment; such is the spirit of our Institute. I return, it is true, to Namur after my visits, because it is in that house that we have our novices and postulants. I do not know, my Lord, if this dependence of the different houses would be according to your views; as all are on the same footing, I could not make any change; my superiors feel as I do about this. Be assured, my Lord, that it would be an extreme pleasure to me to second your projects as far as lies in my power. I omit mentioning to your Lordship certain local difficulties with which I have acquainted M. Sellier.

Whatever the Bishop's former notions had been, the following letter leaves no room for doubt that at this moment he admitted the government of a Superior General. It is dated November 1, 1812.

Either I must have explained myself badly, my dear daughter, or you must have misunderstood me. It was in nowise my design to make you quit Namur and establish yourself at Amiens; but looking on you as the Superior General of your Institute, I would simply ask you to come here to visit your convent, and to make all the reforms in it you think advisable, so that the same spirit may reign amongst you all. Come, then, as soon as possible, so as to consolidate by your presence an establishment which ought to be dear to you as the birthplace of your Congregation, and which I would fain consider its Mother-house (though I do not insist on this).

✠ J.-Fr., *Bishop of Amiens.*

Equally pressing were the messages Julie received from the community of the Faubourg Noyon, who wrote her a general letter calling for her, as she says, *à cor et à cri*. After having taken the opinion of her council and the Bishop of Namur, she was persuaded that God had manifested His Will, and that whatever difficulties might await her, they had to be faced. She writes to Sister Leleu at Jumet that God will send His holy Angel, as He did to Tobias, to show her the way; so she has no fear. " Our good Jesus is our Way, our Life, our Truth." She thinks there is both for and against in this business. The good God will enlighten her about it if it pleases Him. The good Sisters must pray, so that they may all do in all things the holy Will of God, for that is what really matters most. And she ends the letter with one of those short sayings of hers, noble in their simplicity— " Let us do God's work in a manner worthy of Him." But through all the correspondence relating to this affair it is clear that she herself felt the conviction that the proposed reunion would never take place. " What will be the end ? God knows ; this should be enough for me. I have to go ; the councillors all think it is God's Will. . . . . Persevering trust, fidelity in everything ; you must be the good odour of Jesus Christ." And so with closed eyes and her hand tight clasped in that of her good God, she left Namur on November 9, 1812. At Ghent she took up as her companion Sister Catherine Daullée, Superior at Nouveau-Bois. Using this opportunity to give her daughters a grand lesson in religious obedience, she named as temporary Superior, in the absence of Sister Catherine, Sister Angela Witmeere, a virtuous and sensible person, but employed hitherto only in domestic work. She gave her the place of honour at her right hand until she left Ghent, and when the poor Sister entreated to be at least dispensed from giving the conference at Chapter, replied: "Daughter, you will hold the Chapter and you will give the conference. Begin your exhortation with these words:—'He that heareth you, heareth Me, and he that despiseth you, despiseth Me;' those are our Lord's own words, addressed to all who exercise authority in His Name. Afterwards you can make any remarks or give any admonitions to your community which you may judge desirable."

Arrived at Amiens, Mère Julie and her companions hastened to pay their respects to Mgr. Demandolx, who confirmed by word of mouth all that he had written to the Servant of God. On the following day he transmitted to her an official document, formally establishing the dependence of all the houses of the Sisters of Notre-Dame on their Superior General.*

---

* The text of this document runs thus:

"Jean-François Demandolx, by the grace of God and favour of the Apostolic See, Bishop of Amiens, Beauvais and Noyon, etc., to Julie Billiart, religious of Notre-Dame, health and benediction in the Lord. Intimately convinced of the precious advantages which must result from unity of rules, of functions, of custom, of costume, and in general of an entire uniformity among the Sisters of the Association called of Notre-Dame, and thoroughly informed of your wisdom, prudence and other good qualities, We declare that We have recognised

At the same time he addressed the following letter to Sister Marie Prévost:

BISHOP'S PALACE, Amiens, November 17, 1812.

I am forwarding to you, my dear Sister, the Act which constitutes good Mère Julie Superior General of the houses of the Sisters of Notre-Dame now established, or henceforward to be established, in this diocese. I am convinced that no one amongst you will refuse to recognise her as such. In any case, Mère Julie will use her authority towards any who may refuse adhesion to this essential change. His lordship determines nothing with regard to the ownership of the house which you now occupy. But he hopes that you will take no final measures about this house without consulting him. Besides, before any project of removal, you must make sure of obtaining another, either at your own expense or that of the city.

Accept, etc.,

FOURNIER, V.G.

you, as by these presents We do recognise you, as Superior General of all the houses of the Association of the Sisters of Notre-Dame which are, or which in the future shall be, established in Our diocese, and to this effect We give you all the same powers, rights and privileges which have been granted to you in the said capacity or appellation by the Bishops of those dioceses wherein the said Sisters of Notre-Dame have establishments. We recommend in consequence, and furthermore expressly enjoin on each of the Sisters of the Association called of Notre-Dame who are, and who shall be in the future, anywhere within Our diocese, to show to you at all times and in all circumstances the respect, submission and obedience due to their Superior General.

These presents shall be read in presence of the whole Community established in the Fanbourg Noyon of the city of Amiens, and transcribed on to their Register; and the Superior shall communicate them to all the Sisters dispersed in the houses of Our diocese, so that none shall be able to plead ignorance thereof.

Given at Amiens, under Our hand and seal, and countersigned by Our Secretary, Monday, the sixteenth of November, of the year of our Lord, eighteen hundred and twelve.

✠ J.-FR., *Bishop of Amiens.*
By command, etc.,

(Place of the Seal.)   GRAVET, CANON, *Secretary.*

Finally, the venerable prelate sent to Mgr. Pisani the following letter, which is as honourable to himself by its frank acknowledgment of error, as it is to her whose public justification it completed. The original is still preserved in the archives of the Institute at Namur.

My Lord,—I cannot do otherwise than own to you that I have had to reproach myself exceedingly for having followed the pernicious advice that was given me, inducing me to send the good Mère Julie out of my diocese. The harm done by her departure was so serious that I found myself on the point of losing several precious institutions if I had not hastened to recall her, and if you, on your side, had not urged her to yield to my pressing entreaties. Her return has filled me with joy, and I have been as much touched as pleased by the reception she has met with from her former community, and by the holy eagerness with which the Superior whom I had appointed there resigned her post, protesting to Mère Julie that she did so with all her heart, being only too happy to live henceforward in dependence and as the last of her Sisters. All is not yet definitely settled. But I have begun the work by recognising Mère Julie as Superior General of her Congregation. I have forwarded to her the Act of her nomination, not forgetting her title as Foundress, and I now indulge a well-grounded hope that, under the direction of this excellent religious, her Congregation will begin a new life in my diocese. Thus, my Lord, it is to you, after God, that I shall be beholden for the great good which Providence is about to work through her instrumentality. Accept the assurance of the sincere and respectful attachment with which I am, my Lord,

Your most humble and obedient servant,

✠ J.-Fr., *Bishop of Amiens.*

Nothing was now wanting to the complete rehabilitation of the Venerable Julie Billiart in the town where she had been brought into opposition with her ecclesiastical superiors. She had long since forgotten the wrongs done to her, and she now met those same superiors with the utmost openness and cordiality. But notwithstanding all the good will of the Bishop and clergy of Amiens, there were certain grave difficulties in the way. The principal of these was the insolvent condition of the house in the Faubourg. Julie had already heard of this before her arrival, probably through Father Sellier, and had, with her usual activity, sought for a remedy. On her way through Ghent she had spoken to a merchant there, a nephew of M. Duminy, Curé of Amiens Cathedral. He was removing into Picardy, and asked the Foundress, in case she had to part with the house in the Faubourg, to let him have the refusal of it. He went to look at the house, found it suitable, and agreed to pay ten thousand francs indemnity for the improvements made in the building before Mère Julie had been sent away from Amiens. This sum went towards paying the debts of the community. The servant of God sincerely desired to help the good nuns in their embarrassment and to arrange for their future maintenance; but all the resources failed at once. Mme. de Franssu had, at the invitation of Father Enfantin, gone to found an institution of her own at Valence; the boarding-school contained only ten pupils, who rather increased the expenses than otherwise; and the young Superior was apparently wanting in administrative capacity.

Now that she had relieved the Sisters of the Faubourg of their house and the heavy rent due to the Bishop, Julie's next step was to find another dwelling for them. She writes playfully to Mère St.-Joseph: "People are offering me houses on all sides for forty or sixty thousand francs: and I running all over the town to find one for nothing! It is your name, my dear, which gives me this great reputation. The immediate need is to pay the debts. . . . I wait for God to show us what it is best to do."

After a long search, a refuge for the community was found in an old convent of the order of Fontevrault, which went by the name of "The Moreaucourt." A part of the building was still habitable, and it was offered to the Sisters, together with a small allowance, for teaching the girls employed in a cotton factory established close by. For want of anything better Mother Prévost closed with this offer, and about the same time Mère Julie, with a view to the relief of the community of the Faubourg, accepted the proposal of the Count de Rainneville to establish two or three Sisters, to whom he guaranteed a small income, in the schoolhouse of Rainneville itself, six miles from Amiens. Sister Marie Hénocque was named Superior of this little foundation, which opened prosperously.

But the servant of God still hesitated to conclude the reunion between her own daughters and the Sisters of Amiens; in the whole of this affair she moved with the utmost caution, and only step by step. During the three weeks which she passed in

Picardy, she spoke little, but she observed and watched everything, preserving her soul in peace, and holding herself ready to obey the faintest indication of the Divine Will. Without finding in the community of the Faubourg grave defects, she felt at every turn that its spirit was different from that which she had tried to form in her daughters. "God often gave to His servant," writes Mère St.-Joseph, "clear and strong lights." Brief and rapid as their passage was, she yet could not neglect them, knowing well from experience the grace which guided her, and which had so often helped her out of her difficulties; but she would not act upon them without advice.

Sometimes [she said] I see clearly, as if the thing were to be; at other times all is darkness, and I know not where I am. . . . My God, please help me! My good friend, just as I entered the house in the Faubourg, the good God said these two words to me:—*Look at Me, and follow Me.* From that moment I do nothing but look to see where my good God intends to lead me. *

Two days later her words are still more significant and remarkable:

Time is a great master, I prefer to let it pass; it will teach us a good many things. I go quietly on day by day. I wait for the good God, I look at Him, I follow Him. . . . This is the one cry of my heart—"My God, what wilt Thou have me to do? Mary, my good Mother, protect me! I trust that God will bless these dispositions which His Goodness has put into my heart. We have a difficult work in hand; I want prayers, and many of them. When, on

* Letter to Mère Blin, Nov. 21, 1812.

entering that house, as I told you, I met our good Jesus fleeing from Amiens, He saw very well what my repugnance was. . . . . My God, Thou wilt deliver us, if it please Thee!

There is a tradition in the Institute, confirmed by this letter, that at the instant when Julie crossed the threshold of the house in the Faubourg, she had an apparition of our Blessed Lord bearing His Cross and saying to her: " Look at Me, and follow Me; I am the Way, the Truth and the Life." * In saying these words our Saviour seemed to be withdrawing from the convent at Amiens. The servant of God was so habitually reserved with regard to any extraordinary favours, that the Sisters knew very little about this one. The letter to which she alludes in the words "As I have told you" no longer exists, destroyed, as the old Sisters, contemporaries of the Foundress, declared, by Mère St.-Joseph at the command of Julie herself. When, after the death of the Servant of God, she who had so well known and loved her, used to read her letters to the Sisters, she would stop at this passage, saying that Mère Julie had forbidden this " meeting with her good Jesus " to be spoken of, and that the details would be known in heaven.† Charity may have combined with humility to suggest this prohibition; the representation of our Lord departing from the house in the Faubourg might have given an unfavourable impression of the community. The words, " Look at

---

* Process de fama Sanctitatis, first witness, p. 104, ninth witness, p. 108.
† Recollections of Sister Reine Cambier.

Me and follow Me" occur several times in the letters to Mère Blin de Bourdon. And to Sister St. John, Superior of Saint-Hubert, Julie wrote after her return: "I can only tell you one word about the Amiens business; it is this, that I did nothing but follow the good God very quietly."*

Early in December, seeing that matters were provisionally arranged, she returned to Ghent with Sister Catherine. She entered the house at Nouveau-Bois alone, and sent for Sister Angèle and the Counsellors to the parlour, in order to ascertain from them whether the community had been faithful in every detail of religious submission. The report being entirely favourable, Mère Julie reinstated Sister Catherine in her post, saying to the assembled Sisters: "If I had had any complaints, I should have taken Sister Catherine to Namur. I give you back the Superior whom you love so much, because, like good religious, you have been obedient to her whom I put in her place." Lessons like these were not easily forgotten in the Institute. The Foundress returned to Namur on December 11, having been obliged by the severe frost to perform a great part of the journey on foot. It would seem as if in the design of God the sole aim of this visit to France had been her own justification, for hardly had she left Amiens, overwhelmed with testimonies of affection and esteem, than the house at the Faubourg Noyon

* Letter dated December 19, 1812.

collapsed, and its community was forced to disperse. Letter after letter came from Sister Marie Prévost telling her of new troubles. To the Foundress they looked like couriers of Providence announcing its dissolution. The administrators of "The Moreau-court"—for what reason is unknown—withdrew the house and the promised school fees from the Sisters. Soon afterwards M. Duminy's nephew asked to be released from his engagement, as he had found a more convenient residence than the house in the Faubourg. Finally Sister Prévost herself, worn out with all these difficulties, began to long for rest and turned towards her first religious home with the Ladies of the Sacred Heart. Finding that she had only been lent to Notre-Dame, she announced to Mère Julie her wish to return. The Servant of God saw that it was useless to try to keep her, and she did not make the attempt. She simply replied to Madame Prévost that "as things were, the house had dissolved itself, that it was not her doing but God's." There was no chance whatever of keeping it up as a house of education; it had entirely lost the confidence of the public, as Mère Julie had clearly seen when she was at Amiens. Of the Sisters, one or two followed Madame Prévost to the Ladies of the Sacred Heart, and several in very delicate health returned to their families. When the Servant of God had been fully informed of all that had taken place, she wrote to M. Fournier, the Vicar General, to acquaint him with the facts; she pointed out to him the impossibility of maintaining a community at Amiens under the circumstances, and asked to have it suppressed by diocesan authority. The Vicar General replied:

AMIENS, January 7, 1813.

MY DEAR SISTER,—Our Prelate, after reading the letter which you addressed to me, is convinced that the convent at Amiens cannot be carried on for any length of time without contracting fresh debts, so long as there are no more resources to fall back upon than we have at present. He can therefore only approve the step you propose taking. I trust you will always consider the Sisters of Notre-Dame in the other houses as your daughters, and that you will avail yourself of your authority as Superior General to keep, or to dismiss, those who are fit, or unfit, for your Congregation. His Lordship leaves all this to your well-known prudence and charity. Our Prelate was ignorant of Sister Marie's intentions; she did not tell us of them any more than of the debts she had contracted. Do as you think best in her regard according to the judgment you have formed about her. Receive, my very dear Sister, the thanks both of his Lordship and myself for the prayers you addressed to God for us. Accept ours in exchange; they are all offered for your own consolation and for the success of your undertakings for the glory of God and the welfare of souls. I entreat the Lord to continue to shower His blessings upon you. I recommend myself to your prayers, assuring you of the sincere and respectful sentiments with which I am, &c.,

FOURNIER, V.G.*

It was decided that the furniture of the Amiens convent should be sold to liquidate the debts as far as the price would go, the deficit to be supplied by the Bishop. Mère Julie, who had had no share in

---

* Memoirs, vol. iii. p. 192.

the expenses since her departure, held herself aloof; she could not deprive of their daily bread the houses which she had to support, nor place herself in the impossibility of making fresh foundations. The only objects she claimed for herself were the tabernacle and ciborium given to her by Mme. de Franssu; these were restored to her when the affairs were wound up. They are still preserved with religious veneration at the Mother-House, Namur.

The dissolution of the remaining houses of Notre-Dame in France followed close upon that of Amiens. These were Montdidier, Rubempré, Rainneville and Bresles in the diocese of Amiens, and Ambleville in the diocese of Paris. Long before this, in 1811, at the express request of Mgr. d'Aviau, the establishment at Bordeaux had been severed from its affiliation, though the most cordial relations continued to exist between the two Congregations, and the prelate spoke in terms of the highest praise of the Foundress. Early in the spring of 1813, Julie, according to a promise she had made to Mgr. Demandolx, left Belgium in order to make the visitation of her French convents. She went first to Rainneville, thence to Amiens to see the Bishop. From this latter place she wrote to Mère St. Joseph:

I have just come from Rainneville, and found the little community going on fairly well. May God preserve it, if it be His will that it should last; thorns will not be wanting to it. I saw M. de Rainneville, who speaks as founder; and I, on my side, spoke as foundress, not for the temporal prosperity of the house, but in order to uphold the spirit of our Institute in opposition to his demands. My God! what one has to put up with in treating with these gentlemen and ladies, however good they may be! What a large heart one must have to be a Sister of Notre-Dame! What strong medicine one must be able to swallow! This is the grace I ask for all my daughters—that they may be very courageous, very generous.

The little convent at Rainneville had to be given up, perhaps in consequence of the very exigencies on the part of the founders here alluded to. Sister Marie Hénocque returned to the house of the Oratory whence she had come with Mother Prévost; the other Sisters followed Mère Julie. Rubempré, where, it will be remembered, Mère Victoire was Superior, Julie abstained from visiting for reasons sufficiently obvious, which Mgr. Demandolx approved. However, "it happened," say the Memoirs, "that Victoire presented herself at the Bishop's house while he was engaged with the Servant of God. His Lordship, who had received some very unfavourable reports of her proceedings, requested Mère Julie to speak with her and exhort her to change her conduct. Through obedience Julie complied, but, gentle as her admonition was, it was ill received, and when the prelate on her return to him, enquired in what disposition she had found Victoire, she could only reply "Like bronze." His Lordship understood that the erring religious was beyond the reach of remonstrance. Not long afterwards she threw off the mask and abandoned her vocation.

The house at Rubempré was suppressed. At Montdidier the Foundress was received with transports of joy. In spite of the kindness of the excellent Curé, M. Pillon de la Tour, the Sisters were suffering some part of the persecution which had just driven away the Fathers of the Faith and suppressed their college. Their departure too had been keenly felt by the Sisters. The Servant of God encouraged them to remain for the sake of their poor children, and promised to see them again before leaving France. After visiting the convent at Ambleville, which had a very brief existence, she went on to Bresles. The place, situated in her native diocese (temporarily united to that of Amiens), had a special interest for her. Here dwelt the family of the director of her childhood, the holy and learned M. Dangicourt, and it was probably on this occasion that she obtained the portrait of him which is still to be seen at Namur. But unfortunately the foundation was beset with the same sort of difficulties as that at Rainneville; the benefactress of the school, Mme. de Gerville, wanted the Sisters to employ themselves in lace-making, embroidery, and other works not in keeping with their vocation. No human considerations could ever make Julie compromise where the spirit of her Institute was concerned, and she foresaw from that moment that the establishment would not be a permanent one. To a heart like Julie Billiart's, "moulded," as she says in one of her early letters to Françoise Blin, "to feel very keenly," this breaking

of the last threads which bound her to her Picardy
and to France must have been no little pain. To
her burning apostolic zeal it must have been no little
sacrifice that she might no longer scatter its sparks
over the land whose village streets and sunny cornfields had heard her first childish exhortations, and
where she had gathered together her first companions.
But with and out of the pain came to her a supreme
consolation. The visitation of her houses had not in
fact been the only object of this journey. For a long
time she had cherished the project of laying at the
feet of Pius VII., then captive at Fontainebleau, the
homage of herself and of her daughters. The intense
love she bore to the Church and the Pope left her no
rest until she had accomplished this act of filial piety.
On February 16, 1813, she wrote to Sister Godelle :
" I have to go to Paris, and please God I shall obtain
the blessing of the Holy Father for all my good
daughters." Her introduction to His Holiness was
apparently procured through the Fathers of the
Faith. Fathers Sellier and Leblanc both had frequent communication with the persecuted Pontiff,
and we are told by Father Guidée in his Lives
of the Fathers of the Faith that the latter
was especially active in transmitting letters and
pecuniary assistance to the august captive and
to the "black Cardinals." A threat of being
arrested led him at last to seek safety in Belgium, and he retired to the house of a priest
named Kinet at Andennes, between Namur and

Huy.* The foundation of a house of the Sisters of Notre-Dame at Andennes took place immediately after Mère Julie's visit to Fontainebleau, and there is every reason to suppose that Father Leblanc was the prime mover in both these events. Another friend of the Foundress had relations with the Pope. This was M. Danheux, a pious and distinguished layman belonging to Namur. He is known to have made several visits to the captive Pontiff, not without personal risk and great danger of arrest by the Imperial police, who watched very narrowly all who manifested sympathy with His Holiness. M. Danheux held Julie in very high esteem. One of his letters is still kept in the archives of the Institute in which he speaks of " notre sainte Mère Julie." Arrived at Ambleville she took with her as companion a novice named Sister M.-Madeleine Quequet, and proceeded to Fontainebleau. Tradition says she travelled on an ass, she and her companion mounting it by turns. In after years Sister Quequet would often relate the story of this memorable pilgrimage—how she was not told why they were going to Fontainebleau, how when there she was left to take care of the donkey in the courtyard of the palace, and how after a very long time of waiting, Mère Julie came out with her face bathed in tears and whispering : " My daughter, I have seen the Holy Father ; we have wept together over the troubles of the Church." In her hands she

* M. Kinet was brother of M. Lemaire-Kinet, of Ghent, whose family was so devoted to Mère Julie.

HIS HOLINESS POPE PIUS VII.

From an Engraving in Cardinal Wiseman's "Recollections of the Four Last Popes."

clasped a crucifix which the Sovereign Pontiff had given her, and scarcely spoke again during the journey; she was evidently under the pressure of strong emotion. The interview of the Servant of God with Pius VII. took place during the period when, in penance for having momentarily yielded to the perfidious solicitations of Napoleon, he was abstaining from offering the holy Sacrifice. History has recorded the deep sorrow and bitter self-reproach of the holy old man. In that long interview with the Vicar of Christ did Julie's splendid faith and hope lift the courage of the venerable Pontiff, as she reminded him "how good the good God is"? Or did he, looking into that soul, which, in the words of Cardinal Régnier, "united the impassioned heart of a Saint Teresa with the apostolic heart of a Saint Francis Xavier," foresee for her consolation the fruits which her suffering Congregation was destined to bring forth in the future? We do not know. No echo has been borne to us down the long years, save the words occurring in letters written immediately following after the event, between the reserve of whose lines we seem still to feel the palpitation of that first deep emotion.

To Mère St. Joseph she writes:

I am saying nothing of my journey to Paris; it would take volumes! If it please God to give us the grace of seeing each other again, we shall indeed have much to say to each other. . . . I cannot undertake to write about it. My God, what is earth, what is the world?—a place of exile, of banishment! . . . Ah! happy, a thousand times happy, are those who have given themselves up to a life of self-renunciation and sacrifice.

And again to Sister Leleu:

I say nothing of my journey; it would fill a volume. The good God is very good, my dear friend. Say so to my good daughters. I wish I could make myself heard throughout the universe, to invite all men to join with me in blessing the mercies of our Lord.*

* Letters from Montdidier and Namur, April, 1813.

CHAPTER XVI.

RAPID SPREAD OF THE INSTITUTE.

THE tree from which a branch had been so violently severed in France, was giving forth in Belgium vigorous and healthy shoots in great number. As we have seen, three convents already existed there—at Namur, Ghent and Jumet; five more were founded in the lifetime of the Servant of God.

Buried deep in the forest of the Ardennes lies the little town of St.-Hubert, with a population of three thousand souls. It is celebrated for the pilgrimages which for centuries past have been made there in honour of the great Bishop of Liége, whose name it bears. Its beautiful church is dedicated to him, and here sufferers from hydrophobia go to be touched with his relics or his stole. In 1808 this marvel of gothic art was doomed to destruction, but was saved by the generosity of two of the chief citizens, MM. Zoude and Doutreloux. It was this M. Zoude who, as mayor of the town, suggested that the municipality should apply to Mère Julie for some of her daughters to direct the schools. At the express desire of Mgr. Pisani she went to St.-Hubert in the July of 1809, and made arrangements with the local authorities, who offered a house and an annual income of about twenty-five pounds for three Sisters. " With this," writes Mère Blin de Bourdon, "they were provided with the necessary; the superfluous, thanks be to God, has no place in our houses." The Sisters who had just left Montdidier were ready to occupy this establishment, except one who was kept at Namur, as her health was too delicate for the rude climate of the Ardennes. That picturesque district was then almost inaccessible to travellers, and had no regular communication with the surrounding centres of population. The Sisters were two days and a night in reaching their destination.

The Foundress wrote her impressions of the place to Namur. She finds the little house very satisfactory; the two schoolrooms will each hold fifty or sixty children. She and the Sisters have been received with every kind of honour. On the Feast of the Assumption the sub-prefect in full official costume was in the church with his wife, and had made them kneel in his bench. In fact, every one at St.-Hubert loads them with kindness. Divine Providence will arrange all for the best; she had laid it all in His adorable Heart. On the very day when she is writing, the sub-prefect, the mayor and the other municipal authorities will assist with great solemnity at the formal installation of the Sisters.

Mère Julie passed a week at St.-Hubert to establish her daughters at their post and to trace out their line of action, and on her return to Namur continued her instructions in her letters. As they are three in number, she reminds the Sisters, they must represent the earthly trinity, Jesus, Mary and Joseph; and they must honour the adorable Trinity in Heaven by the strictest union, the sweetest charity, the deepest peace. The good seed fell upon good ground; the daughters whom Julie left at St.-Hubert showed themselves worthy of their mother. By degrees the community increased in number, and their good works were multiplied. The attachment of the children to their new mistresses showed itself on one occasion in a naïve and touching manner in keeping with the simple, old-world ways of the quaint little town. It was the end of the summer holidays of 1810, and Mère Julie was herself taking back to St.-Hubert the Sisters who had been making their annual retreat at the Mother-House, as she had to instal a new class-mistress and to introduce her to the administrators. She set off in a hired carriage with her three daughters; when they were about a mile and a half from the town, they were met by all the children, rich and poor, who, on hearing of their approach, had trooped out from St.-Hubert to receive them, and who welcomed them with cries of joy. At the sight of their beloved pupils the travellers got out of the carriage, and, sending on the driver with their luggage, made their entry into the town surrounded by a crowd of happy scholars. The inhabitants had never seen anything like it before and looked on with admiration. But the children had another surprise in store for their dear mistresses. Of their own accord and at their own cost they had prepared a meal for them in the house, of which one of the eldest girls had the key, and they proceeded to usher the Sisters into it with enthusiastic delight. In 1815 a boarding school was opened, which gave some excellent subjects to the congregation. The Superior, Sister St. John, spent forty years at St.-Hubert, where she brought up more than one generation, and was venerated and beloved in no common degree by the inhabitants of the interesting little town.

In November, 1809, the Foundress was invited to Binche by her benefactress, the Baroness de Coppens, who wished to found a school on her estate. She made the journey on foot with a peasant for her guide, God giving her the grace, as she wrote, to keep pace with the good man. The negotiations, however, came to nothing, for the Baroness had made up her mind to have two Sisters living at the château. This Julie refused point-blank, " the good God putting into her mouth what she had to say." One day while she was at Binche, two little girls, one of whom was suffering from a disease of the eyes, came to ask a remedy from the charitable châtelaine. As Mme. de Coppens was absent, the servants were sending the children away.

"What is the matter, my child?" said Julie to the little sufferer.

"My eyes are so bad."

"Come, it is nothing at all. Let us kneel down and say a prayer together." Then she traced the sign of the cross upon the sore eyes with her thumb, and the little girl rose up completely cured, and went home full of joy and gratitude. The story was related to Mère Blin by the daughters of the Baroness, and the miracle was attested by numerous witnesses in the juridical process.*

The same year, in the very depth of a severe winter, the indefatigable Foundress undertook a journey to Breda, by roads so bad that the horses were sometimes breast-high in water. Here again the establishment had to be refused, but the journey had nevertheless served a providential purpose. While waiting in Brussels for the coach to Namur, she felt suddenly and strongly drawn to visit the Countess de Ribaucourt (née Quarré) to recommend to her some poor people at Namur. This lady, who had a great affection for Julie, had just inherited the property and house which the Sisters rented in the Rue des Fossés, and which the Foundress greatly desired to purchase. Julie knew nothing of this, and was therefore much surprised on entering the Hôtel de Ribaucourt to be at once addressed on the subject of the sale of the Namur house. It had fallen to her lot, said the Countess, in the division of the property, and she and her husband wished the Sisters to have the preference over other purchasers. The Servant of God blessed Him that she had

* Memoirs, vol. iv. p. 69.—Informatio, etc., de donis et miraculis in vita, xix. § 29.

been at Brussels just at this juncture; and having ascertained all particulars about the estimate of the house, hastened off to consult Mgr. Pisani and Sister St. Joseph. Two days later, by the advice of the bishop, both the Foundresses started for Brussels; on December 13 the purchase was concluded, and the Institute had acquired its first property. On the return of the two Mothers the whole community assembled to sing the *Te Deum* in thanksgiving that the Lord had provided for Himself a house where He would vouchsafe to dwell in the midst of His humble handmaids— a holy house and a beloved one, whose walls were to stretch out, and whose boundaries were to be extended as the family of Notre-Dame increased and multiplied.

The reader will remember that the last days of 1810 had seen the acquisition of the Nouveau-Bois Abbey at Ghent. The beginnings of what is now one of the most flourishing and best appointed of all the educational establishments in Belgium were marked by extreme poverty. It might indeed be said of Julie's foundations as it was of those of St. Teresa, that each fresh one seemed to lead her Sisters a step further onward in the path of detachment and humility. Crowded together in a small part of the Abbey buildings, excluded even from the church, which was still in the hands of the owners of the workshops, the community of Nouveau-Bois had

to suffer privations of all kinds. For the first
few days they had no seats but two or three
broken chairs left by the last occupants, and no
beds but palliasses thrown on the floor. As to
food, it would often have failed them altogether
had not their Mother, so long as she remained
with them, found their provisions multiplied in
her hands.* She confided the care of the community to the valiant Sister Catherine Daullée,
whose acquaintance we have already made, and
who was replaced at St.-Pierre by Sister Marie
Steenhaut. Perhaps the Foundress had her fears
that the new Superior's courage and mortification
might get the better of her prudence, for before
leaving Ghent she specially recommended her to
watch over her Sisters' health, telling her she
would rather close the house than expose them
to the danger of becoming ill. But when, on the
opening of the schools, the Sisters beheld the
multitude of children who flocked in, eager for
instruction, they felt they could suffer anything
rather than abandon those precious souls. So the
hardships of an extreme poverty were made light
of, and kept, as far as possible, from the knowledge
of the Servant of God. The Sisters indeed counted
all these things joy. Fervour, gaiety and trust
in God, blossomed, as they will always blossom,
under the shadow of holy poverty, and the

---

* Testimony of Sister Marie-Alphonse de Gottal.

daughters of the Venerable Julie were as happy with nothing to live upon as those of St. Teresa were at the Carmel of Toledo, dividing a sardine into three portions and cooking one egg in a borrowed saucepan. Their confidence in God, indeed, was more than once rewarded in a supernatural manner even when their Mother was absent. One day, the annals of Nouveau-Bois relate, the community sat down to table, but there was nothing to put before them save a single piece of bread barely enough for one person's breakfast. The Superior, not telling her Sisters that it was the last morsel in the house, had it passed round, and when they had divided it amongst them, there was still a portion left for the next meal. In the evening of the same day a sack of flour and a sum of money were brought to the door, though the donor knew nothing of the straits to which the religious were reduced. Perhaps it was with some presentiment of the rigorous poverty which for four years her children at Ghent would be called upon to practise, that the Servant of God had put their house under the special protection of that poorest of Poor Clares, St. Colette, like herself a native of Picardy, and whose name, held dear throughout all Flanders, is especially so at Ghent, where she died. She had promised the Saint, moreover, that she would give her name to the first postulant who should present herself at the Abbey. Frances Martens claimed this privilege and, as Sister Colette, kept up for many years the early traditions of the primitive Congregation, dying in her eighty-ninth year at Brussels in 1878.

In the month of May, 1810, we find Mère Julie again at Ghent, when Napoleon and Marie-Louise were making their triumphal entry into the city. The object of this visit was to obtain a provisional chapel for the Sisters at Nouveau-Bois while they were waiting to get possession of the abbey church. Hitherto they had been obliged to attend the parish church of St. Anne, but some pious and charitable friends were occupying themselves with fitting up a chapel for them, and had begged Julie to come and overlook the arrangements.

She writes word to Namur that the priests of the episcopal palace are furnishing the altar, and the Superior of the Seminary is undertaking the expenses of the painting. As for the schools, they are crowded with children, and the lace-making class is flourishing also. The good Curé of St. Anne and the Curé of the Lesser Béguinage are both much interested in the work of the Sisters; the latter is helping them to clothe their poor children. She herself has been to buy stuff to make them all a little uniform, for they have absolutely nothing to put on. All this means a great deal of work, but it is for the good God; He will turn it to His own greater glory and their sanctification. God is raining down alms for these poor children—nearly fifty crowns since Julie has been in Ghent!

Their dirt and ignorance are beyond conception; there are some who made their first Communion two years ago and now cannot even tell you that there is a God! They say no prayers, and know nothing, nothing at all. "My God, how good Thou art to have sent us to help these poor little ones!" Then she speaks of all she has had to do for the Sisters in their poverty. They would hardly believe at Namur how much she has been obliged to spend on absolute necessaries—plates and glasses and spoons: there were only six spoons when she came, and the Sisters had to wait for each other in eating their soup. But they are so gay over it all! and it is such a happiness to be without something!

She thinks the good God must shower down money upon her, for now, after paying for all her purchases, she still finds some in her purse. Blessed be His Holy Name! He will, if He so please, continue to help them like a kind Father. She gives the Sisters of Namur other bits of news—what great preparations are being made in the town for the coming of the Emperor, how she had had the honour of dining with the Bishop, and, best of all, how she is expecting good Father Thomas, with whom she will travel back to the Mother-House. Her old friend and director had, in fact, undertaken to give at Namur the Retreat of which we have spoken in a former chapter.

The dinner with the Bishop alluded to in this letter had been sorely against the will of the humble Servant of God. She had been to Holy Communion in the Church of St.-Bavon one Sunday, and then, after long walking up and down the city in the interests of Nouveau-Bois and its chapel, had gone to call on the Bishop's Secretary to consult him on matters connected with the business. It was midday, and M. Van Schouwenberghe asked her to have some dinner: on her refusal he inquired at what hour she had breakfasted, and Julie was forced to acknowledge that she was still fasting, whereupon the Secretary obliged her by obedience to dine at His Lordship's table in company with several distinguished guests.

At the Convent of St.-Pierre Sister Marie Steenhaut directed the schools in so wise and kind a manner that she conciliated the esteem of every one, clergy, parents and benefactors. The Curé, seeing the effects of the Sisters' influence on the young girls who frequented their schools and workrooms, determined in his zeal to go a step further, and to put under their protection a class of girls who were specially exposed and indeed partially corrupted. He begged the Superior to admit some of these "neophytes," as he called them, as boarders in an unoccupied part of the house. About a dozen were received, and Sister Ursula was entrusted with the difficult task of superintending them. She devoted herself heart and soul to the work, but the results were not satisfactory: the "neophytes" did not appreciate the efforts made to reclaim them. One day, after vainly searching for one of these unfortunate creatures who had absented herself from the general recreation, Sister Ursula discovered her in a tiny attic preparing to hang herself! The horrified Sister was just in time to cut the cord and save her life. Disease had, in a number of cases, made as much havoc in their bodies as sin in their souls, and after a two years trial the work had to be given up. The Servant of God had only permitted the experiment in deference to the wishes of the good Curé; she was satisfied, after the attempt had been made, that God did not ask this sort of work from the Institute, and that it was likely to injure its chief end, the training of youth in the paths of virtue and the creation of houses of education, where children might grow up in all innocence and safety.

In the midst of their works of zeal the Venerable Foundress took care that the Sisters should not neglect their own sanctification:—every summer vacation they renewed their fervour in the Spiritual Exercises of St. Ignatius. In 1810 it was Father Bruson who gave the annual retreat at Nouveau-Bois to the two communities of Ghent. A somewhat characteristic anecdote of the good Jesuit has been preserved. Sister Marie Steenhaut, Superior of the St.-Pierre house, was one day unavoidably detained after the bell had rung and arrived late for the spiritual conference. "Sister," called out Father Bruson, "here you come distracting everybody." The humble religious immediately went down upon her knees, and as the Father did not tell her to rise, remained in this posture during the entire exercise. In the same year Father Thomas, as we have said, gave the Spiritual Exercises at Namur, where the Sisters of Jumet and St.-Hubert were also gathered. On the day of the closing of the retreat the "Maison-Mère" was *en fête;* fifteen Sisters pronounced their vows at the hands of Mère Julie and in presence of M. Minsart as the Bishop's delegate.

Julie herself kept up the sacred fire enkindled in that memorable retreat by him to whom the Institute owed so much. In her wise instructions to the Namur community, in her private counsels, in her letters to the Superiors and Sisters of the secondary houses, burst forth with an irresistible *élan* that double flame which consumed her own heart—love of God, love of souls. Yes! those little souls created to the image of God, redeemed with the Blood of Jesus Christ, how truly, how tenderly, but how supernaturally Mère Julie loved them! She indeed had what Fénelon has called "that divinest characteristic of love—the forgetfulness of self which spends itself without measure, and gives itself without reserve." *Si vis amari, ama*—love is only won by love. But the converse is also true; love such as that which the Servant of God knew how to inspire in her daughters, almost infallibly awakens love in those who are its objects;

—everywhere the pupils of the Sisters of Notre-Dame became warmly and sincerely attached to their new mistresses, a tradition which, thanks be to God, has been preserved to our own day. And Julie rejoiced that it was so; only, she reminds them not to keep the little hearts for themselves. "Turn the tender attachment of your little girls to the greater glory of God," she writes. And again: "Let our only thought be to win souls to our blessed Jesus." Still less was their affection for the children to degenerate into weakness; they are to mingle their gentleness with firmness, so as to ensure respect and maintain authority.

We may fitly insert here some passages from Mère St. Joseph's Memoirs which, treating of the Ghent foundation, admit us to a more intimate knowledge of the spirit which animated the Servant of God in all that she undertook during these last busy years.

Divine Providence [she writes] blessed our Mother's government because she sought only the glory of God. She used to say to those who shared her confidence, that she saw so many palpable effects of God's loving conduct in her regard, that she could no longer disquiet herself about anything; that her one care and solicitude was to know and accomplish the will of God. This was apparent, for she undertook good works boldly and promptly without much troubling about the means of carrying them out. God, when the moment came, gave His blessing to these enterprises, which of course in principle were not imprudent. Neither the darkness nor the difficulty of the way could stop her; it was enough for her to know the goal towards which God wished her to walk. Her habit was to go on blindly, keeping her soul united to God, not seeking to calculate events beforehand, but waiting for, and following, the indications of Providence. She used often to say that all places were the same to her. She gave herself up entirely to the duty of the moment wherever she might be; as soon as it was done she went away. In fact, she considered that a prolonged stay of the Superior-General might be prejudicial to a secondary house. From the time of her miraculous cure her life may be said to have been a perpetual journey. All the while she was frequently ill and without appetite, sometimes passing whole months scarcely eating at all. Yet she never gave up her work or her correspondence. If there was a foundation to be made or a journey to be taken in the interests of God's glory or the well-being of her daughters, it was useless to urge considerations of health to induce her to defer it. Her strength, moreover, was not natural; God seemed to give her fresh supplies as she needed it.

Mère St. Joseph gives us some particulars of the manner in which the Servant of God was accustomed to travel.

She avoided, as far as she could, entering inns; while the horses were being changed, she took a walk. She generally carried her own little provisions and ate alone in a corner of the garden. Sometimes, indeed, she was obliged to appear at the *table-d'hôte*, for she knew how to make herself, according to circumstances, all to all. But what she suffered at times both there and in the *diligences*, from the blasphemies and bad language she was forced to hear, is unspeakable. To know that her God was being so lightly, so repeatedly outraged by His creatures, was torture for a heart that loved and felt as hers did. Often and often have I heard her say that she could not understand why she did not die of grief on these occasions; and it is a fact that she had to make violent efforts over herself to keep from bursting into tears. Sometimes she found an opportunity of expressing her disapproval in words whose zeal was tempered by prudence, and of stopping, for a time at least, the flow of profane language.*

These frequent journeys were no distraction to the Servant of God; she breathed another atmosphere, and the dwelling-place of her soul was in peace. "One beautiful spring day," relates her friend, "on our return from two journeys which we had made together, I said to her: 'It is a pity, ma Mère, but when I have been travelling my imagination is filled for two days with trees, roads, men and women; are you like that, ma Mère?' She answered: 'I never think of them; the moment I am back, everything is effaced from my mind. I have no imagination now.' On the other hand, the most ordinary occurrences served to lift her thoughts above the earth. When, after the retreat of 1810, she had taken her Sisters back to St.-Hubert, she made the long and difficult return journey on foot. On the way she met two good soldiers going to join their regiment at Namur. She found them so courteous and so obliging in accommodating their steps to hers—when they thought of it, be it understood—that she chose to follow them rather than to be by herself on that lonely road. It was a warm September day, and Mère Julie with her woollen habit, her cloak rolled under her arm, and her travelling bag, had hard work to keep up with her

* Memoirs, vol. ii. p. 225.

military companions. One had just been named sergeant and the other captain; they were much elated by their promotion and full of enthusiasm for their profession. Julie listened to the warlike ardour of their conversation and to their glowing expressions of loyalty, and gave silent thanks to the King Who had enrolled her in a more glorious warfare. 'I would give the last drop of my blood for my emperor,' said the young officer. 'And I,' whispered the Servant of God, 'shall I not give to my God whatever He asks of me? Oh! yes, yes, my blood, my heart, my life, my whole being!' She used to tell her daughters afterwards that the martial talk of these brave soldiers had caused her to make many acts of the love of God, and had wonderfully helped her to bear the fatigue of this long forced march. She reached Namur at nine o'clock in the evening in a state of complete exhaustion, having taken scarcely any refreshment during the whole day. A very restless night made the Sisters fear she had done herself harm, but the next morning she resumed her ordinary occupations. 'You have been uneasy,' she wrote to the Superior of St.-Hubert, 'about my journey. The good God took pity on me; I was very tired, but that was all. You know very well that I do not belong to myself, but to God and to His work.'"

At the beginning of the year 1811 Mgr. de Broglie proposed to Mère Julie a foundation at Audenaerde, distant about fifteen miles from Ghent. He offered her there an old monastery, which during the Revolution had been turned into a Freemasons' Lodge. The Foundress went to look at it with the Vicar General and Sister Marie Steenhaut. They were shown the subterranean cave which the late occupants had hollowed out in the garden, their dark meeting-places whose walls were painted with mysterious and dreadful symbols. Glad indeed would the Venerable Mother have been to restore the desecrated house to its former destination; but there were difficulties in the way which made her doubt God's will in the matter; and, in fact, when, committing the decision to the sure guidance of obedience, she laid the reasons for and against before the Bishop, Mgr. de Broglie changed his mind and told her to give up all thought of the foundation. The event proved the guidance of divine Providence. Only a month later the Prince-Bishop was summoned with the other prelates of the Empire to that National Council of Paris by which Napoleon attempted to replace the authority of the Supreme Pontiff. Though the youngest of the assembled Bishops, Mgr. de Broglie distinguished himself among them all by his episcopal firmness and his attachment to the Holy See, and won for himself in consequence the honours of imprisonment and exile. On the night of July 11, 1811, he was dragged from his bed and thrown into the dungeon of Vincennes, where he passed four months in the most rigorous detention. He was then, by the Emperor's orders, exiled first to Beaune, and later, on pretext that he was keeping up a correspondence with his clergy, to the Island of Ste.-Marguerite, near Hyères. Mère Julie never saw her noble protector again. No sooner had she heard of his arrest than " she ordered," say the manuscript Annals of the Institute, " prayers and penances for him and his persecuted clergy in all her convents. Later on, she bade us continue these practices whenever the like necessities should arise. In times of public calamity she wished the whole institute to offer continual supplications to God, to turn aside His anger and draw down His mercies. But when misfortune attacked the Church directly, her zeal knew no bounds: night and day she was to be seen prostrate before the tabernacle, offering herself to God as a victim of expiation for the sins of His people." In the March of 1814 Mgr. de Broglie was able to return to his diocese, where he continued to show the paternal affection to the Sisters of Notre-Dame, often visiting them and presiding at the religious and literary exercises of their pupils. But he was not long left in peace. In 1815 he lifted up his voice against the new constitutional oath, and in the following year against the projects of William of Orange, King of the Netherlands, for the organisation of public instruction. Cited before the tribunal at Brussels, the great prelate was once again condemned to banishment, and his sentence, written in large letters, fastened to the pillory between two criminals in the great square of Ghent.

It has pleased our Lord [wrote the confessor of the faith to the Sisters of Notre-Dame from the place of his exile] to associate me with one of His ignominies by allowing my sentence to be posted up by the hand of the public executioner between two thieves. I felt a holy pride in this, and a great Christian joy. Believe that you are all dear to me in Jesus Christ. I recommend myself to your prayers, and I do not forget you in mine.

Father Leblanc, of the Society of Jesus, his friend and confidant, alone accompanied the persecuted Bishop into France. Mgr. de Broglie died at Paris on July 20, 1821. We have anticipated events in order not to interrupt the course of our narrative. The exile of their friend and protector was a serious loss to the Sisters of Nouveau-Bois. The number of their pupils diminished, and the resources of the fervent community were often at a very low ebb. Sister Catherine bethought herself of a means of increasing them which led to a memorable act on the part of her Superior General. There was at the Abbey a spacious courtyard in which, as they had no garden, the Sisters and children were accustomed to spend their recreation-hour. Now this courtyard was paved with round stones, and it occurred to Sister Catherine that it would be a great gain to remove these and transform the court into a potato-field. The Sisters forthwith set to work—unpaved the court, dug up the earth, planted the potatoes. Unfortunately for the success of the scheme, the Superior had forgotten to ask the permission of Mère Julie. When next the Foundress visited Ghent, she was astonished to find the pavement gone and the first green leaves of the young potatoes sprouting. "What have you done, Sister Catherine?" she exclaimed. "I know you are poor, but are you no longer going to reckon on God's providence? Must the good Sisters be deprived of air and space when already their food is insufficient? Come, we must undo all this. Send for your little pupils; give them an hour's extra play and let them jump and dance on this ill-advised field of yours; the Sisters can then replace the paving stones." No sooner said than done. The nimble little feet trampled down the crop, the Sisters re-paved the court, and the potatoes were forgotten. One day, late in the autumn, as the community were taking their recreation in the courtyard, one of their number perceived some green leaves struggling through the stones. On removing these she found a fine plant with a number of large potatoes. More stones were lifted with the same result. But before touching them the Superior asked Mère Julie what should be done. The Servant of God replied that since the potatoes were there, they might take up all they found; and the harvest thus gathered from the paved field served the Sisters the whole winter through. God had thus marvellously blessed their prompt obedience.

Towards the end of the year 1810 a fresh foundation was asked for by the administrators of the diocese of Ghent; it was for Zèle, a populous country town near Termonde. The Curé offered the Sisters a free house standing in a large garden, and himself undertook all the initial expenses. The exiled Bishop had proposed the place to Mère Julie just before he was taken from his flock, and she wrote from Ghent to ask her Sisters at Namur to offer up their next Communion that "all might be for the greater glory of God." She was quite charmed, as she had been at St.-Hubert, with the patriarchal character of pastor and people, their old-fashioned ways and simple piety. A celebrated chapel of Our Lady of Dolours lent an additional interest to the place. A chronogram over its façade states that it dates back to the middle of the sixteenth century. It contains, besides a lofty marble altar, a fine figure of the dead Christ, and is still a favourite place of pilgrimage for the surrounding villages, while the stations of Maria Desolata, placed just outside and around the Sisters' grounds, are constantly visited by the devout and believing population. "Our Mother," says the author of the Memoirs, playing upon the name of the town, "came back to us tout embaumée de *Zèle*, and tried, as is her wont, to inflame us with her own fire."* The mistresses for the schools were chosen from among the Flemish Sisters, as that language was then the only one spoken at Zèle, and Sister Jeanne Godelle, mistress of novices at Namur, was appointed Superior.

---

* Memoirs, vol. iii. p. 146.

As for the domestic offices, Mère Julie had no one at her disposal, so it was regulated that the mistresses should give whatever leisure time they had morning and evening to manual labour, and that the Superior herself should undertake the kitchen. The delight of the good Curé at the arrival of the Sisters was shared by all the inhabitants, who took it into their heads to testify their joy by firing off salvos of artillery with some old pieces of cannon which belonged to the town. In the midst of these noisy, and to them alarming, demonstrations the Sisters entered their new convent. While the Foundress received the civic authorities, and the future mistresses welcomed the little ones whom their mothers hastened to offer as pupils, Sister Jeanne began her experiments in the kitchen. They do not seem to have been very successful, for Julie writes: "Sister Jeanne treated us on the first day to red cabbage and potatoes burnt nearly dry for want of water. She told us it had all disappeared in the saucepan! Next day I tried my hand; but things did not go much better, because, you see, the burnt potatoes of yesterday tasted much the same one day as another. But it was good to see Sister Jeanne's confidence in her 'début' as cook. 'Ah! ma Mère,' she kept saying gaily, 'it will be all right.'"* The Sisters were soon at home with the good simple people of Zèle; and the Foundress, at her departure,

* Letter to Mère Blin, dated November 19, 1811.

felt that she left there a religious family which would spread the good odour of Jesus Christ. The schools gave every promise of success; a *pensionnat* was before long opened, and work-rooms for teaching lacemaking.

Several other foundations were offered about the same time to the Servant of God, but her zeal was too enlightened to be over-eager, and she declined them until her subjects were more thoroughly formed. "We should lose much," she would often say, "by going on too fast."

Shortly after her return to Namur the Venerable Mother again fell ill from excess of fatigue, and it was some time before she regained her health. She profited by this forced repose to give herself to the religious formation of the younger Sisters at the Mother House. For, as one of her biographers has well said, she was the heart of her Congregation as well as its head, and her example was its living Rule. It was strong food with which she nourished her daughters. Mère St. Joseph tells us that the ordinary subjects of her instructions were the necessity of leading an interior life, of breaking self-will at the foot of the cross, of making meditation a means of conquering the passions, of thorough mortification and abnegation in order to arrive at union with God.

After Namur, the house at Jumet was at that time the most flourishing of the foundations made by the Servant of God. Sister Leleu directed the *pensionnat* with so much skill and success that its reputation stood very high, and even from great distances families would send their daughters to Jumet, for the sake of the solid and practical education given to the pupils there.* The numbers increased so much that additions to the buildings were required, and in 1810 and 1811 Mère Julie made several visits to Jumet to take measures for improving the accommodation. But consolations in this world are not given without crosses, and the cross destined for Jumet was a heavy one to its Superior and to Mère Julie herself. Among the orphans who had been received at Amiens when Mothers Billiart and de Bourdon had first opened their house in the Rue Neuve was a little girl of twelve years, named Madeleine Firmine N——. She entered the orphanage in that memorable February of 1804 when the two Foundresses obliged themselves by vow to devote their lives to the Christian education of youth. While Mère Julie occupied herself with exterior works of zeal, Mère de Bourdon took charge of the inmates of the house, and it was she who prepared Firmine for her first Communion. The letters of Julie from Abbeville and St.-Valéry are full of loving messages to her "dear little girls, to her dear

* The prosperity of the Convent at Jumet has lasted to our own day. Amongst the pupils educated there may be mentioned the Reverend Mother Aloysie Mainy, sixth Superior General of the Institute, universally beloved, and deeply regretted at her death, which took place in June, 1888. Another of the Jumet pupils was Mme. de Dordelot, a perfect type of Christian womanhood in the world, who died at the Castle of Floreffe in 1893.

Firmine and all her little companions who desire with all their hearts to love our good Jesus." This favoured child, the object of so much religious tenderness and care, a witness of Mère Julie's miraculous cure, of many of her supernatural graces, and of the marvellous fruits of her instructions, soon became deeply attached to her kind benefactress. No one had so much power as Mère Julie to restrain the sallies of that ardent and impetuous nature. The young girl grew up to be very attractive both in mind and person, while her intercourse with Mère de Bourdon had given her unusual cultivation and distinction of manner. The holy Foundress was not without anxiety about Firmine's future, and she profited by every opportunity to inspire her with distrust of the world and love of virtue. Firmine knew that no one loved her as her adopted mothers did, she was sincerely inclined to piety, she enjoyed teaching, she believed herself called to religion, and entreated Mère Julie to receive her. She was admitted as a postulant when she had completed her seventeenth year, but her religious life was marked by a certain unsteadiness of purpose, and by fits and starts of fervour. She was unfortunate in being one of the community under Mère Victoire; it became desirable to remove her from Amiens, and when Mère Julie left for Belgium she obtained permission to take Firmine with her. She was sent to Jumet, where she taught the pupils of the boarding-school with great success, and captivated them by her talents and her manners. The praises bestowed upon her by parents and children turned her head; a thoroughly worldly spirit gradually took possession of her till nothing of the religious remained to her but the habit and the name; and Mère Julie after repeated attempts to reclaim this cherished child, was obliged sorrowfully to acknowledge her case was past cure. The Sister herself took the initiative; she wrote to a brother of hers who filled some post at the court of Jerome Napoleon in Westphalia, representing her unhappiness and asking him to send for her. The secret correspondence for some time kept up with him was finally discovered by Sister Anastasie, and Julie made a last effort to keep the erring sheep in the fold, but to no avail. Then the Servant of God prudently resolved to avoid the publicity which the arrival of Mr. N—— would give to the affair by sending Firmine in the charge of a confidential person to the lady at Amiens who had first put her under the care of the Sisters of Notre-Dame. It is hardly necessary to add that the world she so loved played her false when she had returned to it. For years she suffered the privations of extreme poverty, but the Servant of God followed her unceasingly with her prayers, and to them, and to her early religious training at Notre-Dame, she seems to have owed the grace of preserving her virtue in the midst of grave perils and of contracting in the end a Christian marriage.

The blow had been a singularly painful one to Julie's heart. She writes on June 5, 1811, to Sister Leleu :

My dear Daughter,—you have made me anxious; receiving no news of you I began to fear that the shock we have suffered had made you ill. For myself, I cannot get over it, not on account of the loss of a valuable subject, but because of the dangers I foresee for her soul. With regard to ourselves, I believe her departure to be an adorable stroke of Divine Providence. We should perhaps not have had the courage to dismiss her,—I because after all she has told me I feared for her soul, you because you thought no one could replace her with the pupils. Let us acknowledge before our good God that He stands in need of no one to do His work ; I have thought over this in my mind more than once. O depth of the judgments of God ! one is taken, another is left ! Take care of yourself, my daughter, for God's greater glory ; not that I think, any more than you do, that the good God has greater need of us than of the others. Oh ! no, no, my God ! we confess it with all our hearts in Thy holy presence.

* * * * *

Let us pray God not to abandon her. My God ! to have been so long inundated with graces, and to have been so unfaithful ! neither I nor Sister St. Joseph can understand it. One must have seen her, as you and I have done, to realize how far she had gone astray."

The example of Firmine had not been without some influence over the young Sisters who had been associated with her. Julie exhorts the Superior to tighten the bands of religious discipline and to send away a novice with a doubtful vocation. Her words are worth quoting :

In what concerns the schools I beg of you to let everything be submitted to you; have nothing introduced, nothing dropped, without your sanction. Even in secular matters the good God loves this spirit of dependence; how much more in a religious house. Let us show compassion and mercy, but no weakness, or we shall spoil all. When charity is courageous and firm it does no harm, because this sort of charity comes from God, Who is both its principle and its end. I hope, please God, that all will go well in your house, but you must not delay getting rid of Sister E. (the novice). I believe that person's stay with you is not according to the will of God. We must not be so indulgent, my daughter; we might have to pay dearly for it before God. Heli, the high priest, was indulgent, and what a punishment did he not draw down upon himself from the hand of God!

A few days later she announces to the Sisters at Jumet that she will pay them a visit to console them after the trouble they have gone through. "I must go and see you," she writes gaily, "before your cherries are all eaten, and I shall try and bring Sister St. Joseph with me." The two Mothers spent, in fact, a few days with the Jumet Community, where they were consoled to find that, while the prosperity of the *pensionnat* had lost nothing by Firmine's departure, religious spirit had been the gainer. But the penetrating glance of the Servant of God saw that there were still tares among the wheat. Two religious, by name Sister Martha and Sister Frances, whose characters had already given trouble in other houses, had been sent to Jumet in the hope that the wise and kind government of Sister Leleu might reform the insubordination of the one and the passionate and uncontrolled temper of the other. When, at the time of the long vacation, two successive retreats were organised at the Mother House, the Foundress summoned Sister Frances to the first and Sister Martha to the second, trusting that in those days of more abundant and special grace the indocility of their hearts might be overcome. For some reason or other Sister Martha was annoyed at not having been included in the first party, and wrote off a murmuring and disrespectful letter to her Superior General, for whom her affection, though warm, was purely natural. Julie lost no time. Having taken the advice of her Council, she set off for Jumet at five o'clock in the morning, had an interview with the confessor who approved of the expulsion, and in the afternoon herself took back Martha to her family in France. The long journey of some six hundred miles was accomplished, so to say, without taking breath, and is adduced by Mère St. Joseph as a proof of the fortitude of the Venerable Mother. Later on, several members of the French clergy used their utmost efforts with the Bishop of Namur to obtain the readmission of Mlle. L—— into the Institute; but, where the fundamental principles of religious life were concerned the Foundress showed herself inflexible, and Mgr. Pisani fully approved her reasons. Sister Frances also, unable to resign herself to the change of house and occupation imposed upon her by obedience after the retreat, shortly after left the

Congregation, and two novices were dismissed about the same time. One of these last, who belonged to a noble family in Hainault, lived for many years after the death of the Servant of God, *of whom*, say the Acts of the juridical process, *she always spoke as a Saint*. "From time to time," says Mère St. Joseph in detailing these dismissals, "the Lord takes His fan in hand and winnows the wheat of chaff, which is no small grace," and Julie now felt that, like St. Ignatius and St. Francis Borgia, she could congratulate herself on keeping no one in her religious family who was not determined to aim at perfection.*

In the year 1813 we find the municipality of Gembloux applying for a foundation. It had a rapid extension, and in the following year the Sisters removed into the old Benedictine Abbey, founded in the tenth century by St. Guibert, lord of the district, and secularised at the Revolution. The abbey-church contained a very ancient statue, popularly known as *le bon Dieu de Gembloux*, before which Julie, in her visits to Gembloux, loved to kneel; it represented our Lord in His Scourging, and on March 8, 1553, a large quantity of blood had miraculously flowed from it. This house had for its superior the saintly Sister Gertrude—that little Ciska Steenhaut who had clung to "her mother" with such unshaken attachment at Amiens. Hers was no ordinary soul—simple

* Bartoli.

and mortified, so recollected that she seemed hardly ever to lose the presence of God. She was favoured with extraordinary graces and even ecstasies in prayer, and at the same time was of so sweet, amiable, and joyous a disposition that she endeared herself to all who knew her. She had asked our Lord to let her pass as many years in religion as she had lived in the world, and, in fact, having entered the Institute at fifteen, she died at thirty. Another of her prayers, to have her purgatory in this life, would seem also to have been granted, for she underwent terrible tortures. But they never ruffled the peace of her soul, nor shook her childlike trust in God. She died at Gembloux on May 18, 1821, and on the day of her funeral the good inhabitants, in their naïve gratitude, fastened on to the catafalque the touching inscription : " Gertrude, nous te regrettons." Her remains lie in the Abbey grounds in the old cemetery of the monks. During the Processes of 1882 and 1890, a venerable octogenarian presented herself to give evidence before the tribunal—Mme. Bernard de Fauconval, *née* du Ry. She had been educated at Gembloux, and her recollections of the Foundress were mingled with charming reminiscences of her schooldays under Sister Gertrude. " Often," she said, " you might see the abbey walls covered with the inscription : *Vive Julie ! Vive Gertrude !* A deep piety, and an exquisite politeness, reigned among the pupils, who were strictly forbidden to *tutoyer*, and addressed each other with quaint courtesy as *Mademoiselle*. For the slightest want of consideration the most humble excuses were made. The fare was frugal, but we were healthy, and every one was happy. The children met together morning and evening in the oratory, which we called 'Saint Benedict's'; praying like little saints in imitation of their holy mistresses, and singing with them 'cantiques' as the Angels in heaven might have sung." The old abbey, thus twice sanctified, had, unfortunately, to be given up by the Sisters in 1860, as the premises were claimed by the State. It is now a School of Agriculture, and the Community occupy a house built by themselves.

We have already had occasion to mention the foundation at Andenne; it followed close upon that of Gembloux. The interesting little town is full of memorials of St. Begga, daughter of Blessed Pepin of Landen and sister of St. Gertrude of Nivelles. In her early widowhood, St. Begga went on a pilgrimage to Rome, and on her return erected a monastery and seven chapels in memory of the seven great Basilicas, and so to this day the town bears the name of *Andenne-aux-sept-églises*. Encouraged by the Bishop of Namur, by the Abbé Kinet, Vicar of Andenne, and by Father Leblanc, then concealed in the Presbytery there,[*] the Servant of God undertook to open a large school and to give Sisters to teach it. She was cordially welcomed by the Mayor, Baron de

---

[*] See above, Chapter XV.

Loen, and was materially assisted in the good work by the liberality of Baron de Wal, Commander of the Teutonic Order. Struck by the success with which the Sisters managed and taught the little girls, the authorities wanted them to take charge of the boys also, but this the Foundress persistently refused; only allowing the Sisters to teach them their religion and prepare them for their First Communion. The days of the Kindergartens had not yet come, or Mère Julie would willingly have entrusted to the care of her daughters the tiny little fellows of whom, later on, they took charge.

In the spring of 1814 Mère Julie conducted a band of six Sisters to Fleurus. They at once opened a *pensionnat* and an upper-class day school, but their space was too limited to receive poor children. This was a sensible affliction to Mère Julie. "Our Foundress," says Mère Blin, "could not endure to see the poor excluded. . . . 'We ought to have the poor wherever we go,' she said, 'it is they who are the foundation-stone of our edifice.' And so in two months' time, by dint of enquiries and exertions, she found a larger house at Fleurus; she did not consider the price asked for it—which was proportionately high—but secured it without delay in sole view of admitting henceforward her dear poor." She wrote on this occasion: "Our Poor Schools ought to be the first and most important portion of our flock. We can have establishments without boarding schools, but we can have none without free Poor Schools."

Between January and June, 1815, the Servant of God undertook no less than nine journeys in the interests of her congregation. Four new foundations were proposed to her; she was only able to accept two of them. Liége, the city of St. Lambert, the city which was the first to celebrate the Feast of Corpus Christi, had applied in 1810 for Mère Julie's Sisters, and she had gone herself to see the Abbé Neujean, Curé of the parish of St. Nicolas. For the moment nothing could be settled for want of subjects, but the Abbé promised to seek for postulants, and asked how soon he might hope to have the Sisters of Notre-Dame in his parish. "Monsieur le curé," answered the Servant of God, "make the Sacred Heart loved, and you shall have Sisters." The words made an impression on the good priest; he preached devotion to the Sacred Heart, founded a confraternity, which in July, 1814, he affiliated to the Arch-Confraternity in Rome, and won to the Heart of Jesus Christ a number of fervent and devout disciples. Then he claimed from Julie the fulfilment of her promise, and early in 1815 she went to Liége to choose a house for the foundation. She was offered an ancient convent of Recollectines, but so much out of repair and of so sombre an aspect that it was quite unfit for school purposes. No other premises could be found at the time, and the Foundress determined to wait a little longer. But the wars of that memorable year, and then her own illness, prevented her from ever returning to Liége, and the Sisters were not established there till a few months after her death. A little incident is attached to this journey of the Servant of God, which was related at the Process of Information by Sister Theodore, in the world Marie Josepha Paulus, who entered the Institute in 1817 and died at Gembloux in 1887. We give it in the words of the venerable witness herself.

"I saw Reverend Mère Julie once at Liége at the house of M. Neujean, Curé of the Church of St.-Nicolas. I was then about fourteen or fifteen years old. Being the daughter of the sacristan of the parish, I was present when the Foundress arrived, and it was I who opened the door to her. As soon as she entered the Curé exclaimed: 'Oh! how happy I am to see you!' He had previously applied for Sisters, and Mère Julie had promised them on condition that he should establish the Confraternity of the Sacred Heart of Jesus . . . . Mère Julie looked at me as she entered, and then said to the Curé, 'That child will be one of ours.'"

Many years later, in 1834, a niece of this same holy priest entered the Institute of Notre-Dame. She had inherited her uncle's zeal for the salvation of souls, and in 1843 was one of the heroic band of Sisters who, after receiving at Brussels the blessing of Mgr. Pecci, the Papal Nuncio (now our holy Father Leo XIII.), set off to Wallamette in the Rocky Mountains of America to found a house among the savage tribes there. Sister Marie Cornélie died Superior of San José, the central

Convent of California, in 1892, universally esteemed and regretted, having laboured for fifteen years with singular success in the regions bordering on the Pacific.

The good Curé of St.-Nicolas himself lived till 1829. In his necrology the following interesting passage occurs:—

"Reckoning only on divine Providence, he invited to Liége in 1816 a Community of the Congregation of Notre-Dame, an Institute of priceless value for the education of the young, meriting the esteem of all friends of religion and humanity, having its Mother-House at Namur and establishments in many parts of Belgium. The foundation cost him much trouble, but nothing daunted him, for he foresaw how useful the Convent would be to his parish. It has grown and prospered there: besides a boarding-school for young ladies directed on the best and and highest principles and worthy of the confidence of Christian parents—besides classes for externs much frequented by the children of tradespeople, these Sisters teach and train to virtuous living four or five hundred poor girls, to whom they devote themselves with incredible zeal, patience, and charity. such as our holy religion alone can inspire."

M. Neujean's vicar was M. Dehesselles, who later on as Bishop of Namur loved to repeat to our Lady's Sisters that their Foundress was "a Saint and an Apostle."

CHAPTER XVII.

THE WAR.

The Sisters of Notre-Dame, unconnected though they were with politics, could not but be disturbed by the events which preceded the fall of the Empire. A species of religious persecution was going on, which, without being bloody as in the days of the Revolution, was calculated to cause a great deal of suffering and embarrassment. While the courageous Bishop of Ghent was expiating in exile his apostolic firmness, a schismatic priest, the Abbé de la Brue de St.-Bauzille, had intruded himself into the government of the flock left without a shepherd. Usurping the title of Bishop, he made his entry into the episcopal city with the Abbé Maxime de Séguin de Pazzis, whom he styled his Vicar General, on July 9, 1813. Every means was taken to draw the priests of the diocese into the schism, but the faithful clergy of Ghent were not to be moved. In punishment of their resistance, several of the vicars-general, canons and other dignitaries were thrown into prison, among them the President of the Seminary, M. Van Hemme, with two of his professors. The young seminarists whose motto at this time was: "Better to be a soldier than a schismatic," were either carried off to Paris to the prisons of Ste. Pélagie, or made to join a regiment in the Citadel of Wesel. Here an epidemic proved fatal to a great number. Amongst the survivors there were two young men, Messieurs Boone and Van de Kerkhove, who became distinguished members of the Society of Jesus and in after years rendered signal service to the Sisters of Notre-Dame. Mère Julie was able in her journeys to be a medium of communication between some of the persecuted priests. She took messages for them to each other, and did all that lay in her power to assist these confessors of the Faith. Several found a refuge at at Nouveau Bois, and the Sisters profited by their holy ministrations. Father Bruson, however, was arrested just as he was about to give the Community their annual retreat. He was carried off by the police and incarcerated first at Vincennes, and then in the fortress of Pierre Châtel. The schismatics posted up a decree on the doors of the churches in Ghent, forbidding the celebration of Mass by any priest who had not assisted at the processional entry of the Abbé de la Brue. The Sisters at Nouveau Bois attended the Masses of the persecuted priests to whom they gave a refuge, but they did not venture to admit their pupils to the knowledge of this perilous secret.

Above the cloisters of the old Abbey, there is to be seen to this day a small triangular opening which gives access to a loft in which a hiding-place was arranged by the Sisters. In one night, Sister

Catherine, with the aid of another Sister, constructed a wall of wicker-work whitewashed all over; this could be moved at will and the prison had an outlet on both sides of the partition. The Abbés Rensou and Fol, who afterwards became Jesuits, were concealed in this place for a considerable time; many other priests made use of it in passing. During this period of alarms and spiritual privations, Mère Julie made frequent visits to Ghent to encourage and console her daughters.

Greater dangers were at hand; the armies of Europe were daily drawing nearer to Belgium, the battlefield on which their final struggle was to take place. After the battle of Leipzig, many disabled and wounded soldiers of the "grand army" passed through Namur. The citizens vied with each other in assisting these refugees; a committee was formed for the distribution of alms, clothes, linen, &c. In all this Mère Julie took an active part, and the pupils as well as their mistresses prepared baskets of lint for the wounded. Soon afterwards the allied armies entered Namur; the prices of all articles of food rose enormously; corn, already scantily supplied, soon failed entirely. In February, 1814, Mère Julie wrote:—

> We are over seventy in number to feed daily. On Saturday I sent for flour and none was to be got. Very little comes into the town now; it is so sad for our poor people who hold out their empty sacks to us, and who have such need of flour to feed their soldiers! It wrings one's heart

with pity. There is weeping in our town, for all these troops have to be fed with bread, meat and brandy.

Mère de Bourdon writes in her Memoirs :

I cannot pass over in silence the terrors we suffered at the time of the passage of the foreign troops on their way to France. Our good God mercifully preserved us from having to lodge the soldiers in our house, but we were in hourly dread of their forcing themselves in. We had been exempted, it is true, on the ground of the education given gratuitously to all the poor girls of the city; still we could not feel safe, knowing as we did that the men changed their lodgings at will, and settled themselves where they thought they would be best entertained. This kept us always on the alert to exclude intruders and to find favourable moments for the children's entrance and exit. Our Mother had the principal door made as strong as possible with bars and bolts, and this was far from a useless precaution, as was proved by the blows it sustained day and night from the soldiers knocking for admission. We silenced all our bells and kept ourselves out of sight. The excesses which were committed by the military both in Namur and elsewhere were well calculated to alarm us. We placed the picture of Our Immaculate Mother on all our doors, with a prayer which we said daily; our dear Mother assembled us five times a day to recite together five Paters and Aves, with arms extended in the form of a cross. After grace at meals the Psalm "Miserere" was recited; the pupils used to come unsolicited to pray with the nuns for the restoration of peace. In short we did our best to unite ourselves with the petitions sent up for the same end by the whole Church. Happily God found a sufficient number of the just to disarm His anger, to take the rod from His hands, and to give hopes of a happier future.

The traditions which have reached us of those days represent Mère Julie as having been almost ubiquitous :

during the day she watched the doors, especially whenever the children went out, to see that they were not unprotected; for each one she had a word of encouragement and trust; at night she watched again, but this time in Chapel before the Blessed Sacrament, whence she could hear the redoubled blows of the soldiers and marauders as they passed the door. The parents, whose children were in the pensionnat, had no anxiety about their safety while they were under Mère Julie's care. Her solicitude extended to all her houses in these turbulent times.

My daughter [she wrote to the Superior of St.-Hubert], pay no heed to these rumours of war. We have our great Patroness, our good and tender Mother, to watch over us. Put your trust in her, and no harm will come to you. If God is for us, who shall be against us? People have tried to frighten us here at Namur, as elsewhere; but we have placed all our confidence in the Lord. We keep very quiet; we pray as much as we can. We must accustom ourselves to see everything in God. Let us love, let us love Him, my daughter, and cast our care upon His tender providence.

During those days of penury and distress no one knew how the Venerable Mother contrived to feed her Sisters and children. It was thought, and not without reason, that God interposed miraculously in favour of His Servant. One witness relates, though without giving the exact date, that one day Mère Julie sent a Sister to fetch the provisions from the cellar; she returned empty-handed, stating that there was nothing left. "Go back again, my daughter." said Julie, "the good God will make you find what we need." The Sister obeyed, and found in fact just the provisions necessary.*

As soon as the great mass of the troops had passed, the Foundress hastened to visit her houses. At Andenne on April 12, she started for Gembloux on the 22nd; May 3 saw her at Fleurus and Jumet; the 11th at Zèle and Ghent. At the last-named place she was distressed to find the Superior of Nouveau-Bois hopelessly ill. Worn out with work and with the severe mortifications she had imposed upon herself to obtain the cessation of schism, of persecution, and of war, she was now in the last stage of decline. At one and the same time she had the joy of seeing her beloved Mother General and of hearing of the return of Mgr. de Broglie and the proscribed clergy. Two of the priests who were concealed in the hiding-place had been suffering from a contagious disease caught from the dying soldiers. They and the Sister who nursed them were now convalescent, but Sister Catherine Daulleé was going gladly to her eternal rest. When in health, death had always been to her a thought full of terrors, but now that it was near, she met it with earnest longing and the fullest trust in God. She herself begged for the last sacraments, which she received in the community chapel, making the responses to all the prayers of the liturgy, and on the evening of the feast of the Visitation gave up her brave and beautiful soul to God. Sister Mary of

* Witness XIX.—Sammarium, § 37, p. 228.

Jesus (Steenhaut), who knew her well, wrote after her death of the singular examples she left to her community of self-renunciation and humility—a humility which always convinced her that her sins were the obstacle to the prosperity of her house—of her perfect observance of rule, of a life so blameless that many of her Sisters had never been able to detect in their Superior a single imperfection. "She was ripe for heaven," wrote Mère Julie on learning her death, "and I am convinced that from her happy eternity she will be our protectress." Catherine had indeed promised to help from heaven the dear community with which she had gone through so many trials, and for which she had sacrificed her life. She kept her word; scarcely had she breathed her last when new pupils for the pensionnat presented themselves, and from that moment the prosperity of Nouveau-Bois was assured. In the following year the Sisters had the consolation of taking possession of the Abbey Church and restoring God's worship within the walls which had been so long secularised and profaned. The aged Prioress of the Monastery still lived, and begged to bear the expense of some part of the repairs.

God asked another sacrifice of Mère Julie that same year. She had a special affection for a young novice named Sister Thérèsia, the sister of Marie and Ciska Steenhaut, who, when only sixteen, had followed them into the Institute, and whose sweet disposition made her the sunshine and the joy of the house at Gembloux. During the passage of the troops a detachment of Cossacks forced their way into the old Abbey. The terror they caused her occasioned a serious illness. Mère Julie went herself to fetch her, and took her to Ghent, hoping that her native air and the care of her eldest sister would restore her health. But God had other designs for the young Thérèsia ; she died in February, 1815, pronouncing her vows on her deathbed.

Summer brought fresh dangers and sufferings. Napoleon was back in Paris, having escaped from the island of Elba in March. The allied armies overran Belgium. Jumet, Gembloux and Fleurus were almost on the scene of war : Namur was close by. The Sambre formed the line of separation between the opposing forces, who were disputing the passage of the river, and the month of June saw the memorable battle of Waterloo. Mère Julie's uneasiness on her daughters' account was now increased tenfold, and her mental sufferings were aggravated by the first symptoms of the malady which declared itself a few months later. So prompt had been the movements of the French troops that there had been no time to recall to Namur the Sisters of the convents in the greatest danger ; nor indeed would it have been safe to risk their travelling on foot, as they would have been forced to do, through the troops who lined the roads and filled the villages. Equally impossible was it for her to go to them, as she longed to do. Her only resource was prayer, her only support, trust in God. Nor did she pray and trust in vain. Throughout these terrible days the Sisters of Notre-Dame dwelt visibly in the aid of the Most High and abode under His wings in Whom lay their Mother's hope.

The Sisters of Fleurus thus describe their adventures when the French troops were retreating after the battle of Waterloo:—" The unfortunate men, exhausted with fatigue and hunger, went about seeking food. Some of them came to us, broke open the doors, and went straight to the kitchen, where they took all they could lay hands on to satisfy their cravings. Our Sisters, half dead with fright, escaped to the upper floors and fell on their knees in prayer; they heard the men mounting the stairs. There was a statue of Our Lady which could be seen through an open door, the soldiers stopped suddenly before it, turned back quickly, and left the house. They had retreated before the image of her who is terrible as an army in battle array. Hearing them depart, but fearing their return, the Sisters ran down into the garden, got over the wall in the darkness at the peril of their lives—for there was a pond at the other side—and reached at last the garden of a friend and protector, M. Oudart, who took them into his house. But even here there was no security, another troop of soldiers arrived and followed the Sisters up to the loft. M. Oudart obtained help from the police, whose appearance in the loft where the poor nuns were crouched down in a corner, caused fresh alarm. Thanks to the infinite goodness of God," the narrator concludes, "we were saved from all insult, but as for our convent it was ransacked and pillaged from top to bottom. It then became an ambulance, and when we returned to it four weeks afterwards, we found traces of the operations performed on the poor wounded men."

At Jumet, the nuns were protected by a Prussian officer who stayed in their house. A letter from the Superior Sister Leleu is preserved in the archives at Namur, labelled in Mother St. Joseph's handwriting, "Bataille de Mont St.-Jean," the name often given at that time to the battle of Waterloo. The beginning of the letter alludes to the combat which took place at Ligny.

"The good God has taken care of us like a kind Father, but, my dear Mother, I have no words to tell you what that terrible battle was like ! It was close to our house, the good God protected us. Our doors were forced in, the men entered. Herman (a workman belonging to the house) met them and said, ' We have children here, do not make a noise, they will be frightened.' They said ' We will not hurt them : we only want to eat and go away.' Soon afterwards the Mayor sent us a guard and that saved us ; we heard knocking all the night, but no one entered. Our guards behaved admirably, and we paid them all the attention we could. After the retreat had sounded they returned to us for the night; it was happy for us that they did so. The soldiers carried off everything M. le Curé possessed. Our gratitude to God must be eternal, I beg of you to thank Him with us : we have still three men to guard us, Herman and two others. The good God has taken pity on my weakness and has granted me a great confidence and courage for His own greater glory. Come to us, please, as soon as the roads are free.

Sober as it is in its details, the letter of Sister Anastasie Leleu, dated June 24, 1815, cannot be read without emotion even after the lapse of nearly a century, when one thinks of the extreme peril to which the nuns and their children were exposed. "Our gratitude to God must be eternal," writes one of the annalists of the Institute, "whenever we behold the lion of the Field of Waterloo."

The Community of Gembloux were thrown into consternation by seeing the farms around them all on fire, and cannon balls flying through the air. "The day after the great battle," says Sister Gertrude, "the French troops came pouring into the town. It was Sunday morning, and we were hoping to be left in peace, when a terrific noise was heard; the soldiers were breaking in the doors and windows of the Abbey, and beginning to pillage the place. The pupils, who were all with us at the time, screamed and shrieked with terror; we took them up to the top of the house, and sent to the commander for a guard. An officer came with some men, but by this time the invaders had broken and destroyed everything; they had knocked in the tops of the barrels in the cellar, they had taken all our provisions, breaking the locks of the cupboards; the silver spoons and forks of the children, and even the table cloths and napkins were carried off. After these exploits the Frenchmen left us, but it was only to be succeeded by the Prussians, and these, driven to desperation by three days' fighting and neither food nor rest, prepared to pillage in their turn. Fortunately for us our Vicar got us a guard, a good Prussian officer with three men. He spoke French well, and acted towards us like a father. We looked upon him as sent from heaven. He was a religious man, and his conversation was full of piety. Under his protection we were able to rest a little that night. Now that the troops have gone, we have the camp followers and marauders who leave no one in peace. The Mayor has sent us a confidential gendarme to watch our house during the night. He himself has lost everything, his house was pillaged. Our good Curé with his two Vicaires had the same fate; they do all they can to help us, nothwithstanding their own losses."

Mère St. Joseph gives these details of what took place at Namur:—" After the defeat of Napoleon's grand army* nearly all that was left of it, to the number of forty thousand, poured into Namur on the 19th of June. Early the next day, the Prussians were at the gates of the city. All day long firing went on between the conquerors and the conquered, no cannon, however, was used. The French had not more than two pieces, the Prussians had plenty, but the commander was generous enough to abstain from bombarding the town, which would soon have been reduced to ashes. He acted thus, it was said, in return for the hospitality the Prussians had received shortly before in our city. The combat would have

* At Ligny.

been over sooner and the Germans would have lost fewer men by using cannon, but the town would have been destroyed. The allies entered at six in the evening by one gate, while the French retreated at the opposite one. Many attributed the preservation of the town to the protection of the Blessed Virgin. The inhabitants in their gratitude erected an altar in the Cathedral, and there was a solemn service of thanksgiving besides several Masses for the same intention." Mère St. Joseph continues: " I have no intention of writing a history of the war—there are plenty of others to do that—but a history of the care taken of us by the tender Providence of God. It is a just tribute of gratitude which I would offer to His Majesty, and hand down as a duty to those who come after us. Our sisters can never thank God enough for having preserved us from such frightful perils and protected us, like the best and most loving of Fathers." Mère Julie's anxious solicitude during these stormy times is thus described : " Our good Mother was too deeply attached to her daughters, whom she looked on as a precious deposit entrusted to her by God, not to suffer acutely both in her soul and body from the knowledge she had of the dangers to which they were exposed. She bore up under it all with her usual fortitude, she encouraged us and inspired confidence in our hearts while her own was in such anguish. but one could see by the change in her features and even by the first symptoms of an illness which was to be her last, that her sensitive nervous system had been fatally shaken. Her energy never flagged, she watched over everything. She had some of the religious always in prayer before the Blessed Sacrament, and she entered into all the measures taken to help the poor inhabitants and the wounded soldiers. She went herself to the hospitals to visit and exhort the dying, and gave abundant alms."

A few years ago a reminiscence both of the terrible campaign and of their Venerable Mother reached the Mother House of Namur by a somewhat curious chance. In 1891 a French journal published the following article, entitled " A Survivor of Waterloo : "

Among the rare survivors of the wars of the First Empire is Mme. de Valeriola, now residing at Poizat. When a girl she lived with her parents on an estate near Ligny, to which belonged the mill of Bry. On the day of the battle of Ligny Napoleon rested for a little while in this mill, which had been transformed into an ambulance. Here Mme. de Valeriola herself attended on the wounded, both during and after the battle. She relates many details of the fight with the most perfect lucidity of mind. Notwithstanding her advanced age, Mme. de Valeriola takes long walks with the help of her stick. She has had fourteen children, eight of whom are still living. She was brought up in Belgium at a convent of the Dames Françaises founded by some emigrant nuns.

Enquiry proved that the " Dames Françaises " in question were the Sisters of Notre-Dame at Namur, and that the venerable old lady, whose piety is the edification of her parish, had been a pupil of Sister Eulalie and Mère Blin de Bourdon. She at once recognised Mère Julie's portrait, and remembered kissing as a child the crucifix that hung from her large rosary.

As soon as regular communication was restored, Mère Julie, regardless of her indisposition, hastened to visit all the convents which had suffered most from the terrors of the war. On July 6 she was on her way to Jumet and Fleurus; on the 27th she set off for Ghent and Zèle, and a little later she undertook her last journey to St. Hubert and to Picardy. In the course of that memorable year, notwithstanding all her fatigues and infirmities, the Servant of God found time to write numerous letters to her daughters, to re-animate their courage and to give them the last counsels of her mature experience. There is a special *cachet* about the conferences and letters belonging to this period, an ineffable accent of tenderness, and a burning zeal for the perfection of the souls entrusted to her. Her letters distil a very perfume of candour, of simplicity, of deep humility, mingled with an insatiable love of the cross and a confidence in God that has reached heroism. It would seem that, as her end drew nigh, the Venerable Mother was redoubling her efforts to strengthen the foundations of the work God had committed to her, by pouring into the souls of her spiritual children robust virtue, a courage equal to every trial, and the vigorous sap of sound doctrine. The fragments which we detach here and there with reverent fingers from her letters show what was the ideal she had formed of the spiritual character of a Sister of Notre-Dame. Early in the May of 1815, she wrote to the Superior of Fleurus:

In all the unhappy circumstances of the times we live in, we must cleave so strongly to our good God that nothing can trouble us. My heart is ready to melt with gratitude towards God for thus sheltering us under His wings in the midst of all this tumult of war. My God, my God, what thanksgivings of ours can pay Thee for so many benefits? We can only thank Thee worthily through our Lord Jesus Christ, Thy divine Son; oh, yes! we trust to His infinite merits. . . . Ah! my daughters, this is not a time to think of anything but continual prayer. And then confidence, always confidence! We have no motive for fear, we have a thousand for hope.

And again, after the pillage of the convent of Fleurus:

Do not be troubled at your losses; keep very calm and quiet, no one could have foreseen what has happened. Never can you thank God enough for having been preserved from much worse misfortunes. . . . Many times a day my heart flies to you, and this forced delay is no little sacrifice to me. Let us stand firm in all our vicissitudes and trials, seeking only the greater glory of God.

Oh! would to heaven [she writes to the same a little later], would to heaven that we had as much love for God as we have for ourselves! Simplicity is the true way to find God. Let us get ready for death by a life which is all for God and our duty. Grace has its moments, and passes quickly—let us be very faithful to it. . . . Oh my daughter, how much we need to watch over ourselves if we are to acquire the habit of living in God's holy presence, that habit so necessary to our spiritual advancement!

And then she makes them the characteristic

recommendation not to talk to people about all they have gone through :

You have our Lord Jesus in the Blessed Sacrament for your confidant, you have your garden for your recreations among yourselves; that is enough for good Sisters of Notre-Dame.

To St. Hubert she writes :

God asks of us not promises but efforts, sustained persevering efforts ; for a work like ours we ought to have *saints ready-made*, whereas we have all yet to be made saints. At least let us give ourselves to the work with all our heart and strength.

In the summer of the same eventful year the community of Andenne lost their devoted friend and pastor M. Kinet who was named to a more important post. Julie writes :

Here is a trial for you, but, as you say, the good God is our Father, and in Him must be all our trust. God alone! God alone! Ah! happy a thousand times those who lean upon no one but their Lord ; whatever He may send them, they are never shaken. Let us rest in God—He turns all things together unto good for those that love Him. So let us go on our way, ever straight to our good God, leaving Providence to do His work. Life is full of changes ; everything passes, and we along with them ; let us abandon ourselves to God and lean on Him alone.

The house at Fleurus had been much tried in divers ways ; how strong, in the magnanimity of her faith, are the Foundress's words of consolation :

MY DEAR DAUGHTER—God will always be your support and your strength in the midst of the little storms which He suffers to arise. Know this, my child, that if your little convent of Fleurus were not visited by crosses and tribulations, I should tremble, and I should think that it was not the work of the good God. Contradictions, humiliations, persecutions—those are the true mark by which the work of God is to be recognised. Oh! yes, my dear daughter, the seal of the Cross must be set upon it—the cross in yourself, the cross in others, the cross in your children—then our dear Master will know you for His own. But then that cross must be faithfully and lovingly borne. Courage! God will not let His servants be tried beyond their strength; He has said He will not. And again He has said: "I will be with you in tribulation, to bear you up." Found all your hope on God, without restriction. . . . I have the conviction that you understand this doctrine, and that you will put it in practice. I pray God so much for you! What you are going through now is only a little sample. Remember what our Lord Jesus Christ said of St. Paul: "I will show him how great things he must suffer for My Name's sake." So then, do not be afraid of suffering too much; rather be afraid not to be found worthy to suffer for the blessed interests of the good God and His greater glory. . . . Goodbye, my dearest daughter. Let us live by the cross, and we shall die of love.

Lastly, in her letters to Sister Anastasie Leleu, that soul so attuned to Julie's own, the same note rings out.

You tell me that you possess some particles of the true Cross; honour it well, the Cross of our Divine Saviour, for it is the very foundation of our holy Institute. Ask the grace to make good use of your precious relic—let the sight of it strengthen you in God.

Again on November 8:

Courage! Let us all bend to the good pleasure of God. We must have crosses, but do not let us choose our own; let us leave the hand of our good God to give them to us: He knows so well the exact measure of our strength. . . . I think so often of the primitive Church. My God, who are we, that we should even so much as think of the work which Thou puttest into our hands? Poor, miserable things that we are, beginning with her who is scribbling this letter! Never mind, we must always go on along the road where God has set us. Provided we do not want for crosses, all will go well; if we carry the cross as we ought, it will be a strong foundation to our holy Institute. . . . Oh! how different are the thoughts of God from ours. Yes, He began this work with nothing, nothing. . . . He will continue it, and, by His grace He will perfect it. My dear daughter, if we were to talk till to-morrow, we should not have said all there is to say of the goodness of God towards our little Institute. It is the mustard-seed of the Gospel; may it become a great tree and shelter many birds of the air.

Ask, my dear child, for yourself, for all your Sisters, that only true science of *knowing how to carry the cross well*. Ask that I may follow my blessed Jesus to complete death to self.

CHAPTER XVIII.

THE LAST CROSS.

IN the last book of her Memoirs, Mère Blin de Bourdon, after having related with the authority of an eyewitness the wonderful favours bestowed by God on His Servant, adds these remarkable words:—
" Extraordinary graces are usually followed by trials and tribulations. It was in this way that Divine Providence purified our Mother, neglecting nothing that could serve this purpose up to the very end. The last trial of all was perhaps the hardest for her sensitive nature to bear ; and yet it need not trouble or perplex us—rather, we must look upon it as one of those persecutions which God Himself contrives for the sanctification of His elect. The instruments He makes use of to inflict the pain are often actuated by the best and purest motives. Our Mother herself, at a time when neither she nor I had the slightest suspicion of the trouble which was brewing, said to me one day :—' My daughter, I have still another persecution to go through.' I answered, as St. Peter to our Lord :—' No, *ma Mère*, that shall not be ; you have suffered everything at Amiens.' But she rejoined ; ' It was foretold to me that I should be persecuted by bishops, by priests, and by the Sisters —all is not over.' This prediction dated very far

back; it had been made by Father Enfantin, whom God had made use of to cure her."

The cross Mère Julie looked for was to come to her from Ghent. In order to understand what follows, it must be premised that Napoleon, with his extravagant notions of regulating everything himself—even the religious instruction of his subjects—had caused a catechism to be published under the title of "The Universal Catechism of the Empire," in which were inserted the famous Four Propositions of 1682 and other Gallican errors. Mère St. Joseph, in her narrative, says expressly: "It should be observed that Mgr. of Namur not only never introduced this Catechism into his diocese, but we owe it to him that the Government desisted from forcing it on the country."

In Flanders, however, it would seem that these last facts were unknown, and when the Bishops of Ghent and Tournay were exiled from their dioceses, and the Bishop of Namur was left peaceably in his see, he was looked upon by certain persons as guilty of yielding to the desires of the all-powerful persecutor of the Church. But this conclusion was a thoroughly false one; the fact was that Mgr. Pisani happened to be a very old friend of the minister Portalis, who had been able to influence Napoleon in his favour. Moreover, it was part of the Emperor's policy not to interfere with those bishops who had been nominated by himself. Mère Julie was loyally devoted to her chief pastor and superior, and warmly defended his honour and reputation. The suspicions which fell upon him cast their shadow over her, and she had to suffer very bitter treatment in consequence. For the sake of maintaining union in her religious family, Mère Julie felt it incumbent on her to address an explanation of her conduct to the Vicar General of Ghent, M. Le Surre. Mère St. Joseph has preserved the following extract:

> You are not ignorant, Sir, of the troubles which have arisen concerning certain religious opinions and the "Universal Catechism." M―― has put into the heads of the young Sisters at G―― some fears that I should adopt the views of my Bishop, whom they accuse of leaning towards the suspected opinions. I have been for some years past attacked in the extremest manner about him. I can say nothing against my own Bishop; he is my superior, and I have no concern with the matters referred to. But, in Flanders, certain persons have turned against me on account of this; my religious Sisters have been warned about me as if I were likely to lead them into error; in fact, I have borne the most violent attacks without having given any cause for them. M. Van Schouwenberghe[*] has always been my adviser in these difficult moments, he has always possessed my entire confidence, and, thanks be to God, I have done nothing without his counsel.

"Never," adds Mère St. Joseph, "never could I give an idea of what Mère Julie had to suffer about this affair. What teazing, what painful anxiety, what alarms of conscience did they not cause her for things which time and experience have since proved she had no share in. Our Mother loved nothing more

[*] Secretary of Mgr. de Broglie.

than peace, and for the purity of the faith she would have sacrificed a thousand lives. I have seen her tears flow on these occasions, but God, Who dwelt in her heart, soon dispersed the clouds. He led her by the safe road of humility and obedience, and He kept her in such peace that neither in her heart nor in her words did she ever fail in the duties of respect or of charity. The superior whom God had placed over her * was during these painful circumstances the mark for much contradiction from the persons above referred to, and the blow rebounded on our Mother, who was grieved beyond measure at these differences. They acted as if she were concerned in all this, and as if there might be something to fear from her—from her, who had always been so simple and true in her ardent love for Holy Church. I do not know what sort of zeal animated these otherwise excellent persons. I can only say that the charity of our Mother excused everything. 'They mean well,' she used to say."

During a journey to France which she undertook about this time for the business of the Institute, she had an interview with Father Varin on the subject of the accusations brought against her; and in a letter written to Mère St. Joseph from Montdidier we read :

Ma bonne amie,—I went over to Amiens to see our good Father Varin. I was very pleased with the interview. He

* Mgr. Pisani.

takes a very sensible view about past events. He had heard of what I had to suffer at Ghent; he is very far from thinking what you know. The rest I will tell you when we meet.*

There were other causes of pain and trouble. Sister Catherine, the Superior of Nouveau-Bois, had attached herself with some rigidity to the customs observed at Amiens in the beginning of the Institute; she did not distinguish between the Rule drawn up by Father Varin with the Foundress and certain minor regulations for the good order of the community which must necessarily vary with circumstances, especially in a new Institute. The Church herself, the infallible organ of Divine wisdom, maintains her faith and morals intact and unchanged since the day when she emerged from the Cenacle, while she allows her discipline to vary according to the circumstances of time and place. Mère Julie was guided by enlightened and elevated principles; she was, as the Acts of her Process inform us, a model of exact religious observance, but her position as Foundress gave her the right to modify customs according to the exigencies of the work and the development of the Society she governed. In this she acted in perfect harmony with her fellow-labourer, Mère St. Joseph, and with her ecclesiastical superior. Speaking of the customs observed at Amiens, Mère Blin adds:

* Letter 147 to Sister St. Joseph.

These regulations were originally made for certain ladies at Rome, and perhaps some persons misunderstood the case. Our good Mother had no idea of what was passing in the minds of some of her daughters. She used to say to me with perfect simplicity:—" I do not attach myself rigorously to prescriptions of this sort when I see a greater good to be attained." But in the minds of certain Sisters, anxious for what they thought greater perfection, these things were irrevocable. After all, everything happened by the permission of God.

From blaming the conduct of their Mother in secret, the Sisters in question—whose names the Memoirs do not give—passed to open discontent. Then it was that the Foundress laid her difficulties a second time before M. Le Surre. She tells him she has heard from outsiders of the accusations lodged against her as to the alleged non-observance of the Rule at Namur. She points out that the Mother-House, being the nursery and school of the Order, stands on a very different footing from the much less numerous community of Ghent; that at the former place it is necessary to give a great deal of time to the instruction of the young religious; that hence it is impossible that every point of the Roman *Coutumier* should be strictly adhered to. This letter, of which only a fragment has come down to us, would by itself leave us somewhat in the dark; but Mère St. Joseph has let us know what the supposed infractions of religious observance really were, and her words are wholly in praise of the Servant of God:

She did not insist that the same thing should always be done at the same hour if another useful thing presented itself. The chief end of the Institute being the teaching of Christian Doctrine, Mère Julie made no difficulty about intrenching upon what was less important in order to prolong the religious instruction. In fact, she often did so.

At Ghent it appears that the daily exercises followed each other in unchanging order, and that this mathematical regularity was looked upon as essential.

Later on, the line of conduct followed by the Servant of God was acknowledged to be the right one, and in the rules of the Congregation approved by the Holy See in 1844 we find this clause, which exactly meets the case alluded to above:—"Having often experienced that it is not always possible to perform the different exercises in every house at the same hour, they shall sacrifice this religious harmony for the sake of the instruction of children, believing that this will be agreeable to God. They shall gently accommodate themselves to local circumstances, making themselves all to all, as St. Paul says, in order to gain souls to Jesus Christ." The first companion and faithful friend of the Venerable Servant of God thus writes of her at this period of her life :

God gave her all the qualities needed for the work He entrusted to her, and which she so happily accomplished. What intrepidity under all events and accidents! What courage to suffer and to undertake! What calm in the depths of her soul! Who that has gone to her for help with childlike trust has not been supported in her infirmities by the strength of her great soul? All this would assuredly tend to increase our sorrow at the want of confidence shown by some, if we did not clearly see that this trial was specially permitted by God before He took her to Himself in order to purify her by so keen a suffering, to bring out her meekness of heart in all its beauty, and to perfect her other virtues; in a word, it was the finishing-stroke in the fashioning of her soul, the last bitterness in the chalice which she had so nearly drained.*

Nothing pained the Venerable Mother so much as to see some of her most cherished daughters enter into the species of league which had been formed against her person and her authority. Satan can transform himself into an angel of light, and, though grieved, we need not be surprised to find among them the really holy Superior of Gembloux, Gertrude Steenhaut, who, before these clouds arose, had been filled with such singular esteem and affection for the Servant of God. After Julie's death the veil fell from their eyes; one and all deeply deplored their error, and Gertrude tried to repair her fault by drawing up a paper which is at once a record of her Mother's sanctity, and a memorial of her own temptation. After giving many instances of the gift which the Servant of God possessed of reading the minds and hearts of her daughters, Sister Gertrude continues:

In spite of the high esteem in which I held our dear Mother's virtue, the devil, jealous of the glory which my

* Memoirs, iv. p. 61.

entire confidence in her gave to God, and of the profit which
it brought to my own soul, contrived to fill my mind with
darkness and perplexity on the subject of certain exterior
actions of hers ; and what had once seemed to me zeal now
appeared to me to proceed from natural impetuosity and to
lack discretion. What increased, and in fact originated the
temptation, was that some Sisters communicated to me
their own imaginations concerning our General. Seeing
them so fixed in their opinion, I thought it must be presumption in me to think myself more enlightened than they,
and finally adopted their notions. Then, urged on doubtless
by the devil, who had ensnared me by this false mistrust of
myself, I went so far as to confirm some in their opinion.
In short, I know not what spirit impelled me. . . . I can
only say that I had the best intention in the world. . . .

At the present day [she adds], writing after the death of
our revered Mother, I see things in another light : what I
thought exaggerated and extraordinary in her conduct now
appears to add fresh lustre to her life by wonderful examples
of virtues which are rarely seen in persons of her sex. Notwithstanding all the pain she must naturally have felt in
being thus misjudged by her own daughters, she preserved the
most perfect calmness of mind ; she never tried to vindicate
herself, but having at heart the glory of God and the propa-
gation of her Institute, she employed with great prudence the
means which would lead her children to love not herself, but
Truth alone. The more I consider her life, the more persuaded I am that she was guided by the Spirit of God.*

The prejudices which had arisen in the diocese of
Ghent were echoed in that of Tournay, and even to
some extent in Namur itself; some of the clergy
went so far as to suggest dividing the Institute
according to the dioceses, in order to separate the
Mother-House from Flanders and Hainault. It was

* Memoirs, iv p. 93.

then that Mgr. Pisani, at Julie's own request it would seem, gave to the Congregation a special ecclesiastical Superior in the person of his vicar general, the Abbé Minsart. Mère St. Joseph tells us that the Foundress "was enchanted with this episcopal measure," and she adds : "This happened about six months before our Mother's death."

A confidential letter from Mère St. Joseph to Sister Anastasie Leleu, the Superior of Jumet, throws light on this critical period :

You cannot, I think, do otherwise than show our Rule to the Curé, as he asks it and he is your confessor. Since he already rejects the authority of the ecclesiastical Superior of Namur, I hardly know whether it is wise to tell him that arrangements are being made here to get something more stable and fixed.* I believe, my dear Sister Anastasie, that God will allow us to be greatly exercised and tried by good priests as well as by our good Sisters. If each diocese sets to work to govern us after its own fashion, what fine music we shall have! You know well these are just the difficulties we wish to avoid by having the authority of our Superior General recognized by all ; otherwise I do not see how there can be any unity, and there would indeed be great fear that when she is gone, each one would want something different. You and I are the two eldest of the family ; we have seen and known the beginnings of our Society. Others cannot know, as we do, how to appreciate our Mother, but we have seen how long and how gradually she was prepared and disposed for the work she has carried out so admirably. And if we look at the result as a whole, we cannot but see how abundantly it has been blessed despite all the cavilling that

---

* The primitive rule of the Sisters of Notre-Dame, completed by Mother St. Joseph according to the intentions of the Foundress, was approved by Mgr. Pisani in 1818. The approbation of the Holy See was given in 1884.

human weakness and ignorance, helped by the malice of the devil, have never ceased to raise against it. Our Mother is sincerely delighted that all this has been the means of procuring us an ecclesiastical Superior. I believe we may congratulate ourselves on the appointment; but whatever is settled between our Mother and himself must be accepted by the other dioceses, or things will go on badly. I only wish that all had her energy, zeal and forgetfulness of self; there would not be so much fuss made about the trifles she is reproached with, if people could understand the excellence of the qualities with which God has endowed her. I can scarcely believe that the Sisters of Ghent would make any formal complaints of their mother. I thought the displeasure shown by Mgr. of Ghent had originated at Namur;* whatever may have been the cause, God knows it, and that is enough. Our Mother is not troubled on her own account, only so far as the interests of God are concerned; she has no more resentment than an infant. Let us endeavour to imitate her by forming ourselves to the practice of solid virtues. After all, as long as we are on this earth we must be prepared for a host of faults and shortcomings.

In concluding this painful episode, we are bound to say that concord and union were never broken in the Institute of Notre-Dame. After the death of the Servant of God all eyes were opened, her eminent virtue and the wisdom of her government were universally acknowledged : this was very evident when witnesses were examined at the process of Canonization. Never has there been any question since as to the authority of the Superior General, never has any convent of Notre-Dame sought to separate itself from the Mother-House of Namur. The delicate

---

* I.e. on account of Mgr. Pisani, the Bishop.

charity of Mère Julie has deprived us of nearly every document relating to this, her last trial. When we consider on the one hand the numerous and tedious journeys she undertook in the last years of her life to visit her convent at Ghent, her constant anxiety for the welfare of that establishment, with the tender attachment she evinced for her daughters, and on the other hand the contradictions and bitter trials that she suffered from that quarter, the contrast brings out in more vivid light her greatness of soul and heroic virtue. From the lofty summit she had reached, she lost sight of human acts and secondary causes; she saw nothing in all that happened but the fulfilment of the eternal designs of God.

It was in the midst of the troubles just recounted that Mère Julie accomplished a work of charity, unknown at the time to all but Mère de Bourdon, who has recorded it in her memoirs. She brought about the return to the Church of a community of nuns obstinately attached to a schism known as Stévenism. The sect originated with Canon Corneille Stévens, a learned and pious priest but an excessive rigorist; he had refused to sign a formula promulgated by the predecessor of Mgr. Pisani, and the result was that he became the founder of an ephemeral schism resembling what was called in France " la petite Église." The supporters of Canon Stévens called themselves " non-communicants ; " they refused to submit to their Bishop, and acknowledged the Canon alone as their spiritual superior. Some of the clergy joined

this party and set episcopal censures at defiance; it was
not uncommon to find in the same parish two incum-
bents, one appointed by Stévens, the other by the
Bishop, and families were sometimes divided between
the two parties. The first efforts of Mgr. Pisani to
effect a reunion, when he succeeded to the See of
Namur, met with little success. It was only after
the fall of the French Empire that, at the urgent en-
treaty of the Duke of Beaufort, Governor of Belgium,
a generous appeal to the clergy was made which
brought about the extinction of the schism. The
ecclesiastics who had held out, came to offer their submission to the Bishop, and in the end M. Stévens
himself gave in : no one remained outside the Church
except a very few isolated and obstinate sectaries.
Among these was a certain Abbé T——, who was the
spiritual director of some Ursuline nuns at Jumet.
His influence over them was so great that, although
suspended by the Bishop, he continued to exercise
his functions amongst them, and they refused to accept the ministrations of any other priest; it was
under these circumstances that Mgr. Pisani asked
Mère Julie to try and bring back the deluded religious
to their duty. They had been obliged to take off
the habit of their order and dress as seculars, and
they were forbidden to approach the Sacraments.
Mère Julie took Mère St. Joseph with her when she
visited them. Both were well received, and by
degrees their charitable efforts obtained the desired
result; the nuns acknowledged their error, and one

by one made their submission to the Bishop. They were not yet all converted at the time of Mère Julie's death; Mère St. Joseph obtained the last retractation. In 1817 they made a public reparation by following the procession of the Blessed Sacrament with cords round their necks; after this they were allowed to resume the habit of their Order, and to re-enter their convent. Mademoiselle Antoinette Malevé,* who died in 1880, related how consoled the Bishop had been, and how edified the people, by the generous reparation of the penitent nuns. She had heard the Bishop say to her own father (himself a converted Stévenist), "Without Mère Julie and her holy companion, these poor deluded religious would have died in schism." The community, once restored to the bosom of the Church, was ever afterwards distinguished for its piety and regularity. The director who had misled the Sisters did not imitate them in their submission: he sought a refuge in the house of a gentleman at Jumet who, believing his Curé to be unjustly persecuted, gave him hospitality for a time. It was not long, however, before he found out his mistake; he submitted to the ecclesiastical authorities, and shut his doors on the schismatical priest. This unfortunate man died without abandoning his errors, and the young man who had followed him as acolyte ended his days as a free-

---

* This lady lived for years as parlour-boarder with the Ursulines of Namur.

thinker. The Abbé Stévens died in 1828, protesting obedience and submission to the Sovereign Pontiff. The anti-concordat party soon came to an end. None of the clergy belonged to it, and the few adherents that remained in the town of Eecloo (Eastern Flanders), submitted in 1852 to the Sovereign Pontiff and the Bishop of Ghent.

CHAPTER XIX.

THE SOUL OF MÈRE JULIE.

In the lives of the Saints exterior events derive their chief importance from the revelation they afford us of what passes in the hidden depths of their souls.

During twelve years we have followed Julie from town to town, from labour to labour; and it may be that, in the ceaseless movement of this last busy period of her life, we have somewhat lost sight of that "beauty from within" which alone ravishes the heart of the Beloved. It will be well, therefore, to pause for a moment in our story and gather up some of those scattered traits for which the sequence of a biography has not allowed sufficient space, that we may, so to speak, disengage the portrait of her soul from the exterior setting in which we have been forced to frame it.

But before doing so we may try for a few moments to call up again the human countenance and outward person of the Servant of God, as they have been made known to us by tradition and by her pictures. Slightly below the middle height, her erect pose and the simple dignity of her carriage gave the impression of a taller person. Her movements, naturally brisk and active, were regulated by the most perfect modesty;

her manner was easy and unconstrained. There was a winning graciousness and a certain maternal tenderness in Julie which invariably attracted the young, but there was nothing soft or effeminate about her. The most authentic of her portraits now hangs in the convent at Gembloux. It shows a countenance of great intelligence; the eyes frank, deep, penetrating; the features regular; the lips firm-set but wearing their irresistible smile; —a countenance which, without being what men call beautiful, has about it a wonderful charm—a certain mixture of sweetness and strength which was the very mirror of her soul.

But on the living face shone a light which the painter cannot give—the angelic purity which, say the Acts of the Process, made her "seem rather an angel than a woman," and which had won for her the privilege given to some of the Saints, of purifying the hearts of those who came near her. There were times—as during her conferences to the Sisters or after Holy Communion—when her countenance was literally aglow.

The predominating feature in Julie's spiritual physiognomy was surely her ardent charity; a charity which had its source in her deep and lively faith, and found its expression in her thirst for suffering and her zeal for souls.

"Out of the abundance of the heart the mouth speaketh." Many of the Saints have had a motto which gives the keynote of their lives, and expresses the whole bent of their souls. St. Francis of Assisi, the passionate lover of holy poverty, with God alone for his treasure, cried out unceasingly, "Deus meus et omnia!" St. Ignatius Loyola, "Ad majorem Dei gloriam;" St. Francis Xavier, burning with desire to extend Christ's Kingdom, "Amplius! amplius!" St. Aloysius Gonzaga, despising earth and aspiring after Heaven, "Quid hoc ad æternitatem?" St. Teresa, the victim of divine love, "To suffer or to die." Mère Julie's whole soul is poured into that simple and naïve formula which we have found continually dropping from her lips and pen, "Oh que le bon Dieu est bon!—How good the good God is!"

From her earliest childhood it has been her happiness to be all for God, to unite herself to God in prayer, to speak of God to those around her. Divine love grows and burns in her soul as she advances in years; she feeds the flame by long meditations on the Life and Passion of Christ, by her devotion to the Sacred Heart, by daily partaking of the Bread of Angels, and by the constant endeavour —we quote her own expression—"to purify her heart more and more and to *empty it of all that is not God.*" Speaking of those daily Communions of hers, Mère Blin tells us that even when she was travelling it was the rarest possible thing for her to miss one. "However out-of-the-way the place was, she displayed a wonderful zeal, skill and activity in procuring for herself the blessing of Holy Communion;

she discovered means where others would only have seen obstacles. To me it is evident that God marvellously helped her to find the Object of her love." " I know not," the Servant of God used to say towards the end of her life, " I know not how I am able to wait for the moment of Holy Communion, so much do I suffer in body and in soul ; but no sooner do I possess my Jesus than I feel refreshed."

If the Saints in Heaven love because they see, Julie loves here below because she believes ; and her charity is in proportion to her faith. She is, in truth, one of those just who *live* by faith ; faith informs every circumstance of her existence, penetrates her with a sensible and habitual feeling of God's presence, annihilates her at the foot of the altar ; faith makes her see God alone in her superiors even when they humble and try her, in her poor children especially if they are ignorant and abandoned ; in the Sisters of her Institute, to whom she said : " I recommend strongly to all my daughters the practice of living by faith. I hope they will apply themselves with all their hearts to acquire this, and I am always asking it for them of God." She would have " the good God *the soul of their souls*," so that, as she often picturesquely put it, "nothing on earth ought to be simpler than the heart of a Sister of Notre-Dame, which should be like crystal—nay, simpler yet ; for the crystal reflects all the colours of the rainbow, while the heart of a Sister of Notre-Dame should reflect nothing but God alone." It was faith which she defended with such vigorous energy against schism and impiety at the time of the Revolution; faith again which led her to Fontainebleau to the feet of the imprisoned and persecuted Pontiff; faith, too, was what she so earnestly endeavoured to communicate to others by the teaching of the catechism, which she made the chief end and object of her Institute. Faith was her light and her strength in all her difficulties: if there was some difficult thing to be done, some perplexing question to be decided, Julie would not say, "I will think about it," "I will see," but "God will do it for me, God will show me."

Faith is truth; and the truth, says our Lord, makes souls free. This liberty of spirit in the Servant of God is one of the points to which Mère St. Joseph, in her Memoirs, calls special attention.

Our Mother [she writes] was by nature exceedingly ardent and active, full of life and fire; she suffered moreover from an affection of the nerves which generally gives rise to reverie and imaginations. Yet she was absolutely free from such influences; her mind was clear, accurate and singularly free. She was never preoccupied, never lost in her thoughts. No matter at what moment you accosted her, you were sure to find her at liberty; the business on hand was always welcomed by her, if it related to God's interests.

The lively faith which animated her filled her with sentiments of the deepest respect and veneration for bishops and priests; but the simplicity of her soul never allowed her to give way to bustle or anxiety when she was treating with prelates or the great ones of this world. How often have I seen her on such occasions, keeping her mind fixed on God, awaiting the favourable moment, as peaceful under contradiction as though all had gone well with her. And if she were obliged to offer some explanation, it was easy to see by her limpid and facile language, and by the very expressions she used, that she had but one object in view—the glory of God and the salvation of souls.

Her solid faith and her ardent charity were the basis of her unshaken confidence : neither the sufferings of a long and cruel infirmity, nor the privations of poverty, nor the unjust treatment of those who ought to have been her friends and protectors, could trouble the peace of her soul, or shake for an instant the trust she had placed in God alone.

Mère Blin de Bourdon writes:

She excelled in this virtue above all others, and I believe that her confidence in Divine Providence was carried to an uncommon degree. When difficulties, embarrassments and complicated affairs seemed as if they must almost crush her, she went on hoping against hope like Abraham, and pouring all her anxieties into the heart of God. I can even say that I have seen her in the midst of the most trying events assume a more cheerful air than usual. She would say, " I have nothing to do with all that ; it is the good God's business, not mine." Her resource in any specially difficult or knotty point was, not to spend her time reasoning or reflecting, but simply to ask God to show her His will. Although she was careful in all matters of business and took the advice of competent persons, it was in God alone that she put all her trust; many a time she has said to me, " I may well place all my confidence in God, for I have seen so clearly the action of His Providence in a number of perplexing circumstances from which I could never have extricated myself alone. Whenever I am puzzled about anything, the good God comes to help me. I cannot, therefore, be troubled about such matters; you know I am not clever, God must do all.

She wrote to a Superior who was anxious about the future of her school:

Let alone all those merely human views and take those of a lively faith, of faith in God. What a consolation it is to teach little children to know Him! and having no desire but this, what can we fear? Let us do all the good God points out to us, moment by moment, wishing for nothing but what He shows us by His adorable Providence. My dear good friend, hold fast the good God's hand, so that He may lead you, and that you may do all He wants. Leave yourself entirely on one side; be quite sure that by yourself you would, like me, make but a very poor piece of work of it. If we could, once for all, let the good God act, all would go better with us; let us try it in earnest, and do you ask this grace very fervently for me, who from morning till night do not know what I am going to do next.

We are not surprised to find such childlike *abandon* in the hands of God often working wonders. The Bishop of Ghent used to say he was convinced Mère Julie obtained from our Lord whatever she wanted, and we have seen in the course of these pages more than one instance of the power of her faith and trust. We may here add another, which is mentioned in the Apostolic Process. A Sister belonging to the Namur community was one day chopping wood, when she let the axe fall upon her foot, wounding it very severely. The blood flowed profusely, and her companions, in alarm ran to fetch the Servant of God. Julie traced the sign of the Cross on the injured foot, and then said to the Sister: "No harm is done, my daughter; go back to your work. The good God knows you want your feet for His glory." No sooner had she spoken than the Sister rose perfectly cured; so thoroughly was the wound healed that not even a scar was visible.

The work of Mère Julie's life could never have been ventured upon if she had not reckoned entirely on God's assistance. The foundation of the Institute of Notre-Dame, as we read in the reports of the Process, was the outcome of the heroic love of her neighbour which filled the heart of the Venerable Servant of God. "My good Sisters," she used to say, "our vocation comes from God; it is He Who has brought us together, and inspired us to imitate the apostolic life of our Divine Redeemer, by devoting ourselves to the education of poor children, especially of young girls."

It was Julie's wish, as we have seen, that, in order to enable all—even the poorest—to profit by the education given, the schools should be free, and that not only the instruction itself should be gratuitous, but that all books and other requisites should be provided for the children free of cost. When she visited the schools, she showed marked predilection for those of the poor. She would talk maternally with the little pupils, admonishing them about their duties, especially those which concerned their homes and families.

Her charity was not confined to her convent and her schools: it embraced all sufferers; she loved and pitied all, and notwithstanding her own extreme poverty was generous in her assistance to the poor and the sick. " In the beginnings of her Congregation, when she had to go out to market to buy provisions, she always gave away a large portion to the poor; and when some remonstrance was made, she would answer: 'The good God will provide; it is for the dear poor of the good God.'"* When she had pupils whose parents were in difficulties, she found means to assist them under pretext of giving rewards to the children. At Namur the poor remarked that Mère Julie not only assisted them but knew them all by name. In winter her charity led her to deprive herself of her own garments in order to clothe those who, she said, wanted them more than she did.

But she occupied herself with the needs of the soul still more than with those of the body; her chief care in the case of the sick was to help them to prepare for a good death by the reception of the Sacraments; and she particularly recommended the mistresses to inculcate this practice when instructing their pupils, so that these children might one day become the guardian angels of their families by procuring them the consolations of the Church at the hour of death.

Yet, ardent as her zeal was, it was always regulated

---

* Articuli pro constr. Apost. processus, p. 25.

by prudence. Not only did she never undertake any important affair without having first implored light from the Holy Ghost and maturely reflected before God, but she always sought counsel from her superiors and from persons of experience able to advise her. Her admirable spirit of prudence shone forth in the foundation of her Institute and in the rules she drew up for it. Above all it was conspicuous in the long and painful trials she underwent at Amiens, Namur and Ghent; never once in the course of them was she moved to depart from the wise and measured principles on which she acted.

This " bon sens surnaturel," as one of her biographers calls it, guided her in the admission of postulants. She never listened to human motives or the natural desire of extending her Congregation ; but, gifted with no ordinary penetration, and helped by the lights God gave her in prayer, she sought only to ascertain if the aspirant were called by God and had the necessary aptitude.

It may be truly said that Julie possessed all the qualities of a perfect Superior ; as Father Varin said to her, *she had the grace.* Her firmness without harshness, her gentleness without weakness, her equable temper, her thorough straightforwardness, and—not least—her rare good sense, rendered obedience easy, and inspired her daughters with filial confidence and tender affection.

A certain Superior, on giving in, according to custom, the annual accounts of her house, had entered as already spent a sum which, though due, had not yet been actually paid. Mère Julie looked over the books, expressed her satisfaction that they were in order, and the inaccuracy passed unnoticed. But a few days later, on coming out from Mass, she accosted the Sister : " Daughter, your accounts are not exact ; I saw it this morning before God, just as you were going to Holy Communion." The Superior was stupefied, for she had not told any one what she had done.

Such lights were common enough in the life of the Servant of God. On May 18, 1811, the children of the boarding-school at Namur were making their first Communion. Meeting one of the happy band—little Clémentine Hubin—just after the great event, Julie stopped her and said : " My child, the good God is very pleased with you ; He will grant you what you asked of Him this morning—you will be a nun some day." The child was radiant with joy at these words ; she had, in fact, earnestly begged of our Lord as she held Him for the first time within her heart that He would deign to espouse her to Himself among the Sisters of Notre-Dame, though she had told her secret to none but Him.

The prediction was verified : Clémentine became a fervent religious, and died Superior of the convent at Thuin in 1811.

The solid satisfaction I have felt [writes one of the Sisters] in letting myself be governed blindly by our Mother for more than ten years, proves to my mind beyond a doubt that she was led by the Spirit of God. I can say without a shadow of exaggeration that, when she spoke, I felt myself touched to the very depths of my soul.

The same Sister relates:

One day I met her near the refectory. She stopped and fixed her eyes on me for a few moments without speaking a word; then she said to me very gently, "Continue, my child, to occupy yourself with the sentiments which penetrate you now; meditate on these truths, going and coming, as you perform your duties; it will be an excellent means of strengthening you in your vocation." She then repeated the very words of the Gospel on which I had meditated that morning, and which had struck me in an unusual way. The wonderful penetration she showed in discovering each one's spiritual need inspired me with the liveliest confidence in her. She did not often allow us to speak to her about these matters, wishing to teach us forgetfulness of self, but we could easily perceive that one look of hers was often enough to lay open the most secret dispositions of our souls. Another day, after I had meditated before the Blessed Sacrament on these words of St. James, "He who sins not with the tongue, the same is a perfect man," I went to find our Mother in her room. As I entered she said to me, to my great astonishment, "My child, believe me, there is a time to be silent and a time to speak;" and she sent me away before I could explain what I had come for.

Again, on another occasion, I had taken for the subject of my meditation our Lord being despised and sent back from Pilate to Herod. I felt a great repugnance to bear humiliations, and I resolved to expose myself to them in all the little daily occasions which I was likely to meet, so as to combat my self-love. Directly after my prayer, God permitted that some pressing business required me to go to our Mother; she had hardly opened the door before she shut it again, and sent me away without listening to me, having, no doubt, as on so many other occasions, read what was passing in my mind.

Still more striking was this gift of hers when I was hesitating about writing out her daily conferences. I had long wished to do this, but did not venture without permission, and I thought of consulting Mère St. Joseph about it. One day, while I was praying in the chapel with my mind pre-occupied with this design, Mère Julie came up to me, and, giving me a tap on the shoulder, said : " Daughter, do not fail to write out the daily conferences : God asks this of you."

When a Sister committed a fault [relate the manuscript *Annals* of the Institute] and correction was necessary for the sake of example, our Mother sent for her to her room, and put before her in clear and precise terms the gravity of her conduct. It was especially on these occasions that her love for religious perfection, and for all that constitutes the spirit of our holy vocation, was brought home to us. On the other hand, no one ever left her with any feeling of rancour or annoyance; all one's vexation was against oneself. Every one was convinced of the perfect purity of her intention, and that she acted under the inspiration of grace.

It is related of St. Ignatius that he would break off a quiet conversation to address a vehement reprimand to a Father, resuming immediately afterwards his first placidity, as if nothing had disturbed it. Much the same testimony is borne to Julie's possession of her soul; after administering severe and energetic reproof she would pass in perfect serenity to the holy table. Moreover, her frank and generous character prevented her from keeping up any resentment. When once a fault had been acknowledged, there was no fear that she would ever recall it or even let the offender see that she remembered it. Her daughters said of her that she knew how to pour such a healing balm over wounded hearts that no scars were left behind.

If she ever made a mistake, she hastened to repair it. Mère Blin writes:

> It happened on one occasion that some exaggerated complaints had been made of a Sister, which caused our Mother to impose a somewhat severe penance. As soon as she ascertained that she had been wrongly informed, she lost not a moment in acknowledging it, but went straight to the Sister's room and said: "Daughter, you have a right to complain of me; I was deceived by incorrect information about you." She then knelt down and begged pardon of the Sister, who also went on her knees, and they prayed a little while together. Then our Mother rose and said:—"You will soon be convinced, my dear child, that I have nothing whatever against you in my heart." It was the day before the beginning of Mère Julie's last illness that this occurred.

It was but very rarely that the Foundress was betrayed into mistakes of this kind; her perfect uprightness, her clear-sightedness and her consummate experience preserved her in general from such surprises. She knew when to punish and when to forbear, when to wait for the moment of grace and when to give a vigorous push forward. Mère St. Joseph bears witness to the prudence and patience she exercised with regard to cases which needed careful and delicate treatment.

> She would say to me: "It is not time to touch such a one;" for another, "We must wait awhile for her." To others she spoke thus, "As for you, it is God who must work in *your* soul; it is useless to press you before the time, it would only

trouble you. I am not over-anxious about you, as the good God has taken upon Himself to admonish you; when the moment comes, He will make His Will known, and will help you to fulfil it." She used to say to me:—"There are souls whom God guides, so to speak, by Himself, and who hardly need the help of men, save the general observance of the Rule, and of those things which belong to obedience, good order and prudence."

Now and then she met with generous souls ready for any sacrifice; to these she pointed out their path from the first, and they followed it blindly. Thus she led a certain Sister Fidèle, from the very day she entered the convent, by a complete mortification and absolute renunciation of nature. This Sister was a postulant whom the Foundress herself had taken to Ghent. In giving her her religious name, Mère Julie said:—" My daughter, you shall be called Sister *Fidèle;* make yourself worthy to have said to you one day : 'Come, spouse of Jesus Christ ; because you have been faithful *(fidèle)* in the very least of your duties, enter into the joy of the Lord." These words were a continual spur to the young religious, urging her upwards to the heights of religious perfection. After her death in 1835 her Superior did not hesitate to declare that she had never known Sister Fidèle transgress the slightest point of her rule. The good Sister loved to repeat the words said to her by Mère Julie when she received her name.

With all Julie's tenderness and sweetness there was at the back of it an energy and courage which nothing could disconcert; in her it was above all the "valiant woman" that deserved praise:

> Fortem virili pectore
> Laudamus omnes feminam. *

In her virtue there was something robust, manly, militant; a force of soul which she turned in the first instance against herself, to conquer and transform, after the example of St. Francis of Sales, the ardent and impetuous side of her character. Her supernatural strength was a striking contrast to her bodily weakness. When once she had taken a resolve inspired by her knowledge of the will of God and approved by her superiors, no obstacle could daunt her. Mère Blin de Bourdon tells us that this unshaken and invincible firmness in her resolutions proceeded from the following sources: First, she divested herself of all personal inclinations and repugnances; second, she examined the question before God and by the light of the Holy Spirit; she prayed fervently; and lastly, she took counsel. She had even the humility to submit the matter to my judgment. After this nothing could change her. If, when she had made use of all the means in her power she did not meet with success, she was never disconcerted, and the peace of her soul was never troubled."

Wherever obedience or poverty were concerned, the Foundress was extremely strict. "Recommend

---

* Hymn in the Office of the Church for Holy Women.

obedience very strongly to my dear daughters," she writes to a Superior ; " without it they will never be the children of the good God nor mine." A certain novice was about to take her vows. Mère Julie met her one day, and wishing to put her obedience to the test, bade her lock up a room which she had just been cleaning out, put the key in her pocket and not give it up to any one. A moment after she sent the Mistress of Novices to ask for the key, and Sister A., not venturing to refuse her mistress, delivered it without mentioning the prohibition of the General. " Daughter," said the latter when she heard of it, " you shall make your vows when you have learnt to obey." And the novice's profession was put off.

A Superior who had come to make her retreat at the Mother House was found to have a nightgown which, though common enough as to the material, had been edged with a frill. After night prayers Julie summoned the delinquent, and having severely admonished her, burnt the unfortunate garment in her presence ; she then deposed her from her office of Superior, though an excellent religious. Of her own poverty—accepted in her early life with resignation, embraced in religion with holy transport, and practised up to her death with scrupulous care—we have already seen much in the course of her history ; we remember her angelic purity vowed to God from her childhood and guarded by the most vigilant modesty ; her perfect obedience to her confessor and Superiors ; and finally that profound humility which made her look upon herself as the basest of sinners, incapable of doing any good and deserving of utter contempt. She kept ever before her eyes that model of all virtues which she has set before her daughters on the first page of the Rule she gave them: "They who have the happiness of bearing the name of Sisters of Notre-Dame must earnestly strive to copy the virtues of their august Mother."

At the risk of repeating what has already been said, we cannot omit to refer once more to the Notice of the Foundress, dictated by Father Sellier two years before his death.* After speaking of the marvellous gift of prayer and the mysterious state of absorbed recollection in which she passed some hours every day during the years she was nailed to her couch by paralysis, he adds:

To this spirit of prayer Mère Julie joined purity of heart to an uncommon degree; it could scarcely be otherwise, since the higher paths of prayer imply uninterrupted union with God, which is founded on and limited by purity of heart— that perfect purity which supposes entire detachment from self, from creatures and from all that is not God. She would often exclaim with an intensity of feeling which baffles description: "Oh purity of heart! purity of heart!" She wanted to have sacramental absolution several times in the day, but not being able to name any distinct voluntary fault, she could not find a confessor who would consent to listen to her so often. When asked why she was so anxious to approach the tribunal of penance, she would answer: "Ah, it is for the special grace of purification attached to the Sacra-

---

* Father Sellier died at St.-Acheul in 1854 at the age of eighty-two. In 1852 he dictated and signed this paper, now in the possession of the Sisters of Notre-Dame, Namur.

ment, a grace which increases cleanness of heart." A third virtue no less admirable in Mère Julie was her patience. She bore with perfect unanimity all the privations attached to her state of habitual suffering. She was attacked from time to time with sudden nervous spasms followed by complete prostration; but no sooner were these crises over than her countenance recovered its calm serenity. While pitying her suffering, no one could fail to see the supernatural happiness she felt in living on the cross. This existence, so crucifying to nature, was hers for nearly twenty-five years. God tried her literally as gold that passes through the crucible.

Lastly, the source and safeguard of all Mère Julie's virtues was her profound humility. She loved to refer to her humble origin; she seemed always confused at the care taken of her, believing herself unworthy of the slightest attention; she called herself a poor ignorant woman, incapable of being useful to any one and only a burden to those around her. And yet, thanks to her natural good sense and the lights she borrowed from her communications with the Divine Wisdom, she was gifted with singular penetration in the paths of interior life, and in the discernment of spirits. I have known several of our Fathers who used to submit to her the difficulties they met with in the guidance of souls, and even consult her on the direction of their own. I remember, among other cases, that of a somewhat perverse and troublesome *dévote*, who, having heard it said that simplicity was a powerful means of perfection, was seized with a desire to acquire that virtue. When questioned about this person, Mère Julie replied roundly: "Content yourself with her good will; you may very easily make her mad; you will never make her simple." And she was right.

Such was Julie's soul. Adorned with so many virtues, enriched with so many merits, proved by so many trials, she had made good her right to rest from her labours and to break the bonds which held her back from the sight of her Beloved. The hour was at last at hand when the Divine Spouse was to whisper in the ear of His bride the welcome summons: " Veni, sponsa mea, veni. . . . coronaberis." *

* Cant. iv. 8.

CHAPTER XX.

JULIE'S HAPPY DEATH.

Notwithstanding the knowledge which Mère Julie seems to have had of the approaching end of her labours, there was no sign of abated energy in her work. "God and my duty are my sole occupation," she had written at the close of 1815 to the Superior of Jumet; she could not think of rest so long as there was work for God to do on earth. She took advantage of the two retreats of 1815 to give her parting advice to the Sisters of Notre-Dame, who met for the last time around their Mother. There is always something grave and touching about dying counsels; but when they fall from the lips of a saint, these *novissima verba* are doubly beautiful and venerable. The chief concern of the Servant of God was the true spirit of the Institute. "It was not established by human means," she said, "it can neither increase nor be supported, any more than it can be uprooted, by man. What is chiefly important, my dear Sisters, is the preservation of its primitive spirit—the spirit of perfect union, of tender charity, of absolute equality." Like St. John the Apostle, she came back again and again on this mutual charity. "We must be united together," she loved to repeat, "as the stones of a building are united by the mortar.

Charity must be our predominant virtue: the strong must support the weak." And again: "Yes, my dear daughters, be filled with the spirit of Jesus, which is a spirit of love, a spirit of mutual forbearance with faults. O my dearest children, how much I desire to see among you that courtesy, that good understanding with each other, that perfect conformity, which makes people able to say when they see any one of you. 'They are all just like each other.'"

She insisted constantly on this last thought. "A person who sees one Sister of Notre-Dame must be convinced he sees them all. Amongst us there must be no distinction between those employed in household duties and those engaged in teaching. Equality in all things!—no particular affection between those Sisters who come from the same country; but let all unite together like waters which have left their source to flow together in one stream. The recreations should be passed sweetly and gently in mutual communication, in which all the Sisters, though from different parts of the world, speak the same language, so that none may seem strangers where all have but one heart and one soul. Finally, let there be no warm discussions; where there is a difference of opinion sacrifice your own way of thinking in favour of charity."

But there can be no true charity without humility. "We must have humble souls," cried out the Servant of God in words which paint herself; "humble souls are courageous souls, apostolic souls, souls that *go out of themselves*, and those are the sort of souls which our Institute demands."

"My dear Sisters," she said on another occasion, "let our submission to authority be constant and perfect. To me personally you owe nothing, but you owe respect and submission to her who holds the place of God in your regard ; thus considered, your Superior has a right to honour, love and obedience from you, however wretched she may be. If you allow yourselves to criticise her conduct, to reason about her commands or her prohibitions, you are on the wrong road, and you will be severely punished at the Judgment Seat of God." How firmly, in another conference, she inculcated the necessity of "that good, solid foundation of mortification, without which no Sister of Notre-Dame is possible." With what ardour she poured into the souls of her daughters that love of the Cross which, both by word and example, she had preached throughout her whole life, warning them, however, against "those crosses which people forge for themselves, and which are very heavy without being the least meritorious"! With what a burst of almost eloquence she exclaimed one evening : "My dear children, if you have docile and well-prepared hearts, the Holy Spirit Himself will teach you more than I should ever be able to say to you about the dispositions of a true Sister of Notre-Dame. We must have in our Institute magnanimous souls, frightened at nothing, fearing temptations no more than they fear flies buzzing around. Ah! let us not render void the grace of our vocation. A crowd of souls would rise up against us at the Last Day, and would say to us: 'You were the cause of my eternal damnation; if you had been more united to God, you would have won my heart. You passed for a person consecrated to God, but you were so only in appearance.' . . . Do you think, my children, that I justify myself before God? If you have not made more progress in the interior life, whose is the fault? Mine, first and foremost." And the Sister who took notes of this instruction adds that here Mère Julie fell upon her knees before the Sisters and "humbled herself to the very dust."

"God works," she added, "in a soul which puts the reins into His hands; He ennobles it, He divinises it. When one sets about it with one's whole heart, the work is soon done. Do not make bargains with our good God; give Him a free field of action *(donnez-lui à couper en plein drap).* Say to Him:— 'Here I am, my God! cut, sever, spare me not.' . . . And then make war upon your own self-will. . . . Try it, and, by God's grace, you will understand what I say."

At the close of that memorable retreat of 1815 the Venerable Servant of God must have been consoled to see with what perfect union and charity the Sisters gathered from the different houses consulted together about methods of teaching, showed each other different kinds of needlework, and mutually shared the fruits of their knowledge and experience. Their zeal and purity of intention seemed to double their natural abilities, whilst it drew still closer the bonds of religious charity. The blessing of God was manifest.

Her correspondence, as we have seen, continued unbroken. From the time of the re-establishment of the Society of Jesus in 1814 all her letters are signed, " Julie, *called Sister Ignatius*, most unworthy Sister of Notre-Dame ; " they are full of the thought of death.

Say a prayer every day that I, who am getting so old, may have the grace to refer all my actions to eternity. I fear to find myself suddenly surprised by death. . . . A few moments more and we shall no longer exist! Let us never lose sight of that Eye which sees all things, that Ear which hears all things, that Hand which writes all things. . . Keep your lamps trimmed, as wise virgins waiting for the Bridegroom.

On the 7th of December, 1815, Mère Julie had a heavy fall on the staircase leading to the chapel. She fainted and was carried to her room, but, on coming to herself, would only allow the most ordinary remedies, and at once resumed her usual occupations, notwithstanding violent headache and a general *malaise*, soon accentuated by a severe cold.

It was the beginning of her last illness—a long four months of suffering and weakness. But suffering was no stranger to Julie Billiart, and she welcomed it smiling. On the 16th she writes to the Superior of Jumet :

So people have judged me unfavourably! * Ah! how good that is to help me to die to my wretched self-love, and to the esteem of creatures, which I must trample underfoot. Provided that I do what my God asks of me, for His greater glory, for the interests of Him who is my good Father, what matter to me the judgments of men? . . . But as for that of my dear daughter Anastasie! Oh! there are no limits to her charity for her poor Mother; in her eyes, no-one is so perfect as her Mother; and when people say to her this comes from "*ma Mère*," "*ma Mère* said that," all is said. After that, go and see what the good God thinks of it all . . . . . He does not always think like my daughter Anastasie at Jumet! If I had to be judged by you, my daughter, I might expect a very favourable verdict! See how I am joking; a little joke does good now and again.

And all Julie's old self is in the following lines written to the same on December 21 :

Tell all my dear children, especially those who are following our sweet Jesus most closely in the blessedness of His naked poverty and in detachment from self, that I wish them an increase of grace that shall make them reach the poverty of our Saviour as He lies in the miserable crib. Let us try, my friend, to take that road ourselves and to lead others along it, for it is the path our divine Model came to point out to us. I will go and see you as soon as ever I can. If your heart is full, so too is mine. But here is the holy crib of our dear Jesus; I will place everything in it, everything, everything. I believe that before very long we shall see things we should never have dreamed of. Patience! God has His designs: let us adore them with our whole heart. Tell my dear daughters that I hope to find them all at the feet of our sweet Lord in the stable of Bethlehem with the good shepherds. Let us join with each other in doing a holy

* About the dismissal of a novice.

violence to heaven, so as to win the grace of the spiritual birth of the Christ-Child in our souls! Ask it for me especially, my daughter—I need it so much—Oh! yes, more than all of you put together. I shall carry you all, my daughters, to the Cradle of our Blessed Saviour, and put you, each and all, into His Sacred Heart. . . . Who is going to get to the stable first? Let us go there early, dear daughter, so as to secure a place . . . . let us abide in the adorable Heart of Jesus where we can always, always meet, in spite of the fury which hell is arming against us. But, as the Hymn says, "*Je ne crains rien, Jésus est avec moi!*"

Let us do what we can, our very best, to gain a blessed eternity; it is worth the trouble, is it not? . . .

The cross was rapidly doing its last work in the soul of the Servant of God. "I used often to notice on her countenance," says Mère Blin de Bourdon, "an expression of mingled joy and pain. At other times it was all pain, and her glistening eyes told me without words that her soul too was suffering." But she never lost her serenity. The peace of God rested on her emaciated face and lit up the old smile that still came so readily to lips from which words now fell very seldom. In all she said or did it was apparent that her soul was ready to take its flight, that not a fibre of attachment held it to earth. She became extremely weak, and was unable to take any solid food; even liquids could only be administered drop by drop and with the greatest difficulty. On January 14, 1816, she was obliged to take to her bed, first embracing all her daughters as she was accustomed to do before setting out on a long journey, so that they felt convinced she knew she was to die. Indeed, it was the opinion of M. Médard, the Vicar General and ecclesiastical Superior of the Community, as well as of the Sisters, that she had been supernaturally enlightened as to the time of her death. Then, though no one thought her in danger, she at once asked for the Last Sacraments, which, in presence of the weeping community, she received, say the Acts of the Process, with extreme fervour and with the most perfect abandonment of herself into the hands of her heavenly Father. From the age of twenty-two Julie had received Holy Communion daily; she did so still during her last illness, and by a special help from God, even when she could scarcely swallow a drop of water, she was able to communicate with ease, so that, say the Memoirs, almost to the very end she partook every day of that food which was sweetness to her soul. Many priests of the city, penetrated with respect for her holiness, and anxious to enjoy the edification of her virtue, begged the favour of carrying the Holy Viaticum to her.*

"There are persons," remarks Mère St. Joseph, "who keep up their confidence in God fairly well so long as they are in health, but who, when sickness comes, and especially when death is at hand, fall into a state of trouble; but the hope of our dear Mother remained always firm." † She had allowed

* Proc. infor., xxi. p. 248.
† Memoirs, vol. iv.; Proc. infor. viii. de heroica Spe, p. 100.

the ordinary doctor to be called in "for the honour of the house," as she playfully said, and to please the bishop, who had insisted on her taking care of her health; and she submitted, as her Rule requires, with the simplicity of a child to all his prescriptions, though well aware they could do her no good. "We must bear sickness and all it brings with it," she would say to Mère St. Joseph. "This last illness," adds the narrator, "was peculiarly painful and distressing, but with variations which kept the Sisters wavering between hope and fear. The invalid alone never varied, and it was impossible to know whether she preferred to recover or to die. Entirely devoted as she was to the Institute, identified in a manner with the work entrusted to her by God, I think that she would not have refused to re-engage in the combat; on the other hand, she felt that to be delivered from the body of this death and to be with Christ was for her a thing by far the better. I shall never forget the look in her eyes a few days before her last illness as, raising them to heaven, she cried out: 'O my God, how happy a soul must feel when she lays down this burden of the body!'* It seemed as if the old days of Cuvilly and Compiègne had come back; indeed, she had asked of God that, if she might no longer work for Him, He would give her back the sufferings of her youth. She lay in a state of complete power-

---

* Memoirs, iv. p. 7.

lessness and annihilation, often of sharp pain, offering herself continually as a victim of God's good pleasure. She rarely spoke now; only when her daughters wept around her she would say, "Courage, my children! do not be frightened. God will never fail you;" and to those who expressed compassion for her sufferings she would answer with the familiar refrain: "God is our good Father. He is good—infinitely good—the good God!" No desire, no fear, no anxiety, ever once ruffled her perfect tranquillity; "this ineffable peace," as Mère St. Joseph terms it, remained with her till her last breath, nor was it, as her friend is careful to point out, an apathy due to her illness, for she retained consciousness to the very end, but the fruit of God's grace and her own virtue. And she adds that though she herself is firmly convinced that the favours God then bestowed upon His Servant were something very special, yet "had there been nothing else but her profound humility, her invincible patience, her unalterable calm, these were amply sufficient for the edification of those who nursed her or visited her. They were never weary of admiring the peace of her soul, and her immense confidence in the goodness of God, which was its source." The Venerable Mother herself, meanwhile, was penetrated with the sense of her nothingness. "God is taking me out of the world," she would say, "because I am not worthy to carry on His work."* She was fully persuaded

* Testimony of M. Renson, her confessor.

that her death would be no loss whatever to the Institute, but that God would continue to sustain a society of which He alone was the Author. It was not worth while, she said, to trouble about a poor, ignorant peasant like herself. And it is characteristic that she abstained from giving any special advice to her children. Her prayer was rapt and unceasing. A former pupil of the boarding-school at Namur, Mlle. Angélique Goës, bore witness later to the " bursts of the love of God " which used to seize the Foundress before her death, " which was that of a saint."

In the throes of pain which tortured her, her thoughts were absorbed by her suffering Saviour, and, in that contemplation, she seemed, like St. Francis of Assisi and St. Philip Neri, to suffer in the Body of her Lord rather than her own, to lose the sense of her own pains in the thought of those of her Beloved. Her hands constantly clasped the crucifix and pressed it to her heart, while the tears streamed down her cheeks as she gazed upon it. Indeed, in order to obey the doctor, who had ordered rest, she was sometimes obliged to turn away her eyes from the sacred image, being unable to bear the sight of Jesus crucified without bursting into tears and sobs.[*] She had always been thus sensibly affected by the Passion of Christ. Her eyes filled the moment she fixed her mind upon it in meditation. " What! " she would say, " a God reduced to that condition for us miserable sinners! " She never

---

[*] Proc. inform. Summarium, p. 242. Also depositions of witnesses, xvii, and xxix.

made the Stations of the Cross dry-eyed, and one of the witnesses for the cause—an old family servant of Mme. Goëthals of Courtrai, tells how one day she had surprised Mère Julie bathed in tears before the ninth station. "One would have thought," she said, "that Mère Julie was weeping for the sins of the whole human race."* When she fell ill, she had been carried to the bed of Mère St. Joseph, her own little room having no fireplace.

I had in my room [says the author of the Memoirs] rather a fine painting of the taking down from the Cross; and as her eyes often rested upon it, she said to me: "I beseech you, child, take away that picture; I suffer too much when I see it." †

The least sound was torture to her [we still quote from the Memoirs], and she could scarcely bear to be spoken to; but I used often to read her a few lines of the "Following of Christ." One day as I was preparing to do so she stretched out her hand and, without looking at the book, laid her finger on a verse which she could not possibly see, and said: "That is the part you must read." It was this passage: "If thou carry the cross willingly, it will carry thee, and bring thee to thy desired end, to that place where there will be an end to suffering, though here there will be no end." ‡ To obtain the cure of the Superior General Masses, Communions, prayers and penances were continually offered up; large alms were given for this intention; the priests of the different churches begged the prayers of their flocks, the pupils in the schools joined their supplications to those of their teachers in order to obtain the prolongation of so precious a life. As the feast of St. Joseph was approaching, his intercession was particularly implored. Our Mother knew this, and said to me one day,

* Responsio ad animadversiones Promotoris Fidei, cap. iii. de Obstaculis.
† Memoirs, vol. iv. p. 31.   ‡ Imit. book ii. chap. xii. v. 5.

"You must promise to clothe three poor little girls in honour of St. Joseph." "Yes, ma Mère," I replied, "we will do so if he gets us what we are asking him for." "Oh! in any case he will do something; go quickly, and promise him that you will do so; promise it at the foot of our Lady's altar." We promised [adds Mère Blin], and St. Joseph did indeed do something; he obtained for her a happy and peaceful death. †

Feeling her end approaching, she sent to ask pardon of her bishop for any offence she might have given him. Mgr. Pisani, who was too ill himself to visit her, answered: "Why! what has she done? All I have to reproach her with is not taking care of her health; she has killed herself." Then "with great tenderness and humility" she also asked pardon of her assistant for any pain she might have caused her, "though," adds the latter, "she had never really given me any." Up to nearly the end of March this well-beloved "eldest daughter" had nursed her with the most untiring devotion; but God, Who, in death as in life, was fashioning her to the likeness of the Crucified, now deprived her of this consolation. Worn out by fatigue, Mère St. Joseph was in her turn attacked by an epidemic fever complicated with pleurisy. In a few days her state became most alarming; Extreme Unction was administered; on one and the same day the Holy Viaticum was borne to each of the dying Foundresses; and for a moment it seemed that these two, so closely knit together in life, even in death would not be divided. But God heard the prayers of the grief-

* Memoirs, v. p. 11.

stricken community; Mère St. Joseph recovered from the attack, but so slowly that at the death of Julie she was not yet out of danger. Many of the clergy came to visit the Servant of God; the poor, whom she had loved so well, flocked to enquire after her, and prayed fervently for her recovery; and the elder pupils of the boarding-school earnestly besought the favour of being allowed to receive a last blessing from their beloved Mother. For each of these last she had a word of wise counsel. "Palmyre," she said to one of them, "be faithful to the Cross; it will take you to heaven." The prediction was verified; in the heavy trials which fell to her lot, Charlotte-Palmyre Dayeneux found sanctification and merit.* Having heard that one of the children of the Poor School, Thérèse Tasset, who filled the post of errand-girl to the community, was broken-hearted at the thought of never seeing her again, Julie sent for her to her bedside, comforted her with extreme kindness, and gave her her blessing.† On April 2 she sent this message to the teachers of the different classes: "Tell your little girls that I bless them with all my heart; tell them to remember the good God in every circumstance of their lives, and to seek first in all things what will make their salvation secure; the rest shall be added to them."

In spite of her weakness Mère St. Joseph sometimes had herself carried in an arm-chair to the room where her venerated Mother lay dying; but sorrow

* Proc. Infor. Summ., xxi.
† Proc. Apost. de fama. Inter. xxxi. 5th witness.

and prostration hung their weight upon her own lips, and humility as well as pain seemed to seal those of the Servant of God—they spoke little. On April 6 Julie saw that tears stood in her daughter's eyes. "St. Joseph, St. Joseph," she said with affectionate familiarity, "where is your confidence gone to?" In vain the poor Mother tried to master her emotion; unable to suppress her tears, she left the room abruptly without any of her usual expressions of respectful tenderness. On the following evening at about five or six o'clock, though very feverish, she again had herself wheeled to the bedside of Julie, who, lifting up her fingers in gentle reproach, said to her, "The good God was not pleased yesterday," meaning that, as Superior, she should have controlled her emotion in presence of the Sisters. "It was in this way," continues the Co-foundress, "that this dear Mother of mine pointed out my failings to me—many and many a time has she said the same words. Then she spoke again: 'Sister St. Joseph, will you come back again this evening?' 'No,' I answered, 'my fever is too high.' She said no more, and I kissed her; when I saw her again, she was dead."

Nothing could be simpler than that death. Very few even of the Sisters were present at it, for many had been struck down with the prevailing epidemic, and most of the others, occupied all day with the care of the sick or other laborious offices, had been obliged by obedience to take some rest. The dying saint made no external demonstrations; her only request was that she might be buried like a poor person and the last of the Sisters. Then, that she might die stripped of all things, she took a little reliquary of common metal which she wore, and gave it to Sister Eulalie. Palm Sunday was drawing to a close. All at once the feeble voice began to sing very softly and gently her favourite "Magnificat"—to those who listened it seemed as though in the long silent hours she had been recalling all the graces of her life. Soon after, towards eight o'clock in the evening, she lost the use of speech; and we think that no other words could have more beautifully closed the song of praise which Julie Billiart's whole story had been than that canticle of humility and joy in God. Canon Reuson was called and passed the night by her bedside with the infirmarian and two or three other Sisters. On April 8, at two o'clock in the morning, she passed away so peacefully that no one could tell the exact moment of her death, and a mirror was held to her lips to make sure that she had ceased to breathe. It was Monday in Holy Week; the shadow of the crucifix rested upon her death even as it had lain upon her life.

This " blessed death of our dear Mother," as she terms it in a letter written the day after to Sister Marie Steenhaut, was to Mère St. Joseph a terrible blow, and left in her soul a void which God alone could fill. Though her own state made her unfit to move, she insisted on going to look once more on the face of her friend and guide; "then," she tells us, "the features which had been so altered by suffering when we parted, had recovered their usual expression, and the look of pain had given place to a smile."* Beside that body, the tears she shed had nothing of bitterness or discouragement, for through them she looked to the Heaven where she could not but feel that her beloved Mother had become her powerful protectress, and " where," as she said, "she could see better the needs of her children and win for them more abundant help." The deceased, clothed in her religious habit, was laid out in the room where she had died, on a poor bed, beside which on a little table stood a crucifix between two lighted candles. Around the body knelt the Sisters, at once invoking with the utmost confidence the intercession of her who had so often strengthened them in weakness and consoled them in trouble. Her limbs remained flexible, the tints of health returned to her cheek, and her lips were parted with a smile whose beauty struck all beholders—the smile of a child who dies with eyes fixed upon its Father's face. She looked full of life, and on fire with the love of God.†

One of those who prepared the holy body for the grave—Sister Emmanuelle Bonnay, who died at Visé in 1861—had so high an opinion of Julie's sanctity that she used to say : " Our dear Mère Julie

---

* Memoirs, vol. iv. p 19.   † Summ. xxi.

will be canonised some day; I shall not see it, but others will." All the letters and documents in which different Sisters have recorded details of her end bespeak the same conviction of her holiness and her beatitude. In a letter addressed to the community of Montdidier and dated April 22, 1816, we read:

As to the details you ask for concerning her death, I cannot find words to express the faith and love which animated our dying Mother. Her painful illness of three months was borne with the most absolute resignation, and, as you already know, she gave up her soul to her Creator on the eighth of this month. How true it is that the death of the just is like the evening of a beautiful day! There was something heavenly in her countenance, and a certain rosy colour remained in it after death. Her holy life gives us a confident hope that she now enjoys the repose promised to those who walk in the footsteps of their crucified Lord. She had had gall and vinegar given her to drink, and had, as you know, in divers ways, drained His chalice to the dregs. We trust that she has gone to rest from her sufferings and toils.*

In the Annals of the Institute Sister Stéphanie furnishes the following details. After relating the peaceful agony and death of the Servant of God, she adds:

When our Mother had expired, her face instantly lost all trace of pain: she seemed to smile. Canon Renson had not left her since the evening before; he and a few Sisters were present at her last breath; but, in her humility, she would not

* The original of this letter was found at Compiègne in 1891, and sent by Canon de Maindreville, curé of the Church of St. Antoine, to the Rev. Mother General at Namur, where it was authenticated by the Bishop, Mgr. Bélin, on the fifth of October in the same year.

have the community gathered together, nor did she make any of those outward demonstrations which some saintly persons have considered profitable. . . . She had always kept very secret the gifts of God to her soul; she did so to the last. . . . The Sisters embraced their Mother, covering her dead body with their tears. But there was no bitterness in their regrets, for they well knew she was not lost to the Institute she had so much loved; on the contrary we hoped that, being now nearer to the source of all grace, she would obtain a greater abundance of them for her work. If indeed our hearts had not been filled with this confidence that she would sustain the Institute by her credit with God, we might have feared the total ruin of the Congregation.

Then, after mentioning the illness of Mère St. Joseph, the writer proceeds:

On one occasion when M. Minsart had come to visit our Foundresses, to whom he was greatly attached, he made this prediction:—" Mère Julie will die, but Mère St. Joseph will be restored to the congregation." And so it happened.

As soon as our loss became known in the town, many pious persons, who could not obtain the privilege of seeing the holy remains because the public were not admitted, sent rosaries and medals to touch the body, and begged for pieces of her clothing or of anything which the Servant of God had used. Each Sister had the consolation of receiving some fragments of her garments, and we wear them with the same sentiments of veneration and of confidence which we bore her in life.

It had been decided that the townspeople should not be indiscriminately admitted to venerate the mortal remains of the Servant of God, but that this favour should be granted only to the clergy, the friends of the house, the pupils and their parents. But it was impossible to keep to this regulation;

the crowd was so numerous, that, as we learn from the letter to Montdidier already quoted, the great gate of the Rue des Fossés had to be thrown open in order to satisfy their devotion. Some of the pupils of those days, who now reckon among the most precious memories of their childhood that of having venerated the remains of Julie Billiart, appeared as witnesses in the Juridical Process. One venerable old lady, Mme. Nihotte, said :—" I have often seen Mère Julie ; she was greatly beloved by the children on account of her kindness. . . . At the time of her death I was a day-scholar at the convent; we all went to see her, and to kiss her feet. Many people, too, from the town came to venerate her mortal remains. She was not changed by death : I can still see her features, bright and fresh-coloured as if she had been alive ; people said to each other :—' She is a Saint. See ! her features are not altered.' " *

Félicie Minet stated :—" I saw Reverend Mère Julie Billiart after her death. I remember distinctly that the children touched her body with their rosaries. Her reputation for holiness was very great, and every one in the town was talking of the good she had done."†

Other witnesses recalled their impressions in similar terms. In fact there is no more glorious testimony to the memory of the Venerable Servant of God than that given under oath at the various " Processes " by

* Fol. 608.   † Fol. 409.

her former pupils. One mentions her faith, her trust in God, her love for the poor; another her amiability and wonderful kindness; a third her boundless charity. Mme. de Bernard de Fauconval, whose tender reminiscences of Gembloux and Sister Gertrude the reader will not have forgotten, tells of her ecstasies, her visions, her miraculous cure, and dwells on the firmness of her rule, her vigilance, and the reputation for holiness which she enjoyed. To this last fact a chorus of voices testify. "Mère Julie," says Mme. de Saegher, "was loved and venerated *as a Saint*;" and Colette Cambier, known in the Institute as Sister Reine, relates that when a child she could not take her eyes off the Venerable Mother's face, and that once, after watching her during Mass, she had cried out joyfully to her teachers: "Now I know how the Saints say their prayers."

On hearing the news of the death of the Foundress Mgr. Pisani, though seventy-three years of age and extremely ill at the time, wrote the following letter to Sister Eulalie:

My dear Child in Christ,—I heard with the deepest sorrow of the fatal stroke which has just separated you for a time from your estimable and holy Mother, Sister Julie. This is the moment for showing heroic courage and resolution, full and entire submission to the decrees of God, always just even when severe. Tell all your Sisters and pupils how much I am concerned for their affliction; what adds to my own is that I am still unable to go and see you on account of my weak health, and a long and troublesome cold which I am trying to get rid of before the ceremonies of Holy Thursday and Easter Sunday. However, I am sure that my Vicar

General, Monsieur Médard, will have gone to console and strengthen you in this difficult crisis. May God preserve Mère St. Joseph to us; I am afraid she will sink under this terrible blow, but I trust that God will take pity on your community, which is so useful and fervent, and will leave us that good Mother. I have no doubt that Canon Renson assisted Mère Julie in her last moments; it was a source of great regret to me not to have been able to see her and be edified by her virtue during her illness. I had several times offered the Holy Sacrifice for her recovery, knowing how necessary she was to your work. God did not hear my prayers; may His Holy Name be ever blessed and His paternal will accomplished!

I am, my dear child, entirely devoted to you and your Sisters in union with our Lord Jesus Christ.

☩ C.-F.-J., BISHOP OF NAMUR.

In the midst of these painful circumstances Monsieur Médard, the Vicar General, redoubled his kindness and attention to the much-tried community. On the very day of the decease of the Servant of God he assembled the Sisters, and, having expressed his sympathy for their affliction, he spoke in praise of their Foundress, saying that he had never met with so pure a soul, and that he was certain she already enjoyed the sight of the God she had loved so much.*

On account of the offices of Holy Week the funeral of the Foundress had to be hastened; it took place on Wednesday, April 10. Mère Julie's express wish, as we have seen, was that she should be buried simply, like the other Sisters, but the Bishop would not hear of complying with this humble request. He

* Proc. inform. xxii.

even went so far as to undertake the expense of a walled vault, over which he placed later a tombstone with an epitaph. The Venerable Servant of God was therefore interred with great solemnity; but the most touching pomp of her funeral was the long file of pupils and Sisters who followed their Mother and their Foundress to her last resting-place. This touching cortége numbered over four hundred, and made a great impression on the public. Besides these, a large number of persons assisted at the interment: the church was crowded, and during the solemn Requiem, in which many ecclesiastics took part, several Masses were going on at the side altars.

The obsequies took place in the Church of St. Joseph, to which parish the community belonged. As soon as the funeral set out, all the bells tolled: the shops were closed along its route, and the circuit of the town was made to satisfy the devotion of the people. Every child in the long procession carried a taper. In a letter sent to Montdidier we read:

The whole population, as well as the Sisters and children, followed the funeral to the grave, a thing not customary in this country, but granted to us by the civil authorities. Our ecclesiastical Superior, a venerable old priest of saintly life, followed the coffin accompanied by eighteen young men bearing torches.

The body of the Venerable Julie was interred in the common cemetery of the town, close to the great Calvary which, later on, was destroyed when the cemetery was transferred to another locality in the interests of public health. More than one person accidentally passing through Namur between the 8th and 10th of April, 1816, has testified to hearing in the streets exclamations of "The Saint is dead! The Saint is dead! We have lost a Saint!" In other places also witness was borne to her sanctity. At Montdidier, where she was well known, the greatest sympathy was shown for the Sisters in their sorrow; the parish priest announced her death to his flock in words which showed the esteem in which she was held. "We recommend to your prayers Mère Julie, Superior General of the Sisters of Notre-Dame, who died at Namur on the 8th of this month in the odour of sanctity, after a life consecrated to the glory of God and the service of her neighbour. Her Sisters are inconsolable for her loss, and their tears are her highest praise. Although St. Augustine says that to pray for the Saints is to do them a wrong, still, faithful to the decrees of the Sovereign Pontiffs, who wish us to pray for those who die within the pale of the Church, and not to cease praying for them, however firm may be our belief that they are in the bliss of Heaven, until the Church has pronounced her verdict, and inserted their names in the catalogue of the Saints, faithful to this rule, I say, I shall sing the *Libera* after this Mass, and on Friday at the accustomed hour shall offer the Holy Sacrifice for the venerated deceased, whose death, there can be no doubt, was precious in the sight of God."

As soon as Mère St. Joseph had recovered, Monseigneur Pisani hastened to visit the community. The pious Bishop reminded the Sisters in eloquent language of the merits of their Foundress. "Mère Julie was one of those souls who do more for the Church in a few years than hundreds of others, good though they may be, without her apostolic spirit, can do in a century. You have sustained a great loss in the person of your Mother, but she watches over you from Heaven, and you will feel her protection still more efficaciously than when she lived with you. You will behold her in Heaven with the triple crown of a virgin, an apostle and a martyr. Her reward is great because she did much for God."

Among the letters of condolence which were addressed to her, Mère de Bourdon preserved three on account of their special value: the first is from Monseigneur Demandolx, Bishop of Amiens:

It would be impossible to say, Reverend Mother, how much I was affected by the immense loss you have sustained through the death of your good Mère Julie. You know what my sentiments were towards her, and what a high opinion I had of her virtue. She is gone to receive the reward of her fidelity, and I could not allow myself to regret for an instant the happiness she is enjoying in Heaven. Her patience and resignation in her last illness formed the crowning act of her sacrifice. Let us always keep her example before our eyes as an encouragement to us in the trials we may have to endure. I know I am speaking to Sister Blin, to Sister St. Joseph, to the true friend of Sister Julie. Remember that you take her place in my sentiments towards her, and that I still have for your Congregation the same attachment I expressed to her. I hope that you continue on the same good terms with your venerable Bishop. Present my respectful compliments to him, and never doubt of my kindly feelings toward you.

☩ J.-F., BISHOP OF AMIENS.

Amiens, May 3, 1816.

Father Thomas wrote on May 6, 1816 :

I heard at the same time of our good Mère Julie's death and of your illness, and I am certain that her loss affects you more than your own danger. However good those who remain in a community may be, it is exceedingly difficult to fill the place of a Superior of such merit as hers when God has taken her to himself. I am uniting my prayers with yours most heartily for the soul of our good Mother, although her singular virtues give us reason to hope that she is with God. I should blame myself if I lost sight of the important services she rendered me in the stormy period we passed through together. I always considered her a good counsellor and never repented following any advice she was kind enough to give me. I know nobody to whom I am under greater obligations, and I am praying to God with all my heart to reward her for my sake and that of so many others who were helped by her wise counsels.

On May 8, 1816, Father Varin wrote from Paris to Mère St. Joseph :

What a blow our Lord has struck, dear Rev. Mother, in taking from us our good Mère Julie! but how adorable are His designs! He had given her to your little Society in a manner which showed His power and His goodness. He has recalled her to Himself now, when she has fulfilled all the purposes He had in view. I am persuaded that the work of which she was the instrument in God's hands, far from suffering from her loss, will receive renewed prosperity by her intercession ; for who can fail to have recourse to her prayers? If they had such power over the Heart of God while she was in the place of her exile, how much more must they have now that she is in the heavenly country, in the bosom of her God! Could we, in fact, think otherwise of that good Mother, than that she who on earth lived for love alone, must be destined to love God for all eternity? This ought to be for you, dear Mother, who take her place, a motive of consolation and confidence. Yes, she will be more useful to you in heaven than on earth; she will give you palpable proofs of her credit with God; she will obtain for you the lights and graces of which you stand in need for the confirmation and extension of the Lord's work; and all your children will join you in acknowledging that their good Mother is a powerful protectress. Convey my good wishes to your community, and accept the assurance of the respectful and invariable attachment of your devoted servant.

Two years after the death of the Venerable Mère Julie, March 2, 1818, Father Varin wrote again to Mère St. Joseph, now Superior General of the Institute:

It is a real consolation for me to hear news of you and of your numerous community. The memory of its early days has made it so dear to me that it never leaves my heart and mind; I offer it every day to the Eternal Father in union with His Divine Son in the Holy Sacrifice of the Mass. I must mention a thought which constantly occurs to me. Have you not collected the details of the life of our good Mère Julie? I obliged her in the early days of your Society to write some memoirs of her life; she began, in spite of her dislike for the task, but did she either continue or keep what she had written? I have strong doubts about it. However that may be, it seems desirable that some one should gather together all that was most remarkable in her life and most fitted to excite admiration for the mercies of our Lord over that holy soul. Do me the favour of telling me what you think about this; it seems to me that for the glory of God and the good of your Society it is proper to preserve the memory of your Mother and of the particular graces bestowed upon her. Although I am unknown to the greater number of your Sisters, they are not less dear to me ; so pray assure them of my sincere good wishes, and believe always in the perfect and respectful attachment of your ever humble and obedient servant,

VARIN, S.J.

It was in response to the desire of Father Varin that Mère Blin de Bourdon wrote the Memoirs which have been so freely made use of in this Life.

CHAPTER XXI.

"HER SEPULCHRE SHALL BE GLORIOUS."

THE Saints do not die; for to exchange a land of exile for one's native country, to cease to suffer in this vale of tears "that we may reign with Jesus Christ and enjoy the perfect happiness of heaven, cannot be called death."*

Not only are they in heaven "plunged in the immense ocean of light eternal and of the eternity of light,"† but they live on here below by the memory of their virtues, by their kindly, loving and miraculous intervention in what passes on earth, by the perpetuity and the progress of the good works they have begun, by the solemn worship paid to their name.

We would in no way anticipate the judgment of the infallible Church concerning the life, the the virtues and the miracles of the Venerable Servant of God Julie Billiart; but the Cause is already introduced, and it is no difficult task to prove from the Acts of the Process itself, this glorious survival of the humble daughter of the poor peasant family of Cuvilly, exalted now in proportion to the heroic self-annihilation of her life.

---

* Council of Trent, Sess. XXV. De invocatione, veneratione et reliquiis sanctorum.
† St. Bernard on the Love of God.

Scarcely had the Venerable Mother breathed her last, when thousands of voices were everywhere uplifted to proclaim her blessed. On April 22, 1816, the Sisters of Namur wrote to those at Montdidier:

> People are coming from all sides, through veneration, to ask for things which she used. Here and everywhere there is a general cry that we have a saint in heaven, since we have, with our own eyes, seen the sick recover their health by coming to pray devoutly at her tomb.

The Sisters living at the time are unanimous in their account, though with some differences as to details, of an extraordinary occurrence which took place at St.-Hubert on the very night of the Venerable Mother's death. Sister St. John, the Superior of the house, had neglected to execute an order given by the Foundress. During the night of April 7, she suddenly heard the curtains of her bed shaken, and looking, saw before her Mère Julie, who said in a grave tone: " My daughter, when did you do what I recommended you?" "Oh ! *ma Mère, ma Mère,* forgive me, " cried Sister St. John : believing that the Superior General had come to St.-Hubert without announcing her visit, she rose hastily from her bed, but there was no one in the room. Much impressed with what she had seen and heard, she related it to the Sisters on the following morning, and it was only two days later that the post, then very slow in the Ardennes, brought the news that the Venerable Mère

Julie had died on the very same night on which she had appeared at St.-Hubert.

This incident, and several others not less extraordinary, contributed to spread among the sisters of Notre-Dame a filial devotion towards Mère Julie, "whose protection of the Institute," wrote Mère St. Joseph, "daily manifested itself in a real and solid manner." Their pupils and many pious persons united with them in imploring the intercession of the Servant of God in their troubles and in their temporal as well as spiritual needs. Mère Blin de Bourdon, elected Superior General by plurality of votes, June 2, 1816, made it her chief care to maintain in the Institute the spirit of Mère Julie, to keep alive her influence and to honour her memory. By order of the Bishop of Namur M. Médard, the Vicar General, composed and placed on her tombstone this epitaph:

> Here rests the body of the most virtuous MOTHER JULIE BILLIART, Foundress and Superior General of the Sisters of Notre-Dame, who died holily at Namur, April 8, 1816, aged 65 years. She consecrated the most precious moments of her life to the instruction of youth and the formation of those excellent houses of education, rightly considered the bulwarks of religion and morality. She founded the establishments of Amiens, Ghent, Bordeaux, Namur, Chartron, Montdidier, Rubempré, Jumet, Saint-Hubert, Zèle, Andenne, Gembloux, Fleurus, etc., and after having exhausted her strength by her excessive labours for the glory of God, she fell asleep in the Lord, as much regretted by those who survived her, as admired by those who knew her.
> R.I.P.*

* When the cemetery of the town was changed, those who wished to do so, were allowed to take away the tombstones of their friends. The

The Reverend Mère St. Joseph summoned to Namur to act as her assistant and superior of the Mother-House Sister Anastasie Leleu, whom we have seen governing the convent at Jumet with so much wisdom and devotedness. Sister Anastasie wished to direct in person the erection of the tombstone. and accompanied by two or three Sisters, and two workmen whom she could trust, she went to the cemetery. To fix the stone firmly, it was necessary to uncover the four little walls which surrounded the grave; the coffin was laid bare before them. Seized with an intense longing to behold once more the mortal remains of their beloved Mother, the Sisters gave a sum of money to the sexton, who was present, to induce him to retire to a distance; then they ordered the two workmen to lift the lid of the coffin. Tears of love and devotion filled their eyes as they gazed upon the body of the Venerable Servant of God lying before them in the freshness and colour of life, without any sign of corruption, the limbs flexible, and bending as they reverently touched and moved them. "When it was uncovered," said Francis Mottiau in his judicial evidence, "The body of Mère Julie lay just as it was while she was living; it did not smell, it was without blemish, her garments were dry. Looking upon it,

---

Sisters of Notre-Dame took the stone which covered the original grave of their Foundress and placed it in the garden of the Mother-House. It is now in its right place, built into the wall of the annexe of the Chapel of the Sacred Heart of Mary, where lie the remains of the Venerable Servant of God.

we believed there was in the sight something extraordinary; that she was with God, that she was a saint."

"She had in her hands an ivory crucifix that had been put there when she was buried," says the Reverend Mère St. Joseph in her autograph narrative, "the same crucifix which she had so often kissed and pressed to her heart: they took it away, for it had become doubly precious to us since it had thus been in the hands of this faithful Servant of God. They took also her large rosary, and part of the cloth which covered her."

"They made me replace the lid of the coffin immediately after," continues Mottiau in his testimony; "I myself screwed it down."

The gravestone was then put upon the tomb, but only lightly cemented, for the Sisters had already conceived the idea of taking possession of the venerable remains. Sister Stéphanie tells in the Annals of the Institute that the Reverend Mère St. Joseph received the crucifix and other relics of her holy friend upon her knees, shedding many tears; they were kept with the greatest care in a room near the sacristy.

The cemetery where the mortal remains of their Venerable Mother lay, became a place of pilgrimage for the Sisters who accompanied the pupils in their walks; the children themselves loved to go there. The fact was known throughout the town, and excited no surprise.

In 1815 Belgium had become part of the dominions of William I., King of the Netherlands. Already certain acts of his government had caused the more clear-sighted of his subjects to fear that the Catholics of Belgium had little but severity and oppression to expect from the stranger king. Mère St. Joseph and Sister Anastasie, therefore, submitted to the judgment of several prudent persons their project of carrying away in secret to the Mother House the body of the Foundress. It was a bold undertaking, but if they gave it up they would deprive themselves of the consolation of possessing these precious remains, the source of blessings for the Mother House as well as for all the Institute. It had never been the custom for the Sisters to go out often; all could not accompany the pupils in the walks they were allowed to take, and, moreover, if the cemetery were changed or profaned, they would run the risk of losing for ever the relics of the Servant of God.

They obtained at last a verbal permission from Monseigneur Pisani—who, however, took upon himself no share of the responsibility,—the approval of M. Médard, the Vicar-General and ecclesiastical superior, and the advice of M. Hauregard, who warned them to act with the greatest possible prudence.

In the spring of the year 1817 Mère de Bourdon built at the bottom of the garden at the Mother House, at the right hand side, a vault forming the crypt of a little Oratory, in which, in order to hide the real destination of the edifice, a statue of the Blessed Virgin was erected.

All being ready, on the evening of July 27, 1817, Sister Anastasie and her companions went once more to the cemetery, as if to pray there. They gave some money to the grave-diggers to get them to move the tombstone, and after that to go away, leaving the Sisters to satisfy their devotion. This time they opened the coffin themselves, found the body in the same condition as in the preceding year, without any sign of decay; only there was, they remarked, at the ends of the fingers a tendency to dry up, and there issued from them some drops of very clear oil. They took the body just as it was, wrapped it in the linen cloths they had brought for the purpose under their cloaks, and, under cover of the darkness, succeeded in depositing it safely in the Mother House without exciting the least suspicion.

Canon William Colson, a former professor of Sacred History at the Seminary of Namur, at his judicial examination, gave the following testimony: "The body of Mère Julie, buried in the cemetery of the town, was taken to the Mother House some little time after her death. M. Hauregard, then a lawyer and member of the town council of Namur, later on a Canon of the Cathedral, seconded the Sisters in its removal." Several of the older Sisters bore witness to the same fact.

If no document existed to prove that the translation of the body of the Venerable Servant of God was permitted and even approved by the Bishop of Namur, the part which M. Hauregard took in it is proof sufficient. He was a grave and learned man who enjoyed the full confidence of his Bishop, and was raised in 1823 to the dignity of protonotary apostolic, through the intervention of Monsignor Nazalli, the nuncio at Brussels.

The mason Francis Mottiau declares in his deposition that a priest had told him and his fellow workman Léanne to open without fear the coffin of the Foundress if they were asked to do so, giving them to understand that some day a part of her remains would be sent to Rome. * This shows, beyond the fact of ecclesiastical intervention in the translation itself, that the idea of a judicial inquiry had already entered into the minds of those who had known Mère Julie.

We were fortunate enough [says Mère St. Joseph in her written declaration] to succeed in bringing the body to the Mother House. It was entire and incorrupt when it was placed in the vault, fifteen months and eighteen days after her death. The movement that was necessary to take it out of the coffin, to bear it from one place to another, to put it in a new coffin, left it absolutely entire. There came from the body, which was still heavy, a quantity of oil, which stained the winding sheet and other cloths, and even the floor of the room where it was (for a moment) laid. †

Sister Stéphanie tells us that "the entrance to

* Sum. xxiii. De miraculis post obitum. Test. IV, fol. 116, et seq.
† Procès-verbal of the Reverend Mother St. Joseph, declared authentic by the episcopal authority of Namur.

the vault is at the right of the little chapel near the door." When the Sisters, who came to Namur for the retreat during the holidays, saw the chapel and learned what was there, Sister Jeanne, Superior of Jumet, and Sister Gertrude, Superior of Gembloux, were all the more struck by it, as one day when she was with them in the garden during recreation, Mère Julie had said to them : "This is the place in which my miserable body will one day rest." It was the very spot on which the chapel stood. These two Sisters had never spoken to any one of the prediction. Mère St. Joseph forbade the professed Sisters to give any exterior signs of their affection and veneration for their Foundress, and it was decided that the novices should be told nothing of the treasure which the chapel contained.* To this secret, so religiously kept, may be attributed the fact that devotion to the Venerable Mère Julie was not widespread outside the Institute. But the Sisters among themselves had the greatest confidence in their beloved Foundress. In 1818 Mère St. Joseph composed for their private use a series of invocations in the form of a litany, in which she recalled to the minds of Julie's daughters the virtues which their Mother had practised under their very eyes. She calls her a virgin profound in humility, most obedient, most patient, full of confidence in God, inflamed with divine love, a martyr in desire, a mirror of true piety, &c., &c.,

* Annals, vol. i. p. 118.

CHAPEL SHRINE OF THE VENERABLE JULIE BILLIART AT NAMUR. GARDEN OF THE MOTHER HOUSE, NAMUR.

and begs of God that He would be pleased to give to the Sisters of Notre-Dame through the intercession of their Mother, a constant courage to overcome the obstacles to their salvation and perfection. The well known devotion of the Sisters of Notre-Dame to the Mother of God shielded from suspicion the frequent visits of the professed Sisters to the chapel in the garden, and we know from the judicial proceedings, from the traditions of the Institute, from the writings of the first Sisters, that the religious never ceased to invoke the aid of their Foundress on the spot where her mortal remains were laid.

In 1842 the vault was opened. The action of the water which had penetrated the vault at the time of the rising of the Sambre and the Meuse, had broken the coffin, the flesh had crumbled to dust, and the bones were disjointed. They were collected and placed in a smaller chest. Another flood in 1880 determined the ecclesiastical authorities to allow the construction of a tomb at a higher level, and there since December 14, 1882, the relics of the Venerable Servant of God have lain.

It would be impossible to relate in detail the the favours obtained at the tomb or by the intercession of the Venerable Mère Julie. We must content ourselves with the summary given by the advocates of the cause:* That these miracles

* Namurcen. Beatificationis et Canonizationis Servæ Dei Juliæ Billiart, *Positio super dubio: an sit signanda commissio introductionis causæ:* de miraculis post obitum, p. 103.

are numerous is very clearly stated by the thirty-second witness in the Process at Namur. "I have in my possession," he says, "and I have read more than two hundred attestations concerning favours obtained by the intercession of the Venerable Mère Julie, given by persons who have been the object of them since her death, but especially during the last twenty years: sickness healed, help granted in temptations or other difficulties, protection in case of fire, vocations obtained or strengthened, conversions, &c."

Witnesses are not wanting to prove that her charitable assistance has been granted even to those who had neglected to invoke her aid. Such was the experience of a former pupil of Notre-Dame, who, for a long time forgetful of her duty, was recalled to the path of virtue both by interior warnings and by a wonderful apparition. A little child, a great-niece of the Venerable Mother, was saved from injury by calling on her name just as she fell under the feet of a cart horse.

Many others afflicted with sickness of different kinds, already reduced to the last extremity, have been restored to health by the simple invocation of her name. One of the most remarkable cures was that of Louis Waelens of Ruddervoorde, who, after twenty-eight years of acute suffering from a disease of the stomach, was instantaneously healed when, invoking Mère Julie, he placed a relic of her upon the seat of the disease.

But as the Postulator of the cause remarks, "the rapidity with which the Institute of the Venerable Servant of God has spread, shows how pleasing the work has been to God, and how powerful is the protection with which from her throne in heaven the Venerable Foundress continues to assist it."*

The Congregation of the Sisters of Notre-Dame possessed, in the year 1896, 109 convents, of which 51 are in Belgium, 18 in England, 1 in Scotland, 38 in North America, and 2 in Belgian Congo.

So many virtues practised during life, so many favours granted after death, afforded such strong proofs of the sanctity of Julie Billiart, that it could not be rashness to claim for her the honour which the Church sets aside for the blessed in Heaven.

An ecclesiastical tribunal was set up by episcopal authority in the dioceses of Namur, of Malines, of Beauvais and of Amiens, to proceed to collect canonical information concerning the virtues, the reputation for sanctity, and the miracles of the Servant of God. With a view to the beatification and canonization of Julie Billiart this preliminary process was sent to Rome, where it was subjected to a rigorous examination by the Sacred Congregation of Rites. It is from these authentic sources, and from these judicial testimonies given under oath, that the promoter of the cause and the Advocate of

* Mgr. Virili, Articuli pro construendo apost. processu, No. 219.

the Faith have drawn the elements of a discussion which must dissipate all doubt and bring out the truth in all its lustre.

Meanwhile postulatory letters were addressed to the Holy See from all parts of the world. Some of these letters bear the signatures of imperial or royal personages, of the Emperor of Austria, Joseph Francis I., of the Empress Dowager Mary Anne, of the Queen of the Belgians, of Francis II., King of Naples, of the Countess of Chambord, of Prince George, Duke of Saxony, the Grand Duchess of Tuscany, Charles III., Prince of Monaco, and, to represent France, two pious princesses of the House of Bourbon, Princesses Marguerite and Blanche of Orleans. The following is the letter addressed by the two last to the Sovereign Pontiff, January 25, 1884 :

MOST HOLY FATHER.—Prostrate at the feet of your Holiness, we unite our voices to those of the daughters of Mère Julie Billiart, Foundress of the Institute of the Sisters of Notre-Dame of Namur, to implore of you earnestly the introduction of the cause of this heroic Servant of God. It was in France that Mère Julie was born, that she laboured and suffered and taught the Catechism, even at the peril of her life. It was amongst us that she founded her Institute. As Frenchwomen and daughters of St. Louis, we take greatly to heart the interests of this holy cause, petitioned for with the greatest earnestness by England and Belgium. May Mère Julie, when thus held up to public veneration, protect the faith of children, everywhere menaced by so many dangers, and inspire other souls with generosity equal to her own.

Not less earnest than these royal personages in their petitions for the introduction of the cause were the Cardinals of the Holy Roman Church: Cardinal Howard, Bishop of Tusculum, Cardinal Deschamps, Archbishop of Malines, Cardinal Manning, Archbishop of Westminster, the Cardinal Archbishops of Toulouse, Algiers, Sens, Rheims, Rennes, Paris, Lyons, Dublin, Toledo, New York, Quebec, Sydney, the Patriarch of Jerusalem, and Monseigneur Goëthals, Archbishop of Hieropolis, Vicar Apostolic of Western Bengal, whose name is so intimately connected with the history of Mère Julie and the Institute of the Sisters of Notre-Dame.

It is consoling to see with what unanimity the Catholic episcopate in France, in Belgium, in England and in America proclaim the heroic sanctity of the Servant of God. Amiens also unites its testimony to that of Namur, and thus completes—if this indeed were necessary—the solemn rehabilitation of the once persecuted and exiled Mère Julie. "The result of the depositions received in the process of information," declares the Chapter of Amiens, "proves that the reputation of sanctity of the Servant of God was acknowledged during the time that she dwelt in this city; that the memory of her faith, of her unalterable patience, of her zeal, left a great impression on her contemporaries, and on the few witnesses surviving who were called upon to give their depositions.

It was here that God began to favour Julie

Billiart with extraordinary graces, by curing her of the paralysis which kept her for long years nailed to a bed of suffering. It was at Amiens that this humble peasant girl, without preparatory study, with no other learning than that of the crucifix, of prayer and of ardent zeal for the glory of God, laid the foundations of a teaching order, which could not have spread throughout several kingdoms of Europe, and even as far as America, without a marvellous intervention of Providence. We may indeed cry out with the Royal Prophet, "A Domino factum est istud, et est mirabile in oculis nostris."

The same sentiments of veneration are expressed by the priest and people of Cuvilly, "which had the honour of giving to the world the saintly Mère Julie Billiart."

There are few religious orders which have not united their voices to the Institute of the Sisters of Notre-Dame to implore, for the Servant of God, the honours which the Church renders to the Saints. Among others, as the postulatory letter of the Very Father Beckx attests, the Society of Jesus does not forget that it was Father Varin and Father Thomas who decided the vocation of Julie Billiart and supported her in her trials.

Among the Congregations of women we single out those that were most nearly connected with Mère Julie by the relations which they had with her or with her children—the Carmelites and the Sisters of the Visitation, the Dames du Sacré-Cœur, so faithful to the spirit of Mère Barat, and the Sisters of the Nativity of Valence, founded by Madame de Franssu, the generous friend of her days of trouble at Amiens.

Can we fail to admire the ways of Divine Providence as we behold the manner in which God has been pleased to exalt the humble? A poor country girl reduced to extreme poverty, for long years a prey to sickness, unknown, despised and persecuted, is glorified by God, placed in the ranks of the heroes of the Faith, and while they await the final decision of Holy Church, is proclaimed "Blessed" by the voices of sovereigns, of princes of the blood royal, of cardinals, of archbishops and bishops, of divers religious orders of men and women, and of the most illustrious amongst the nobility of every country—the families of Rochefoucauld, de Broglie, Croy, Caraman-Chimay, Ligue, Hohenlohe, d'Ursel, Stolberg, Talbot, Clifford, etc.—a long list, at the end of which we cannot without emotion see the names of Blin de Bourdon, de Franssu, de Beaussier.

Above this concert of praise, the voice of the Sovereign Pontiff has already made itself heard. On June 25, 1889, His Holiness Leo XIII., upon receiving the favourable report of the Sacred Congregation of Rites, deigned to ratify the decision of the Cardinals and to sign the commission for the introduction of the cause. The opening words of the Pontifical decree sum up the praises of the Servant of God: "In the evil days in which the last century closed and our own began, flourished the Venerable Servant of God, Julie Billiart, *an eminent labourer in the harvest of the Lord.*" *

Since that time an important step has been taken in the cause. Leo XIII. had named for the process of Beatification as Cardinal Relator, His Eminence Gaetano Aloisi Masella, Prefect of the Sacred Congregation of Rites. At the prayer of the Roman Postulator, and at the proposal of the said Cardinal, the Sacred Congregation in its session of February 27, 1890, approved the writings of the Venerable Mère Julie. According to this decree, ratified and confirmed by the Sovereign Pontiff on March 14, 1890, " nothing has been found in the writings of the Servant of God Julie Billiart to prevent the canonical proceedings for her beatification and canonisation."

In the same year, owing to the exertions of Mgr. Virili, the indefatigable and devoted Postulator of the Cause, the Apostolic Process *ne pereant probationes*, on the life, the virtues and the miracles of the Venerable Servant of God, was begun : this was followed, in 1891, by the Apostolic Process *de fama sanctitatis*, and the Cause is at the time at which we write (May, 1898,) advancing gradually to a conclusion.

Meanwhile, the fresh miracles wrought by the inter-

---

* Superioris saeculi labentis nostrique ineuntis luctuosis sane temporibus, insignis in messe Domini operaria effloruit venerabilis Dei serva Julia Billiart.

cession of the Servant of God will hasten, we may hope, the hour when the humble Julie, already glorified in heaven, shall be proclaimed Blessed upon earth and placed upon the altars of the Church, that the faithful, reading her story, may lift up their voices for her in the words which will most fitly close these pages,

"Ah! que le bon Dieu est bon!"

THE END.

www.ingramcontent.com/pod-product-compliance
Lightning Source LLC
Chambersburg PA
CBHW022147300426
44115CB00006B/390